DEDICATION

THE HUAWEI PHILOSOPHY OF **HUMAN RESOURCE MANAGEMENT**

Published by
LID Publishing Limited
One Adam Street, London WC2N 6LE

31 West 34th Street, 8th Floor, Suite 8004,
New York, NY 10001, U.S.

info@lidpublishing.com
www.lidpublishing.com

A member of:

BPR
Business Publishers Roundtable

www.businesspublishersroundtable.com

Copyright licensed by Huang Weiwei and arranged with
Shanghai CEIBS Online Learning Co., Ltd.
Dedication is translated from the original Chinese edition
以奋斗者为本：华为公司人力资源管理纲要

Editor-in-Chief: Huang Weiwei
Editorial Board: Yin Zhifeng, Lv Ke, Hu Saixiong,Tong Guodong,
Gong Hongbin, and Wu Chunbo

Printed in in P.R China by Beijing Congreat Printing Co., Ltd
ISBN: 978-1-910649-51-0

Cover and page design: Caroline Li

DEDICATION

THE HUAWEI PHILOSOPHY OF **HUMAN RESOURCE MANAGEMENT**

HUANG WEIWEI

YIN ZHIFENG, LV KE, HU SAIXIONG, TONG GUODONG,
GONG HONGBIN, AND WU CHUNBO

LONDON   MONTERREY
MADRID   SHANGHAI
MEXICO CITY   BOGOTA
NEW YORK   BUENOS AIRES
BARCELONA   SAN FRANCISCO

Resources can be exhausted; only culture endures. Huawei does not have any natural resources to depend upon. What we do have is the brainpower of our employees. This is our oil, our forest, and our coal. Human ingenuity is the creator of all wealth.

— **Ren Zhengfei**

EPILOGUE

This book was compiled based on Huawei's internal training material for managers *Human Resources Management Philosophy (On Value and On Managers)*, a writing project led by Huawei Rotating CEO Hu Houkun, also the director of the editorial board. Li Jie and Lv Ke are the deputy directors. The other members of the editorial board for *On Value* are Huang Weiwei, Yin Zhifeng, Tong Guodong, Hu Saixiong, Gong Hongbin, and Wu Chunbo, with Yin Zhifeng and Shen Shengli serving as executive editors. The other members of the editorial board for *On Managers* are Huang Weiwei, Hu Saixiong, Yin Zhifeng, Tong Guodong, Gong Hongbin, and Wu Chunbo, with Hu Saixiong and Ma Yueyong serving as executive editors. Chang Min and Li Shiwen have also contributed to these two parts.

Human Resources Management Philosophy (On Value and On Managers) was approved in January 2011. Since then, it has been used as training material at the Huawei Senior Management Seminar. As of June 2014, 64 sessions have been held for over 4,000 middle and senior managers. Based on their own experiences, these managers have extensively discussed many of the topics and key points mentioned in the book. While deepening their own understanding of Huawei's HR management philosophy, they have also helped refine the structure of this book. We would like to extend special thanks to these managers.

The initial English translation of the book was produced by Rong Hui. Following this, a Huawei translation team, led by Zhang Linyan, reviewed the accuracy and readability of the English translation, and made revisions as needed to ensure the translated text was faithful to the original Chinese, in both content and style, especially the speaking style of Huawei CEO Ren Zhengfei. In addition to Zhang Linyan, the translation team also included He Yanghong, Feng Wenchao, Du Xiaolian, Guo Yanjuan, Xu Tiantian, Chen Xiahuan, Sean Upton-McLaughlin, Gary Maidment, Philip Hand, and Niva Whyman. The final English text was confirmed and finalized by Huang Weiwei.

Editorial Board
April 29, 2016

PREFACE

After nearly three decades since its inception in 1988, Huawei has emerged as a leading player in the global communications industry. People often ask how Huawei has caught up in the global high-tech race to become what it is today. This book answers this question. Huawei's growth is attributable to its core competencies, which are built upon its core values: staying customer-centric, inspiring dedication, persevering, and growing by reflection. When 150,000 knowledge workers are gathered together, the importance of HR management becomes abundantly clear. In fact, it takes precedence over technology and capital.

Huawei values traditions. In 1996, we began drafting *The Huawei Charter*. Today, we have come far enough on our journey to write this book. We have set our thoughts down here to systematically compile the company's management philosophy and policies. By doing so, we can examine our traditions and gain new insights. We also hope to shake off our reliance on individuals and increase the continuity of our management system. Both actions can help enrich innovation in the future.

This book comprises two parts: Part One, On Value and Part Two, On Managers. Part One has three chapters: Going All Out to Create Value, Objectively Assessing Value, and Fairly Distributing Value. Objectively assessing value is the basis of fairly distributing value. The purpose of both is to motivate employees to go all out to create value. Part Two has a structure that reflects Huawei's systems and priorities for managing managers. This part focuses on managers missions and responsibilities, as well as requirements for their conduct. Developing strong managers is the most unique part of Huawei's HR management system. This area is also the main focal point for Huawei executives. Even so, Huawei's managers remain the bottleneck for its future development.

In contrast to *The Huawei Charter*, this book contains excerpts from speeches and articles by Huawei's founder and CEO Ren Zhengfei. These are complemented by resolutions from the company's Executive Management Team (EMT). Remaining true to the original text, the source of each excerpt is also provided, thus increasing the value of this book as a research reference. The editorial board has designed logical structures and topics for each chapter so that both the content and focus are presented as clearly as possible.

The content for each topic in every chapter is arranged chronologically, running from the year of the company's inception to December 2013. This enables readers to understand how Huawei's HR management philosophy and policies have evolved. It also illustrates the continuity of Huawei's core values, upon which its HR management system is built. The core values of an enterprise are like the DNA of a living being.

When drafting *The Huawei Charter* years ago, the editorial team suggested that the charter should answer three questions: Why is Huawei so successful? Can Huawei's past success ensure greater future success? What else does Huawei need to do to achieve greater success? Today, these three questions remain in the continually evolving *Human Resources Management Philosophy.*

In China, few people know how to manage a global high-tech company like Huawei. There is a lack of experience and mature management systems for us to learn from so we must turn to Western companies for guidance. We must then apply what we have learned and summarize our own experiences; otherwise it would be difficult to learn how to manage such a large company. This book provides a valuable reference for training Huawei's managers. By having it published, we hope to collect feedback from people outside of Huawei so we can refine its message.

Editorial Board
May 20, 2014

CONTENTS

PART ONE

ON VALUE

All enterprises are benefit-driven. This requires a fair value distribution system preceded by objective value assessments, which in turn need to be underpinned by a positive culture.

To expand, an enterprise must develop a wolf pack. Wolves have three key characteristics: a keen sense of smell; a pack mentality; and tenacity.

– Ren Zhengfei

GOING ALL OUT TO CREATE VALUE

The most basic goal of an enterprise is to survive, and to survive sustainably. Enterprises that outlive their competitors prove to be the best. As survival is so important, an enterprise must never stop exploring how it can survive, why it needs to survive, and what value it can create. To survive, an enterprise must have customers. To win customers, it must better satisfy their needs and create value for them. Then what is value? In economics, value reflects an enterprise's current and potential capabilities to make profits. Simply put, value equals sustainable growth. That is how Huawei understands value.

Value creation is to some extent a paradox: The more selfish an enterprise is, the further it moves away from its goals. Conversely, if an enterprise tries as hard as it can to create value for others, it thrives and grows. Knowing this well, Huawei CEO Ren Zhengfei believes that Huawei only exists to serve its customers.

So how is value created? In Ren's view: "Resources can be exhausted; only culture endures. Huawei does not have any natural resources to depend upon. What we do have is the brainpower of our employees. This is our oil, our forest, and our coal. Human ingenuity is the creator of all wealth." The most valuable resources that an enterprise can ever have are people – they have huge potential to create value. This idea seems so simple that most people take it for granted. But it is the simplest ideas that make the greatest enterprises.

Creating value should be the focus of all corporate activities, including HR management. The major goal of HR management is to encourage employees to go all out to create value, both for customers and the enterprise. Whether this goal can be achieved depends on how employees' contributions are assessed and how the value created by the enterprise is distributed, including surplus value. So, creating value, assessing value, and distributing value have emerged as the most critical and difficult tasks in HR management. As assessing value concerns objectivity and distributing value concerns fairness, HR management is all about being objective and fair. If these two issues are resolved, the goals of individual employees will be aligned with those of the enterprise. In that case, there will be an inexhaustible source of motivation to create value.

Chapter One mainly describes Huawei's perspectives on value creation. Chapters Two and Three discuss the policies and principles that Huawei follows to assess and distribute value in an objective and fair way.

1.1 Managing Human Resources to Create Value

1.1.1 What is value?

By maintaining fast-paced growth, Huawei provides its employees with opportunities for personal development. Our increasing profits enable us to compensate employees generously and attract global talent to join the company. So, in this sense, a steady growth rate is necessary to inspire passion across the company. *(Ren Zhengfei: How Long Can Huawei Survive, 1998)*

To achieve growth, an enterprise must create results for its customers, capital providers, and employees. Therefore, it is essential to satisfy customer needs, and cultivate employees who are passionate and work hard to meet these needs. We should base salaries on employees' real contributions and potential to contribute continually, and base bonuses on short-term contributions. We should also emphasize individual contributions to capital. Any increase in headcount should be accompanied by added value. An enterprise must satisfy its customers, as this is the basis for its survival. It must also satisfy its shareholders, as this is the purpose of their investment. The enterprise must satisfy its value contributors, and value the contributions of dedicated employees, as they are the driving force behind sustainable growth. *(Ren Zhengfei: Guidelines for Human Resources Management Transformation, 2005)*

We have brought together over 100,000 employees to make Huawei a company with increasing corporate value, and this is an indicator of its overall strength. Revenue is not everything, and current financial statements may not accurately reflect real value. In fact, corporate value needs to reflect current and potential profitability. That is why Huawei focuses so much on sustainable growth. *(Ren Zhengfei: Effectively Managing Corporate Value to Pursue Sustainable Growth, 2012)*

1.1.2 Survival is fundamental to an enterprise

Survival is our most basic goal and we must have markets to survive. If there are no markets, we cannot achieve economies of scale. If there are no economies of scale, costs cannot be low. If we have neither low costs nor high quality, it will be hard for us to compete and our company will definitely decline. *(Ren Zhengfei: Standing Against Pride and Complacency and Being Mentally Dedicated, 1996)*

The purpose of improving our managers is to help our company survive. To survive, we must demote those who hinder the company's growth, and eliminate conduct that is not conducive to our development. This is the only approach we can take. *(Ren Zhengfei: Highly Skilled Employees Are the Wealth of Our Company, 1999)*

At Huawei, we must never stop exploring how we can survive, what we need to survive, and what value we can create. To survive, we must enhance our core competencies, because they will make our company bigger and stronger. *(Ren Zhengfei: Survival Is Fundamental to an Enterprise, 2000)*

Personally, I do not have great ambitions. What I think about most is what to do and how to do it in the next two or three years to help our company survive. I place more emphasis on short-term management improvements than long-term strategic goals, because survival is fundamental to Huawei. Short-term improvements to management should be guided by the long-term goal of enhancing the company's core competencies. With this in mind, we will not get lost in the midst of short-term management improvements, and our short-term and long-term goals will not contradict each other. As a result, our core competencies will improve, and we will discover what we need to survive and what value survival brings. *(Ren Zhengfei: Survival Is Fundamental to an Enterprise, 2000)*

The survival of an enterprise depends on the enterprise itself. If it does not survive, it is not because others do not allow it to – it is because it cannot find a way to carry on. Survival doesn't mean dragging out an ordinary existence or simply existing for the sake of existing. To survive is not easy and to thrive is even more difficult. This is because we are always facing a constantly changing environment and a highly competitive market. This is further complicated by interpersonal relationships within our company. An enterprise can survive only if it constantly improves. *(Ren Zhengfei: Survival Is Fundamental to an Enterprise, 2000)*

Being big and strong temporarily is not what we want. What we want is the ability and resilience to survive sustainably. *(Ren Zhengfei: Huawei's Hard Winter, 2001)*

For the past ten years, I've worried about failure every single day and paid no attention to success. I have no sense of pride or superiority, just a sense of urgency. This might be the reason for Huawei's survival. If all of us try to figure out how we can survive, we may survive for a much longer time. No matter what, we will fail one day. Please be prepared for that. This is my unwavering point of view because it is a law of history. *(Ren Zhengfei: Huawei's Hard Winter, 2001)*

We need to point out that survival is fundamental to an enterprise. Huawei does not exist to pursue fame. We want to be down-to-earth. I hope that you will adopt an appropriate attitude toward old and ordinary products. Don't always aim to develop cutting-edge technologies. We are not scientists. We are businessmen with an engineering background, and our job is to develop products that sell well and generate profits. *(Ren Zhengfei: Corporate Development Should Focus on Meeting the Current Needs of Customers, 2002)*

We need to adapt to market changes and apply flexible tactics and strategies. Our ultimate goal is survival. (*Ren Zhengfei: Acting According to Universal Laws, Giving Full Play to Core Teams, Constantly Improving Per Capita Efficiency, and Working Together to Survive Hard Times, 2002)*

Huawei does not have any external resources to depend upon. What we have is the diligence and perseverance of our employees. We must eliminate anything that undermines our internal vitality and innovation. This is critical for us to survive fierce global competition. No enterprise will always succeed when faced with this. Changes occur frequently in industry. To survive, many global companies have to downsize; and some even disappear. The road ahead is not easy and is full of uncertainties. We cannot guarantee that our company will survive over the long term. Therefore, we cannot promise our staff that we will offer them lifelong employment. We will not tolerate lazy employees, either. If we do, it is unfair to those who work hard and make real contributions. Nothing is free. We have to earn a happy life through hard work. Dedication is the only way to succeed. We have to rely totally on ourselves to create a better future. *(Source: Notification on the Status of the Human Resources Management Transformation, 2007)*

The goal of any enterprise is to make itself more competitive, build trust among its customers, and survive market competition. To provide excellent customer services, we have to recruit excellent employees, and these employees must work hard. To remain dedicated over the long term, they must be paid fairly and stay healthy. *(Ren Zhengfei: Speech at the Mid-year Meeting of the Marketing & Sales Department, 2008)*

1.1.3 The goal of all corporate activities is business success

Huawei is a results-driven company and all our efforts are focused on achieving our goals. Our corporate culture serves our goals of generating value and business returns. *(Ren Zhengfei: Excerpts from Q&A with New Graduate Employees, 1997)*

Huawei's first core value is about what the company pursues. A popular view today is that enterprises should pursue maximum profits. However, what Huawei pursues is quite different. We do not seek maximum profits. Instead, we keep our profits at a reasonable level. What do we pursue? We strive to become a global leader and provide quality services for our customers. *(Ren Zhengfei: How Long Can Huawei Survive, 1998)*

Rather than seeking maximum profits, we will set profit goals that are sufficiently high but also reasonable in different stages based on our need for sustainable growth. *(Source: The Huawei Charter, 1998)*

As a company, Huawei pursues profits and fulfills its corporate social responsibilities. If a company wants both profits and fame, it will be a disaster. *(Ren Zhengfei: Speech at the Shanghai Research Center, 2007)*

I think the only criterion for success is achieving business goals. That is something we must always bear in mind. *(Ren Zhengfei: Speech at the Shanghai Research Center, 2007)*

Business success is the ultimate measure of the value of any technology, product, solution, or business management approach. *(Source: EMT Meeting Minutes No. [2008] 041)*

Maximum profits are not what we pursue. In fact, maximizing profits will bleed the future dry, which in turn will harm our strategic position. So everyone needs to bear this in mind: We must unlock our own potential, lower operating costs, and deliver high-value services to our customers. We must also curb our greed and lower our profit margins to increase benefits to our customers and suppliers. *(Ren Zhengfei: Speech at the EMT ST Meeting, April 2010)*

An enterprise needs profits to survive. But we only pursue reasonable profits. We have to ensure that our partners can also earn reasonable profits, so we can build a robust industry chain. *(Source: EMT Resolution No. [2011] 052 On Correctly Understanding Staying Customer-centric)*

1.2

Source of Value Creation

1.2.1 Huawei's success depends on customers' success

We aim to help our customers realize their vision in the field of information and communications; we also aim to become a global leader through hard work and perseverance. *(Source: The Huawei Charter, 1998)*

The interests of customers are actually where our survival and development lie. Therefore, we prioritize services when developing our company, and customer satisfaction is the base criterion for measuring our work. *(Source: The Huawei Charter, 1998)*

Our sustainable development relies on whether we can meet customer needs. *(Ren Zhengfei: The Focus of High-level Visits Should Be Marketing, 2000)*

An enterprise must make profits to survive. Profits can only come from customers. Huawei's survival depends on meeting customer needs, providing products and services that customers want, and receiving reasonable rewards. We need to pay our employees and investors, and only our customers pay us. If we do not serve our customers, who do we serve? Huawei only exists to serve its customers because they determine the company's destiny. Therefore, the key to our growth is customers, not one specific entrepreneur. *(Source: Huawei's Core Values, 2007)*

1.2.2 The dialectical relationship within value creation

I love my nation, and I also love my company and my family. Of course, I love my family more than my employees. That is the truth. We can unite our employees only by telling the truth. We need to give meaning to our employees' work, and make them realize how their work contributes to their country. We also need to avoid empty talk and encourage our employees to start small, such as helping people around them and improving themselves. Working for one's country and for one's family are the two engines that we need to start at the same time. *(Source: Out of Chaos, 1998)*

Huawei only exists to serve its customers. The only way for us to survive is to maximize value for customers. Some companies serve their shareholders and maximize shareholders' interests. I don't think it's wise to do so. In the United States, many companies have fallen because of this. There are also companies that aim to maximize benefits for their employees. That is not wise, either. You might know that it has been years since Japanese companies raised their employees' salaries. Therefore, we must be dedicated to maximizing customers' interests. To me, high quality, good services, and low prices maximize benefits for customers. When their benefits are maximized, they will stay loyal, buy more of our products, and help us survive. We must change our organizational structures, processes and systems, service modes, and work skills based on this purpose. *(Ren Zhengfei: Speech at the First Quarter Meeting of the Technical Support Department, 2002)*

We work hard for ourselves, but we also contribute to society. These two aims are reconciled through customer service, without which there is nothing but empty talk. *(Ren Zhengfei: Speech at the Mid-year Meeting of the Marketing & Sales Department, 2008)*

Huawei's Board of Directors has made it clear that its goal is not to maximize the interests of shareholders or stakeholders (including employees, governments, and suppliers). Rather, it embraces the core values of staying customer-centric and inspiring dedication. *(Ren Zhengfei: Clarifying the Rotating CEO System Under the Leadership of the Board of Directors, 2012)*

1.3

Elements of Value Creation

1.3.1 Huawei creates value through labor, knowledge, entrepreneurship, and capital

At Huawei, we believe that value is created through labor, knowledge, entrepreneurship, and capital. To build our value distribution system, we must redefine the elements for value creation, and break away from the traditional economic theory stating that labor creates value. The four elements we have identified for value creation – labor, knowledge, entrepreneurship, and capital – lay the foundation for our value distribution system. *(Ren Zhengfei: Seizing Opportunities, Adjusting Management Systems, and Meeting Challenges, 1997)*

In the hi-tech field, we need to redefine the role that knowledge and entrepreneurship play in value creation. We cannot simply emphasize the role of labor, especially manual labor. In hi-tech companies, manual labor only accounts for a tiny part of the total workforce. For example, at Huawei, about 40% of our employees work in R&D, 35% in sales and marketing, and only 15% in manufacturing. Of this 15%, less than 10% are manual laborers. In this case, who creates value? We can no longer say that labor creates value. Instead, we need to emphasize the role that knowledge and entrepreneurship play in value creation. *(Ren Zhengfei: Seizing Opportunities, Adjusting Management Systems, and Meeting Challenges, 1997)*

1.3.2 Labor

At Huawei, employees can earn high salaries by using their knowledge and working with integrity. If they can earn money in other ways, then there is a problem with our management system. We have to develop a culture that encourages employees to work with integrity and continuously improve. *(Ren Zhengfei: Being a Manager Means More Responsibility, 1996)*

Being mentally dedicated is different from working hard, as the latter usually involves having no goals. We need to cultivate a team of mentally dedicated managers. Even if they are not as technically skilled as others, they can easily catch up if they try their best. When we are building our organization, we need to cultivate this type of team and promote employees who are mentally dedicated. *(Ren Zhengfei: Minutes of the Report by the Transmission Department of the R&D Department, 1996)*

I believe everyone present is a hard worker, but I don't know whether all of you are mentally dedicated. These are two totally different things. To become a senior manager, you need to be mentally dedicated. Hard work alone does not make a good manager. *(Ren Zhengfei: Building the Development and Pilot Department to Act as a Sieve, 1996)*

Some employees are irresponsible. They often find excuses, like processes have changed, or new rules have been issued, so they can avoid doing what they are supposed to do. In other words, they are not mentally dedicated. When someone is in need, we should try our best to help them solve their problem. We cannot simply ask them to solve the problem themselves. Being mentally dedicated is completely different from working hard, and we need to differentiate the two in performance appraisals. *(Ren Zhengfei: Being Mentally Dedicated and Trying Your Best to Successfully Complete Your Work, 1996)*

Many people work hard but lack mental dedication. Scientists, entrepreneurs, and successful business people are always mentally dedicated. They endure tremendous pressures just to do a little better than others, for example, to make a scientific breakthrough, seize greater market share, or offer a lower price. Some of them are wealthy, but this does not mean they are not mentally dedicated. Compared with hard work, mental dedication may be more easily misunderstood, but is more valuable. We need to consider the difference between the two when appraising employees' performance. *(Ren Zhengfei: Speeches During the Early Years of Huawei, 1996)*

Integrity and competence are the basis for long-term employment at Huawei. *(Ren Zhengfei: Key Points for Management, 1999)*

What is dedication? It includes every effort we make to create value for customers and to improve our capabilities, no matter how trivial they are. All other efforts that do not serve this purpose are not dedication. *(Ren Zhengfei: Deepening our Understanding of the Corporate Culture of Staying Customer-centric and Inspiring Dedication, 2008)*

Dedication is how you create value for customers. If you scrub coal to make it white but don't create customer value, you cannot say you're dedicated no matter how hard you work. For instance, if you work overtime and spend 14 hours doing something that could be done in 2 hours, it does not mean you are dedicated. In this case, you are creating no additional value and incurring additional costs that will be passed on to customers due to the extra electricity used and free evening snacks consumed. *(Ren Zhengfei: Remarks at a Meeting with Staff of the Kenya Representative Office, 2008)*

We cherish all employees who remain dedicated and contribute more than they cost regardless of their country of origin or seniority. *(Ren Zhengfei: Speech at the EMT ST Meeting, 2009)*

Working 40 hours a week will only make you ordinary – you will never become a successful musician, dancer, scientist, engineer, or business person. If you often sit in cafes like others do, you will never catch up. *(Ren Zhengfei: The Market Economy Is Best for Competition; Economic Globalization Is Inevitable, 2009)*

1.3.3 Knowledge

In the knowledge economy, the way we create wealth is totally different from the past. Information networks have changed people's mindsets and fully unleashed their creativity. As a result, wealth is now mainly created through knowledge and management. In other words, people now come first. This is something that we need to study. *(Ren Zhengfei: How Long Can Huawei Survive, 1998)*

In the knowledge economy, the way enterprises survive and grow has changed significantly. The role that knowledge – including intellectual property rights and technical expertise – plays in value creation outweighs that played by capital, which used to be the dominant element of value creation. Today, capital needs to rely on knowledge to retain and add value. *(Ren Zhengfei: How Long Can Huawei Survive, 1998)*

In some hi-tech industries, the human brain – the so-called knowledge capital – plays a more important role than monetary capital. That is why we need to emphasize knowledge and labor. *(Source: Out of Chaos, 1998)*

We prioritize increasing human capital over increasing financial capital. *(Source: The Huawei Charter, 1998)*

1.3.4 Entrepreneurship

We should have the courage to take risks and pick ourselves up again in difficult times. With such courage and confidence, we can develop new markets and new technologies. We need to help our employees develop their acumen and vision in business and technology, enable them to stand out through trial and error, and cultivate a new generation of employees. Trial and error is a great way to success. You can succeed as long as you try. If you don't try, you will not have a chance because fortune favors the bold. *(Ren Zhengfei: Speeches During the Early Years of Huawei, 1991)*

Initially, Huawei relied on its founders to seize opportunities despite insufficient resources. Their dedication, vision, and courage have made the company bigger and stronger. *(Ren Zhengfei: Fitting in the Team and Developing Together, 1997)*

According to Professor Howard H. Stevenson from the Harvard Business School, entrepreneurship is "the pursuit of opportunity without regard to resources currently controlled". This is clearly reflected in the early years of Huawei when it was a typical company run by an entrepreneur. Huawei owes its success to three factors. First, we remain focused on our strategy and are not distracted by random opportunities. Second, we fully utilize both internal and external resources. Any organization depends on resources for its development. You may not control all resources, but what matters is whether you can mobilize them. Third, we focus our limited resources on a very specific area to make breakthroughs. *(Ren Zhengfei: Seizing Opportunities, Adjusting Management Systems, and Meeting Challenges, 1997)*

We have to make it clear that our company's development relies on our customer-centric management system where survival is our bottom line, rather than on the decisions of an entrepreneur. When such a system is in place, the soul of an enterprise is no longer an entrepreneur; it is customer needs. Customers are always there, so the soul of the enterprise will also be there. In an article I wrote ten years ago, I quoted Confucius: "Time goes on and on just like water flowing in a river, never ceasing day or night." Once a levee is built along a river, water can flow continuously. Management is also like a flowing river; when a customer-centric management system is in place, supervision is less necessary. To me, an enterprise is most likely to thrive when its entrepreneur does not play a big role. Continuing to admire the entrepreneur will propel the enterprise into its most dangerous and hopeless time. *(Ren Zhengfei: Living with Peace of Mind, 2003)*

It does not matter if leaders are not tech savvy; they should have a clear vision, set clear business goals, and think strategically. They should not just see problems from a technical perspective. *(Ren Zhengfei: Speech at the Shanghai Research Center, 2007)*

What is the job of a leader? To focus on the most important issue and the factors that influence the issue, and then figure out where to go. *(Ren Zhengfei: Speech at the PSST[1] Managers' Meeting, 2008)*

The role of a leader is to set a clear direction and let others follow. *(Ren Zhengfei: Speech at the EMT[2] ST[3] Meeting, March 29, 2013)*

I believe thought leaders should be able to play a leading role in defining value distribution and global strategy. They should focus on management philosophy rather than specific management approaches. Strategic leaders shape the future strategic landscape. Business leaders concentrate on major issues. And senior experts develop systematic plans. *(Ren Zhengfei: Speech at the EMT ST Meeting, March 29, 2013)*

1.3.5 Capital

The development of our company relies on capital, which can come from two sources. One is to sell stock in the open capital market to raise money; the other is to accumulate capital on our own by expanding scale and increasing profits. The former is an easier way to get money, but it comes at a price because investors may interfere with our system. Our current system is based on labor, not on capital. We recognize high performers, and reward them with higher salaries, more shares, and other incentives. This system is not mature, and to some extent, relies on the personal charisma of our executives. Therefore, we still need to keep working on this system and institutionalize it. Regarding fund raising, we need to balance the two sources rather than prefer one over the other. *(Ren Zhengfei: Finding a Balance and Growing Together, 1994)*

Based on our success with products, we can explore how to obtain capital and mobilize more resources based on an ownership system. The transition from product-based to capital-based operations depends on our technological, marketing, and management capabilities as well as on timing. We have to make ourselves strong before we expand, and be prepared before we seek out opportunities. *(Source: The Huawei Charter, 1998)*

Capital-based operations and external expansion should help enhance the company's potential, increase profits, and create a united organization and corporate culture. Going public should help solidify the foundation of our established value distribution system. *(Source: The Huawei Charter, 1998)*

While we were drafting *The Huawei Charter*, Ren frequently mentioned that high-tech enterprises were smart to use the concept of knowledge capital during their start-up period. There are two types of capital: knowledge capital and venture capital. The former needs to be translated into the latter, which in turn needs to increase steadily. Otherwise, the enterprise may not endure. Venture capital comes from both the enterprise itself and external investors. During value distribution, we need to think about the role of venture capital and find a new path: translating labor, knowledge, and the entrepreneur's management contributions and risks taken into capital. We must not distribute all the value we create. We need to save some to reinvest in our company and help it grow. *(Source: Out of Chaos, 1998)*

Thanks to the large quantity of talent we have in China, we have gained a unique competitive advantage – low R&D costs. We are expanding our network equipment business, and building world-class marketing, sales, service, R&D, and management platforms. Based on these platforms, we are cultivating our managers, developing new businesses, and earning profits through the capital-based operations of these new businesses. *(Source: EMT Resolution No. [2007] 021 Guidelines on Global Competition Strategies)*

---

[1] PSST: Products & Solutions Staff Team; a platform which R&D organizations use to make daily business decisions, conduct operations, and perform management.

[2] EMT: Executive Management Team; the highest authority at Huawei, which is responsible for the company's operations and customer satisfaction; the company CEO is the chairman of the EMT.

[3] ST: Staff Team; a platform which business departments use to make daily business decisions, conduct operations, and perform management.

1.4 Cultural Factors That Support Value Creation

1.4.1 Inspiring dedication

Huawei is united by its corporate culture, which is built upon its organizational methods and mechanisms, rather than individuals, markets, or technologies. Huawei has established effective mechanisms that encourage collective dedication. *(Ren Zhengfei: Promoting Collective Dedication to Develop the High-Tech Industry, 1996)*

Huawei is a results-driven company, and all our efforts are focused on generating business returns. Our culture is purely corporate, not political or anything else. Our corporate culture is based on service because only service generates business returns. There are many types of services: after-sales, research, production, and upgrades that occur before the end of the product lifecycle. Therefore, we prioritize services when developing our teams. We can earn customers' trust only by providing quality services. The power of trust is infinite and inexhaustible. If one day we no longer need to serve customers, we will have to shut down our company. Therefore, service is the lifeline for our company and for us as individuals. *(Ren Zhengfei: Resources Can Be Exhausted; Only Culture Endures, 1997)*

To shape a corporate culture, we need to build a platform where our thinking is unified. We need to have a clear corporate culture in place before further delegating authority. If we had delegated authority in recent years before reaching a consensus on our corporate culture, Huawei might have fallen apart. *(Ren Zhengfei: Resolutely Implementing ISO9000, 1997)*

Thought and culture are very important for corporate management. The culture a company promotes is shown in its premises. For example, one of our premises is that knowledge is capital. Another is that we value dedicated employees and reward them accordingly. Our premises must be decided at the corporate level, and proven through application. *(Ren Zhengfei: Thought and Culture Are of Utmost Importance to Corporate Management, 1997)*

The most important issue for a corporate leader is to create and manage the corporate culture. The major talent of any corporate leader lies in his or her ability to shape culture. People are driven by material needs. However, if people are only driven by material needs, they will argue over little things, be unwilling to cooperate, and have no ambition. The role of culture is to help people move beyond their basic material needs, pursue higher-level needs such as the need to fulfill themselves, and unleash their full potential. During this process, people cooperate with each other, and earn respect and recognition. These needs are the foundation of effective team operations. *(Ren Zhengfei: Seizing Opportunities, Adjusting Management Systems, and Meeting Challenges, 1997)*

Huawei must strike an overall balance. To achieve this, we need to rely on our corporate culture. If there is no consensus on corporate culture across an organization, there will be no overall balance. The Chinese philosopher Confucius once said, "Follow your heart without breaking rules." We are not restraining you, but requesting that you strike an overall balance: to correct yourself, adjust yourself, and make progress. Self-adjustment is not realized by the leader. The leader is like the head of a wolf pack, and his main job is to secure opportunities. After opportunities are secured, the wolf pack automatically strikes an overall balance. This is a culture-based integrated propulsion system that develops on its own. *(Ren Zhengfei: Speech at the Meeting for the Fourth Revision of The Huawei Charter, 1997)*

The word "dedication" has many connotations. We value dedicated employees and reward them accordingly. Dedicated employees include not only employees, but also investors. These investors put their money in our company, and share the risks and liabilities. They are also dedicated. These are two types of dedication, and they share the same goal – to make money. *(Ren Zhengfei: Comments to Staff of the Kenya Representative Office, 2008)*

Staying customer-centric, inspiring dedication, persevering, and growing by reflection: These are the core values that we have established over the past two decades. They are the essence of our corporate culture. *(Ren Zhengfei: Managers Should Live and Pass on Huawei's Core Values, 2010)*

We stay customer-centric and inspire dedication. Some people may argue that these are merely marketing slogans. I disagree. What is wrong with dedication? We have learned this principle from our country's slogans, including Dedication to the Four Modernizations, Dedication to National Prosperity, and Dedication to Better Hometowns. What else should we advocate if not the principle of dedication? As a private company, Huawei can only measure employees' dedication with money. We distribute shares and bonuses to employees who are dedicated. Yet, employees should not work for bonuses and shares alone, otherwise our core values will weaken. We encourage dedication and motivate dedicated employees with monetary incentives. Over the past two decades, we have learned the ideas of staying customer-centric and inspiring dedication through trial and error. We might have applied these ideas unconsciously in the past. But now, we are applying them consciously. Our corporate culture also includes persevering and growing by reflection. *(Ren Zhengfei: Success Is Not a Reliable Guide to Future Development, 2011)*

1.4.2 We will toast those who succeed and offer a helping hand to those who fail

This marketing and sales department slogan is well-known throughout the company. It means we will celebrate no matter who wins and help those who are in need. This has shaped our corporate culture. *(Ren Zhengfei: Maintaining Technological Leadership to Expand into New Areas, 1996)*

The next era will be characterized by collective dedication and collective success. Everyone on a team should be a good team player: You cheer for your teammate when he does a good job, and help him if he fails. That is what teamwork is. *(Ren Zhengfei: Speech at the Opening Ceremony of the Technology Summer Camp, 1996)*

The main goal of our expansion is sustainable growth. We aim to align with international management standards over the next ten years. During this growth stage, we will gradually reduce the influence of the entrepreneur and strengthen professional management. We must create a corporate climate where individual charisma, a spirit of leadership, and personal influence combine to promote and guide our company's development. Our corporate climate is an important management resource as it touches the majority of our employees. A favorable climate helps develop a superb team of managers with common values and governance capabilities. It also promotes corporate development in a wider scope. This dominant corporate climate is reflected in *The Huawei Charter* that we have developed and identified with. *(Ren Zhengfei: Shifting From the Realm of Necessity to the Realm of Freedom, 1998)*

We must encourage collective dedication. Our appraisal and incentive mechanisms should incorporate our customer-centric culture and our fine tradition of "toasting those who succeed and offering a helping hand to those who fail." Our incentive mechanisms, such as adjusted performance statistics and adjusted performance appraisals, will ensure that benefits are shared between field offices and back offices, and between operating teams and support teams. *(Source: EMT Meeting Minutes No. [2008] 021)*

I think collective dedication is the core of Huawei's corporate culture. If you want to develop yourself to the fullest, you need to be a good team player and communicate effectively with others at different levels. These are the key things needed to do a good job and contribute to the organization's success during critical moments. *(Ren Zhengfei: From "Philosophy" to Practice, 2011)*

1.4.3 The wolf spirit

To expand, an enterprise must develop a wolf pack. Wolves have three key characteristics: a keen sense of smell; a pack mentality; and tenacity. We must create an environment that encourages employee dedication. When new opportunities emerge, a group of leaders will stand out and seize them. *(Ren Zhengfei: How Long Can Huawei Survive, 1998)*

We target the strongest competitors in the world, and gradually catch up with and overtake them. Only in this way can we survive. Therefore, in the R&D and marketing and sales fields, we must establish an organization and mechanism that facilitates the survival and development of "wolves" – aggressive managers. We need to attract and develop a large number of aggressive managers who are eager for success and growth, and motivate them to develop a sense of smell as keen as that of wolves. They must remain united and do whatever it takes to seize opportunities, sell products, and increase market share. In addition, we need to develop a group of Bei[4] who are good at coordination and can support the operations of wolves. In this way, the wolf and the Bei can collaborate to achieve synergy. During operations, the Bei is integrated with the wolf and can help push the wolf forward. However, such an organizational development model does not suit other departments. *(Ren Zhengfei: Establishing an Organization and Mechanism That Facilitates Enterprise Survival and Development, 1997)*

---

4   The "Bei" is a legendary animal from Chinese folklore. The Bei is much like a wolf; the major difference between these two animals is that the wolf has long front legs and short hind legs, while the Bei has short front legs and long hind legs. Working together, the wolf and the Bei will flourish.

1.5

Two Wheels of Value Creation

1.5.1 Management first, technology second

The success of companies like IBM and Microsoft can be attributed more to management than to technology. Some companies have failed even though they were better than Huawei. They failed because they did not pay attention to management. Management is something that cannot be bought with money. *(Ren Zhengfei: Speech at the CIMS⁵ System Report Meeting of the Management Engineering Business Department, 1997)*

What counts as a contribution? It's not only about doing a job: debugging, programming, or whatever. Managing a job is also a contribution; as a matter of fact, it has even broader and deeper implications. In a team, there must be someone who acts as the organizer or manager. Does an organizer or manager necessarily contribute less than an ordinary employee? Definitely not. In principle, an organizer contributes more than those who do the actual work. Of course, there are instances where a small number of experts can contribute more than a manager. However, most experts should be placed under managers. *(Ren Zhengfei: Speech Before the Appointment of New R&D Managers, 1997)*

The most obvious characteristic of Huawei's transformation from the start-up phase to the growth phase is strengthening management and developing professional managers. In our start-up phase, we focused on both product and market development. In our growth phase, we aim to strengthen management. This will provide you with great opportunities. *(Ren Zhengfei: Fitting in the Team and Developing Together, 1997)*

For an enterprise, core competency means more than a competitive edge in technologies and products. Progress in management and services is far more important than technological progress. We have felt this strongly over the past decade. Management brings synergy among people, technology, and capital. Without services, management will have no direction. *(Ren Zhengfei: Innovation Is an Inexhaustible Driving Force Behind Huawei's Growth, 2000)*

In all companies, management comes first and technology comes second. Without first-class management, advanced technologies will weaken. With first-class management, even second-class technologies will advance. *(Ren Zhengfei: Comments at the Meeting with New Employees of the 22nd Session of 2000)*

Future challenges will not relate to technologies or products, but rather to basic research, innovation, and corporate management. The biggest challenge we face right now is internal management – to build organizations, processes, and IT systems that can promptly adapt to market demands and meet customer needs. If such a management system is not in place, problems will arise as our company expands. To avoid a decline and prevent employees from slacking off, we must constantly motivate our organization to maintain its vitality. We should also keep our organization under control at all times, but not so much that it loses vitality. What matters is a balance between motivation and control, and it needs to be constantly adapted to changing dynamics. *(Ren Zhengfei: Huawei's Opportunities and Challenges, 2000)*

We must not go crazy over technologies. I once analyzed the factors that might lead to the failure of Huawei and Lucent, and concluded that we must focus on customer needs rather than product technology. *(Ren Zhengfei: Comments to Staff of Avansys, 2001)*

Our goal is to meet customer needs, which can be achieved through new technology. New technology is a means to an end, not an end in itself. *(Source: Huawei's Core Values, 2007)*

The expansion of the internet into new areas has led to technological transparency and management improvements. The internet has also narrowed gaps between companies. In the future, managerial excellence will be the key to remaining competitive. We must set ourselves apart from our competitors in management. *(Source: EMT Meeting Minutes No. [2008] 028)*

Over the next three to five years, Huawei will face two possible outcomes: becoming a market leader or collapsing. It is possible for us to become a market leader, but the major obstacle is that we have focused more on business development than on organization building and manager development. We have not done well in the areas of organization building, process development, and manager development. For this reason, we need to make some changes in the next three to five years. If our efficiency can improve by 30%, we will become very successful. *(Ren Zhengfei: Speech at the EMT ST Meeting, May 2009)*

As a high-tech company, we think technology is important but management is more important. The key to corporate management is to integrate elements based on market needs. The value of management lies in the effective integration of all market-oriented resources and elements such as capital, technology, talent, markets, R&D, manufacturing, and industry chains to help the company compete successfully in the market. This is also a goal of management. Many enterprises have the required resources and elements, but those that integrate these resources and elements effectively are more likely to succeed. *(Ren Zhengfei: News Release, 2009)*

What is the downside of engineers being managers? Engineers-turned-managers tend to neglect management and emphasize technological innovation to the extent that they make products that no customer wants. We should not always prioritize technology. We must also emphasize management and shift our focus from technology to business. A project manager must be a business leader, not a technical expert. *(Ren Zhengfei: Speech at the EMT ST Meeting, June 2012)*

The company moves forward on two wheels. One is the business model and the other is technological innovation. *(Source: E-mail No. [2012] 35 Minutes of the Meeting Between Mr. Ren Zhengfei and Staff from the 2012 Laboratories)*

1.5.2 Our concepts of customer-centricity and technology-centricity are intertwined

Looking back on Huawei's history over the past decade, we can see that it is nearly impossible to survive in the high-tech sector without technological innovation. In this area, there is no time to lose because you will not survive if you fall behind. *(Ren Zhengfei: Innovation Is an Inexhaustible Driving Force Behind Huawei's Growth, 2000)*

Years of development have taught us the importance of prioritizing customer needs. By providing solutions, we can meet customers' needs for cost-effective services with high added value to help them boost profitability. Only after customers have become profitable will they buy our products. *(Ren Zhengfei: Staying Close to the Customer by Going Where You Are Most Needed in the Field Office, 2001)*

In the past, we developed products behind closed doors and touted them by pitching their advantages to customers. This work mode was feasible in a seller's market with huge demand, and we grew comfortable with this mode. But things are different now. If we continue to produce what we believe are "good" products without paying attention to customer needs, our products won't sell well. We need to clearly understand that prioritizing customer needs is the right path for Huawei's survival and development. *(Ren Zhengfei: Speech at the PIRB⁶ Product Roadmap Review Meeting, 2003)*

We have to understand the importance of prioritizing customer needs and stick to it. This is the right path for Huawei's survival and development. Customer needs are our lifeline, and we must give them enough attention. *(Ren Zhengfei: Speech at the PIRB Product Roadmap Review Meeting, 2003)*

Our future development goals are oriented towards customer needs. What is the difference between prioritizing customer needs and prioritizing products? It is in essence the difference between putting others first and putting ourselves first. At Huawei, technology-driven growth is slowing down, whereas customer-driven growth is accelerating. This phenomenon is in line with the laws of social progress. *(Ren Zhengfei: Speech at the Third Quarter Meeting Regarding Marketing in China, 2004)*

We must constantly innovate products and solutions based on customer needs. Customers' business success is the ultimate measure of the value of any cutting-edge technology, product, or solution. When it comes to making decisions on product investment, we prioritize customer needs over technology. We can maintain the competitiveness of our products and solutions only through continuous innovation based on an in-depth understanding of customer needs. *(Ren Zhengfei: My Thoughts on a 100-Year-Old Church That Survived the Wenchuan Earthquake, 2008)*

We must increase our technology-centric strategic investments to maintain a leading position in the industry. After all the talk about customer-centricity, it is possible that we go from one extreme to the other and ignore our forward-looking technology-centric strategy. In the future, our concept of technology-centricity will be intertwined with our concept of customer-centricity. We will be customer-centric when developing products, and technology-centric when developing next-generation architectural platforms. *(Ren Zhengfei: Speech at the EMT ST Meeting, March 31, 2011)*

We have two principles for innovation. First, we must emphasize value. We must not innovate for innovation's sake; rather, we must innovate to create value. Second, we must be more tolerant of failures in innovation. *(Source: E-mail No. [2012] 35 Minutes of the Meeting Between Mr. Ren Zhengfei and Staff from the 2012 Laboratories)*

We will increase forward-looking strategic investments and continue augmenting technological advantages to lead industry development. We must increase our technology-centric strategic investments to maintain a leading position in the industry. *(Source: Corp. Doc. No. [2012] 081 Guidelines on the Analysis of the 2012 Business Environment and Key Business Strategies)*

---

5 CIMS: Computer Integrated Manufacturing System.

6 PIRB: Product Investment Review Board; later changed to IRB for short.

1.6 Reducing Reliance on Three Elements

1.6.1 Reducing reliance on technology, capital, and individual employees

We are currently considering how we can systematically develop the company. At present, we rely heavily on technology, capital, and individual employees. As we move forward, we need to reduce this reliance in order to shift from the realm of necessity to the realm of freedom. *(Ren Zhengfei: Victory Is Inspiring Us, 1994)*

We are trying to reduce our reliance on technology, capital, and individual employees in order to shift from the realm of necessity to the realm of freedom. By using technology, humans can free up their hands. We need to apply technology to management. Advanced management softwares and documents can help us rebuild Huawei if a crisis occurs. Management, though abstract, is a kind of treasure. In the past, we were not clear about how to define treasure. After eight years of development, we now have an initial idea of what treasure is – it is our management and documents. *(Ren Zhengfei: Speech at the Work Report Meeting of the Management Engineering Business Department, 1997)*

Management effectiveness can be evaluated based on how much we rely on individuals. I do not mean that a system should be created to reduce reliance on employees. Rather, I believe organizations themselves need to become less reliant on individuals. Why are Western companies able to operate smoothly even though their staff mobility rate is much higher than ours? The reason is that these companies have adopted management systems such as ISO9000 and MRP II. It does not matter if anyone leaves the company, because new employees can learn their jobs quickly by working under systems that accurately give orders, send plans, or enable manufacturing. At Huawei, we still have a long way to go regarding management improvements. Our goal is to align with international management standards in three to five years. *(Ren Zhengfei: Speech at the Work Report Meeting of the Management Engineering Business Department, 1997)*

The goal of transforming management and implementing management policies and regulations is to sustain Huawei's development by reducing our reliance on technology, capital, and individual employees. *(Ren Zhengfei: Corporate Development Should Focus on Meeting the Current Needs of Customers, 2002)*

1.6.2 Shifting from the realm of necessity to the realm of freedom

One management view holds that, "The best management control model can help attain goals even in the absence of control." That is what the Chinese philosopher Lao Tzu called Wu Wei, or non-action, which means governance without intervention. That is the purpose of *The Huawei Charter*, and that is the best we can hope for in management. *(Ren Zhengfei: Speech at the Meeting for the Fourth Revision of The Huawei Charter, 1997)*

Our employees have to understand the company's development rules, and explore ways to apply non-action in management. I believe we can shift from the realm of necessity to the realm of freedom as long as we work hard. *(Ren Zhengfei: How Long Can Huawei Survive, 1998)*

What do we mean by "freedom"? Freedom means setting rules and making things work by simply following the rules. For a train, freedom means traveling on the tracks and reaching the destination without being derailed. Freedom comes from the knowledge of natural laws. It is the opposite of necessity, which is the result of a lack of knowledge or mastery of natural laws. *(Ren Zhengfei: Shifting From the Realm of Necessity to the Realm of Freedom, 1998)*

Good mechanisms and processes will greatly accelerate our company's progress. As the saying goes, "A good river flows forever." Huawei's core values are clearly "circular". How long can Huawei survive? The results can speak for themselves. "Circular" refers to a continuous cycle. We are constantly optimizing our mechanisms and processes. After a strong circular mechanism is formed, we will gradually separate the operating mechanisms of our company from human factors. The company will continue to operate very well even when a critical person leaves. Operating mechanisms and business processes are the key factors that will determine how long Huawei can survive. *(Ren Zhengfei: Loosening the Soil for Growth, 1998)*

Huawei used to be a small company that relied on individual heroes. Now it has become a relatively large company supervised by professional managers. To achieve professional management, we must inevitably reduce the influence of heroes, especially the influence of leaders and founders. Process-based professional management is the only way to improve efficiency and reduce internal management friction. *(Ren Zhengfei: Mission and Responsibilities of Professional Managers, 2000)*

An enterprise must follow rules and constantly seek truth (laws) during its operations and management. Rules include natural laws and social norms. What we must do is to understand these rules and follow them. *(Ren Zhengfei: Survival Is Fundamental to an Enterprise, 2000)*

CHAPTER 2

OBJECTIVELY ASSESSING VALUE

Value assessments focus on assessing the contributions employees have made in creating value for customers and the company. The purpose is to ensure the company is objective, and lay the foundation for fair value distribution. To objectively assess value, a company needs to have objective assessment criteria underpinned by a positive culture.

Core values are the guidelines Huawei uses to objectively assess employees' work attitude. Clear and challenging goals and tasks are the criteria it uses to objectively assess their work results. When assessing employees, Huawei prioritizes the competence and potential they have demonstrated in their jobs over their academic degrees.

To ensure that value assessments are objective, Huawei prioritizes results and responsibilities. As CEO Ren Zhengfei stated, Huawei has only one value assessment system. The focus is on fulfilling responsibilities. What is the aim of responsibility fulfillment? The answer is providing effective services for customers, ensuring customer satisfaction, improving Huawei's core competencies, and implementing corporate strategies. The goals are creating value for customers and contributing to the company's business success. Huawei uses this value assessment system to measure the performance of its employees, level by level, and thus resolve internal conflicts.

The major challenges Huawei faces in assessing value are balancing short-term and long-term contributions, in-process contributions and final results, and measurements and assessments. The overriding guideline for value assessments should be the following: Anything that cannot be measured is not manageable. Therefore, Huawei needs to figure out quantitative criteria or identify facts that can support the measurement of long-term contributions, contributions made during the process, and employees' sense of responsibility, so as to establish an objective foundation for subjective assessments. If contributions to creating value over the long-term are not recognized, the company will have no future.

It is worth noting that during performance appraisals, Huawei focuses on results and responsibilities supplemented by tracking of key events. These events are used to identify, measure, and assess responsibilities. This approach is especially suitable for appraising the performance of middle and senior managers. It is also helpful for identifying future leaders.

This chapter introduces Huawei's value assessment system from three perspectives: orientations and principles, methods and criteria, and common misconceptions about value assessments.

2.1	# Orientations and Principles of Value Assessments

2.1.1 Prioritizing results and responsibilities

To improve customer satisfaction, we must establish a value assessment system that is oriented towards results and responsibilities rather than competence. Our enterprise is results-driven, so we must provide customers with products they like. Huawei's value assessment system, including performance appraisals for middle and senior managers, must be redesigned to focus on results and responsibilities. *(Ren Zhengfei: Speech at the Meeting on the Project Report for the Value Assessment System for Junior Employees, 1998)*

Our current competency & qualification (C&Q) assessment system is in fact a type of value assessment system. Wouldn't it be problematic if we promoted competence-based value assessments? Would we still need to include responsibility and service as the basis for value assessments? If certain employees don't fulfill their responsibilities or fail to provide required services, we will not recognize or pay them generously, no matter how capable they are. I have criticized staff of the R&D department several times because there are problems with their approach to value assessments. They consistently recognize accomplishments in technology rather than contributions to results. If the latter type is not recognized, how do they know whether or not employees who modify a screw or wire should be given a high reward? This type of value assessment will inevitably increase costs and decrease productivity. So we must avoid this, institutionalize successful approaches through our value assessment system, and ensure these approaches endure. Only this can ensure a bright future for our company. *(Ren Zhengfei: Remaining Fully Committed to Products, 1998)*

We must improve the company's core competencies, build a process-based and up-to-date management system, and reinforce a value assessment system based on results, responsibilities, and key events. *(Ren Zhengfei: Key Points for Management, 2001)*

While implementing a performance-based appraisal system, we also need to track key events. We must investigate every error to figure out what has gone wrong and what we can do to improve. We should identify good managers during this process. I think that both performance-based appraisals and the tracking of key events are very important. We must identify and cultivate managers at all levels based on successful decisions, particularly those made in the process of achieving goals. We should also summarize project failures, but identify good managers via these projects. We should avoid using results as the sole basis for appraisals. *(Ren Zhengfei: Huawei's Hard Winter, 2001)*

Fairness is the most important aspect of appraisals. To ensure fairness, we should focus on performance. The purpose of key events is to produce results, which means that key events should be results-oriented. We must therefore focus on both performance and results in appraisals. The playing field is level when everyone is measured against results. *(Ren Zhengfei: Continuously Improving Per Capita Efficiency and Building a High-performance Corporate Culture, 2004)*

We cannot simply measure competence when assessing and promoting employees. We also need to look at performance and results. The assessment of integrity is largely influenced by managers' personal preferences and the limitations of their perspectives. Performance and results are concrete and objective. We have requirements relating to responsibilities and results for all our senior managers. We always look at results before reviewing the actual process for producing them and examining whether key events reflect competence. *(Ren Zhengfei: Speech at the Meeting to Convey the Main Ideas of the Human Resources Conference, 2002)*

I think the key event-based appraisal is important, but we cannot base our conclusions solely on a certain event. We must appraise employees through multiple rounds and multiple inputs. We must not set key event-based appraisals against appraisals that focus on results and responsibilities. I am not interested in the key events of employees who achieve no results. *(Ren Zhengfei: Speech at the Training Session for Managers, 2003)*

We must stick to an appraisal system that is oriented towards results and responsibilities. Managers at all levels only serve for fixed terms, and must achieve specific goals. Those who fail their work report assessments will be removed or demoted. We will implement an accountability system that covers managers at all levels. Those who fail to complete their tasks must be held accountable. Appraisals will not make outstanding employees leave. Even if they suffer setbacks temporarily during appraisals due to internal or external factors, they will eventually be recognized if they continue to work hard. In addition, we must stick to fixed-term contracts for employees. This will allow new people to come in and replace those who are no longer fit for their positions. We must check the key events of those who have done their job well to identify future leaders and give them opportunities for further development. *(Ren Zhengfei: Speech at the Training Session for Managers, 2003)*

Appraisals for all levels of managers must be oriented towards results and responsibilities. We will gradually roll out a pilot program for key event-based appraisals for middle and senior managers, especially senior managers, to improve their leadership and influence. *(Ren Zhengfei: Key Points for Management, 2003–2005)*

We must stick to an appraisal system that is based on results and responsibilities. Managers who fail to meet C&Q requirements must be demoted, removed, or dismissed. Our company will not always succeed amid increasingly fierce market competition. We therefore cannot tolerate a bloated organization or unqualified managers. *(Ren Zhengfei: Continuously Improving Per Capita Efficiency and Building a High-performance Corporate Culture, 2004)*

Huawei's value orientation focuses on results and responsibilities rather than competence. Managers must have successful field experience. One's competence will be recognized only if it helps contribute to the company. The playing field is level when everyone is measured against results. *(Ren Zhengfei: Speech About Employee Skills Exams, 2009)*

We must remain dedicated. The tortoise in *The Tortoise and the Hare* is a symbol of persistent effort – this spirit must endure at Huawei. This tortoise spirit also means that our efforts and dedication should be sensible. We don't need employees who are too excited because this does not create extra value. Instead, we need controlled passion that allows our employees to work hard and methodically. Value creation must be the yardstick that we use to measure everything we do. *(Ren Zhengfei: Applying the Spirit of the Tortoise to Catch up with the Dragon Spacecraft, 2013)*

2.1.2 Emphasizing contributions

In our compensation system, we base compensation and rewards on employees' contributions and ability to contribute continuously. We can provide more opportunities for employees who are capable of leading and uniting people, but we will not promote or reward them until they have made contributions in their new roles. We don't give anyone a pay raise simply because he or she has potential. *(Ren Zhengfei: Guidelines for Human Resources Management Transformation, 2005)*

In our appraisal system, we emphasize contributions, productivity, and results. The value created by employees can be direct or indirect, tangible or intangible. *(Ren Zhengfei: Speech at a Meeting for Directors of HR Branches, 2005)*

Only contributions that create value for customers count. We must eliminate redundant work that does not create value for customers and dismiss employees who pretend to work hard but create no value. *(Source: EMT Meeting Minutes No. [2008] 018)*

2.1.3 Focusing on business value

Our goal is to cultivate business people, not scientists. As a result, our value assessment system must focus on results rather than on competence. *(Ren Zhengfei: Speech at a Meeting with New Hires, 1997)*

Huawei's ultimate goal is to hit its financial targets. The business performance of product lines, regions, and departments will be reflected ultimately in their short-, mid-, and long-term financial targets. *(Source: EMT Meeting Minutes No. [2006] 030)*

Providing effective services for customers is the direction we should follow at work. It is also one of the criteria for value assessments. Departments, processes, and employees that cannot create value for customers are redundant. *(Ren Zhengfei: Speech at Huawei Market Conference, 2008)*

2.1.4 Focusing on the most important issue

A serious problem at Huawei is that we are not appropriately assessing employees. For instance, the production department tests assembly line workers on *The Huawei Charter*. Those who don't do well in the exam may be dismissed. This is ridiculous. If junior employees take their work seriously and adhere to work ethics, they are following *The Huawei Charter*. *(Ren Zhengfei: Speech at the Meeting for the Fourth Revision of The Huawei Charter, 1997)*

Management includes three important elements: improving quality, reducing costs, and increasing overall productivity. Business units have three goals: higher potential, higher profits, and consistency in overall corporate interests. If we fully unleash the potential of business units, they will increase profits. It is therefore a good sign if Huawei employees want to join our subsidiary, Huawei Telecommunications. *(Ren Zhengfei: Remarks at a Meeting with Manufacturing Staff of Huawei Telecommunications, 1997)*

By establishing business units, we aim to put in place a resource-sharing system and develop new sources of growth. When making decisions on appraisal elements, we need to decide which need to be controlled and which do not. The following considerations are essential: (1) enabling independent operations and expansion; (2) focusing on key factors and establishing a unified and effective system for adjustments, controls, and appraisals. Regarding key factors, we must study how to facilitate their growth rather than manage them rigidly or let them get out of control. Enabling independent operations allows expansion. If business units don't grow faster than the parent company, there is no need to establish them. There are many success stories in various countries that we can learn from. *(Ren Zhengfei: Meeting Minutes About The Huawei Charter (III), 1997)*

From its inception, Huawei has never pursued perfection. If we do this, we will lose our momentum. We need to implement policies once we understand their major components, and gradually optimize them during implementation. One feature of Huawei's corporate culture is that we don't pursue perfection when we have new sources of growth. If we do, then we cannot generate growth. Therefore, we do not need perfect policies, but rather ones that are practical and feasible. *(Source: Out of Chaos, 1998)*

During the appraisals of employees and managers, we regularly assess their performance, work attitude, and competence based on clearly defined goals and requirements. Performance appraisals focus on improvements, and should be specific. Appraisals of an employee's work attitude and competence focus on long-term performance, and should be general. *(Source: The Huawei Charter, 1998)*

We must not consider too many indicators at the same time, and should instead stay focused. Currently, our main focus is on office and travel expenses. We should not adopt a one-size-fits-all approach when reducing expenses. Instead, we should ensure that office and travel expenses are kept at a reasonable level and used effectively. *(Ren Zhengfei: Speech at the EMT ST Meeting, 2006)*

Our appraisals of ordinary employees are too complicated, and some lack specific goals. Employees should learn their jobs well and be appraised based on how well they have done their jobs. Currently, they are burdened by too many appraisals. We must reduce this burden by removing appraisal elements that are unrelated to employees' core work. *(Ren Zhengfei: Speech at the UK Representative Office, 2007)*

We must eliminate complex HR appraisals. Some managers ask employees to fill out many work report forms when they are not working in the same office. This is sometimes reasonable; for example, in the case of work logs for sales personnel. However, some managers don't have many subordinates but still ask them to complete work logs every day. This increases costs. I think it is a waste of time and money to do this simply for the sake of doing it. I will make sure that the Human Resource Management Department is made aware of this problem. We must get rid of complex appraisal systems. We have to make it clear that the purpose of appraisals is to help achieve business success. It is not worth conducting appraisals merely for their own sake. *(Ren Zhengfei: Speech at the PSST Managers' Meeting, 2008)*

Appraisals must not be too frequent and we must not spend too much time on them. If we don't focus on working hard, we will face many problems in the future. *(Ren Zhengfei: Speech at the EMT ST Meeting, 2010)*

The theme of appraisals should be simple and clear; they should not include too many dimensions or elements. In the past, more than 30 items were included in our appraisals, which made employees simply follow convention. This is not what we want. The major purpose of our appraisals is to motivate employees to create value and contribute to the company. There is no need to assess anything else. *(Ren Zhengfei: Speech at the*

Meeting Regarding the Report on the Pilot Program for Absolute Appraisals of Junior Employees in Operational Positions, 2012)

Performance appraisals should not contain too many KPIs. Key event-based appraisals are used to select managers. There is no need to consider key events during bonus assessments as long as the final goal has been achieved. If an outstanding employee is assessed using too many KPIs, he or she might feel discouraged and will only focus on hitting KPI targets. Therefore, the number of KPIs must be reduced. *(Ren Zhengfei: Remarks at a Meeting with Staff of the Guangzhou Representative Office, 2013)*

2.1.5 Differentiating assessment criteria based on job levels

We require our junior employees to be pragmatic, and provide those who are pragmatic with appropriate rewards and positions. If we overemphasize the wolf-like aggressiveness required in middle and senior managers throughout the company, we will be unable to lay a solid foundation for overall development. Likewise, if we overemphasize the pragmatic attitude required in junior employees throughout the company, the company will stagnate and lose its vitality. We seek to strike a balance under most circumstances, but must take different approaches on this issue. *(Ren Zhengfei: Speech at the Meeting for the Fourth Revision of The Huawei Charter, 1997)*

We must adhere to two principles when establishing appraisal criteria for junior-level positions: First, we must focus on performance and assess employees based on their work results. Second, we need to make it clear that employees must be assessed only on the fields they work in. We must have a management mechanism in place to prevent junior employees from straying from their specific fields. For employees with a Master's degree or PhD, we advocate diverse capabilities with a focus on specific fields. However, we encourage junior employees with lower-level academic degrees to love what they do and become experts in their given fields. *(Ren Zhengfei: Speech at the Meeting on the Project Report for the Value Assessment System for Junior Employees, 1998)*

The focus of employee appraisals must vary with job levels, responsibilities, and customer needs. To ensure sustainable corporate growth, executives must strive to achieve long-term performance goals, contribute to the company's long-term interests, develop teams and a pool of potential managers, and raise leadership capabilities. Middle and senior managers must strive to achieve mid- and long-term performance goals, effectively implement business plans, manage teams, and develop managers and employees to continuously boost team performance. Junior and middle employees must strive to achieve short-term performance goals, standardize activities for achieving goals, complete tasks, and continuously improve performance. *(Source: Regulations on Performance Management at Huawei (Provisional), 2007)*

We need to learn from the experience of our industry peers and assess whether our senior managers' long-term goals are reasonable. Appraisal criteria should vary with managers' levels. We also need to build an appraisal system that balances the short-term and long-term goals of junior, middle, and senior employees. Appraisals should direct senior managers towards achieving their current business goals, and more importantly, towards achieving long-term goals. To prevent senior managers from focusing solely on short-term goals, we must take improvement measures such as integrating annual appraisals with mid- and long-term appraisals, linking on-the-job work reports to exit interviews, and combining supervisor comments with committee comments. By studying and formulating specific solutions – for example, job management, bonus incentives, and non-monetary incentives – we will optimize our incentive mechanism for senior managers and direct them towards achieving long-term goals. We also need to optimize the accountability mechanism for senior managers. *(Source: HRC[1] Meeting Minutes No. [2010] 053)*

We prioritize work results over job skills when appraising junior employees' performance. *(Ren Zhengfei: Speech at the Meeting Regarding the Report on the Pilot Program for Absolute Appraisals of Junior Employees in Operational Positions, 2012)*

We should urge administrative teams (ATs) to delegate authority, improve team training, and increase supervision over execution. The authority to approve the deployment of junior and middle managers will be delegated down from the AT of a division. Managers will manage two organizational levels below them, except key positions and special positions. Manager appointment procedures will also be optimized. The authority to approve organizational restructuring will be delegated down from divisions, and the pace of delegation will be controlled based on specific scenarios. The authority to take disciplinary action against economic violations of the

Business Conduct Guidelines (BCGs) committed by employees and managers below a certain level will be directly delegated to the Disciplinary and Supervisory Sub-committee of the HRC. Offices of ethics and compliance (OECs) at all levels can be authorized to handle non-economic violations and internal conflicts. *(Source: EMT Resolution No. [2012] 042)*

We must ensure the separation of authority when appraising executives' performance. To that end, we will adopt an authorization mechanism in which rotating CEOs appraise the performance of BG^2 CEOs and presidents of the Joint Committee of Regions and the Group Finance Management Department. The Executive Committee under the Board of Directors will appraise the performance of heads of other level-1 organizations. *(Source: Executive Committee Resolution No. [2012] 002)*

2.1.6 Prioritizing goals

People normally value success over achieving goals. This is the incorrect management approach, because overemphasizing success prevents employees from taking on challenging tasks. Therefore, we have adopted a goal-based appraisal system. If an employee achieves a goal, but does not develop a successful product, managers should be held accountable. Individual employees should be recognized and promoted if they achieve their assigned goals. If we merely emphasize success, employees may not commit themselves to making the best possible products. As Huawei is a young company that lacks experience, many of our products do not reach the production stage. However, R&D engineers who develop these products still receive promotions, salary increases, and bonuses. These engineers are not at fault, as the decisions are made by managers. This helps establish a favorable internal mechanism to drive our development. *(Ren Zhengfei: Seizing Opportunities, Adjusting Management Systems, and Meeting Challenges, 1997)*

The problem of unequal rights and responsibilities will always exist, because it is difficult to clearly define the responsibilities, rights, and interests of a department during the course of development. This is a very common problem, especially when the company is developing rapidly. Our managers are inexperienced, because most of them have been promoted from professional positions. Their management skills and attitudes still need improvement. I think it's not good for a department to assert that something is not its responsibility, or to divide responsibilities too clearly. A department that does so is not looking at issues from the company's perspective. Our goal is to resolve problems rather than divide responsibilities. *(Ren Zhengfei: Remarks at a Meeting with Employees, 2000)*

At the end of last year, we reviewed a document on payment collection and cash flow management. The document proposed that internal responsibilities should be clearly defined for different departments on a case-by-case basis. At the EMT meeting, I completely opposed this idea, because it would result in nothing but internal conflicts. Instead, we just need to assign responsibilities to different departments proportionately. The collection of payments increased notably in the first half of this year, indicating that this approach has begun to bear fruit. All our efforts should be focused on productivity rather than on the division of responsibilities. In future appraisals, all departments must undertake responsibilities and share benefits based on achieving ultimate goals. Setting phase-specific appraisals without considering end-to-end processes is not permitted. *(Ren Zhengfei: Speech at the Mid-year Market Conference, 2006)*

[1]   HRC stands for Human Resources Committee. It is one of the four committees under Huawei's Board of Directors.

[2]   BG stands for Business Group. Business Groups were established by Huawei from the customer perspective during its organizational transformation in 2011.

2.2 Methods and Criteria for Value Assessments

2.2.1 Attaching equal importance to sales revenue, profits, and cash flow

In performance appraisals, we must attach equal importance to sales revenue, profits, and cash flow to support continued survival and development. If we simply pursue greater sales, things may get out of control; if we only focus on profits, we may compromise our future; and if we don't evaluate cash flow, we may only have book profits, which are not actual profits. Cash is to a company like rice is to a person. Without cash for even a few days, Huawei will starve to death. *(Ren Zhengfei: Speech at the EMT ST Meeting, 2006)*

We should not overemphasize any single indicator in our appraisals, because doing so will not guarantee our company's sustainable development. If we only focus on sales revenue, some regional offices and product lines will do whatever they can to get strategic subsidies and price cuts. We usually see this behavior in incompetent sales people and managers, because they can only sell products at low prices. That way, the more we sell, the sooner we will perish. Focusing on profits alone will not work either. We may easily hit profit targets, such as 10 billion US dollars or more, if we abandon our long-term strategic investments, for example, by laying off R&D employees. However, doing so would be at the expense of our future. Therefore, we should assign appropriate weights to sales revenue and profits during appraisals. Emphasizing both sales revenue and profits is not enough. We also need to strengthen cash flow management. We may have good contract terms, high prices, and high book profits, but if customers make payments years later, we may have no cash on hand and will gradually collapse. Therefore, it is critical to control and manage cash flow. *(Ren Zhengfei: Speech at the Mid-year Market Conference, 2006)*

In the first two decades since Huawei's inception, the market was large and profits were high. At that time, we focused on scale as it guaranteed profits. However, we have adjusted this practice. Now, we require every representative office, every region, and every product line to focus on positive cash flow, reasonable profits, and improvements in employee efficiency. I believe significant changes will take place over the next three years. If we continue to be scale-oriented, the company will spin out of control. Hitting our profit targets should be our ultimate goal. *(Ren Zhengfei: Remarks at a Meeting with Senior Managers at PMS, 2009)*

2.2.2 Setting departmental KPIs based on the company's strategic goals

KPIs should be based on our strategic goals, and departments must not set their own. Every department should play its part in increasing product coverage, market share, and growth rate. Our strategic goals can be achieved only after they are broken down into management and service targets. This can be compared to flood control in China. Provinces along the Yangtze River should not seek to control floods separately, but work together to achieve the overall goal. *(Ren Zhengfei: Do Not Be a Temporary Hero, 1998)*

All employees should share responsibility for achieving the goals critical to the company's survival and development. Otherwise, it will be impossible for us to succeed. So we have now adopted a new KPI system under which all employees share the pressures of crises. We will disband departments and demote managers that do not involve themselves in this process. *(Ren Zhengfei: Speech at the Q3 Marketing Meeting, 1999)*

By asking all our senior managers to sign a Personal Business Commitment (PBC), we've broken down the company's KPIs level by level. We focus on results and responsibilities during appraisals, and jointly share the pressures from market competition. *(Ren Zhengfei: Work Report to the Board of Directors Regarding the Completion of the 2003 Business and Budget Goals, 2003)*

Teams in each department must share departmental KPIs rather than setting their own. Individuals need to play a part in fulfilling department responsibilities. We must clearly define responsibilities while strengthening synergies. *(Source: EMT Resolution No. [2005] 010)*

2.2.3 Contributing more than you cost

We must emphasize each individual's contributions to the increase of capital. Each additional employee must create additional value. *(Ren Zhengfei: Guidelines for Human Resources Management Transformation, 2005)*

We distribute value based on individual contributions rather than individual needs or the industry average. In addition, we need to work out a reasonable ratio between compensation for labor and capital gains. *(Ren Zhengfei: Guidelines for Human Resources Management Transformation, 2005)*

Don't measure ordinary employees using standards for managers – we only select those who identify with our core values and contribute more than others as managers. However, we only require ordinary employees to abide by the company's rules and regulations, and pay them based on their contributions. We will ask those who contribute less than what they cost to leave. *(Ren Zhengfei: Adapting the Appraisal System for Managers to Challenges Facing the Transforming Industry, 2006)*

Everyone must fully understand what role they can play in contributing to our company's total value. If they can't add value or contribute, their roles are not needed. Per capita efficiency is a broad concept. It can't resolve all our problems, and we must therefore shift to improving efficiency and focus on input-to-output ratios. The same is true for contributions. If we solely focus on contributions, everyone will claim that they have contributed. The point is whether your contributions are greater than your cost, and add value to our company. Every process, every position, and every meeting must add value. *(Ren Zhengfei: Speech at the HRC Meeting, 2009)*

We only value employees who are good at their job and contribute more than they cost. As to those who are not competent in their current job but have a very positive work attitude, we can move them to lower-level positions with lower salaries if they are willing to accept such an arrangement. We will retain those who contribute more than they cost and dismiss those who don't. *(Source: EMT Resolution No. [2009] 016)*

2.2.4 Increasing per capita efficiency through sustainable and profitable growth

We need to optimize our organizational structure and adjust our workforce structure. In the next one to two years, we will have to downsize support functions and reduce the number of support staff. This may help us dramatically increase our per capita efficiency. *(Source: EMT Meeting Minutes No. [2008] 037)*

We need to analyze the necessity of each position from field offices to the HQ based on our processes, remove all redundant process activities and organizations, and consolidate departments with overlapping functions. To enable functional departments to provide better support and services for field offices, we will replace HQ staff who don't have field experience with those who do. *(Source: EMT Resolution No. [2009] 002)*

Sustainable and profitable business growth is a major way to increase per capita efficiency. Measures taken to do this must support business development. We need to constantly improve organizational efficiency and mobilize existing human resources, instead of simply laying off employees. *(Source: EMT Resolution No. [2009] 002)*

Per capita efficiency should increase at the same pace as business scale. Excessively low requirements for per capita efficiency will inevitably lead to a bloated organization. We should not set the same improvement targets for per capita efficiency across the company; instead, we should set targets based on the development and management needs of the company, business units, and support functions. Then we can ensure the required staff are in place to promote sustainable development for our fast-growing businesses, and increase the per capita efficiency for our mature businesses or businesses where growth is sluggish. Moreover, we should boost per capita efficiency in the HQ and support functions. *(Source: EMT Resolution No. [2008] 029)*

Starting in 2009, we need to ensure that headcount grows at a slower rate. During staff planning and management, we should focus on raising efficiency – both organizational and individual efficiency – to ensure that we fully unleash the potential of existing employees. We should rely on effective management instead of simply increasing headcount to support business development. *(Source: EMT Resolution No. [2008] 029)*

During our current organizational restructuring, we should prioritize market opportunities over per capita efficiency. It doesn't make much sense if we only emphasize per capita efficiency. The reason is this: Based on our business performance this year, per capita efficiency will increase as long as we don't recruit new people. But in this case, we may not achieve much business growth. The measures we take to increase per capita efficiency must also support sustainable growth. So we need to think strategically and focus on business growth rather than merely on per capita efficiency. Otherwise, we will be doomed to fail. *(Ren Zhengfei: Speech at the Regular Meeting of the Reserve Pool, March 25, 2009)*

We need to maintain a flexible HR management system. And we also need to make adjustments and transitions while expanding and moving forward. We can't afford to stop in order to change. *(Ren Zhengfei: Speech at the Regular Meeting of the Reserve Pool, March 25, 2009)*

When I say we shouldn't increase headcount, I mean that we need to downsize support functions and reduce the number of support staff. However, we should make sure we have enough employees for our field teams. Also, when downsizing support functions, we have to make reasonable decisions based on facts. *(Ren Zhengfei: Speech at the Regular Meeting of the Reserve Pool, March 25, 2009)*

2.3 Misconceptions about Value Assessments

2.3.1 Basing compensation on academic degrees, cognitive abilities, length of employment, interpersonal relationships, or pretense of hard work

As a company, we pursue business success rather than advanced technology. This is different from academic research at universities. Those who you think are knowledgeable may not earn good money at Huawei, but those who you think are not so knowledgeable may be paid well. The reason for this lies in our value assessment system, which is different from that adopted at universities. Our system is based on business success whereas theirs is based on academic achievements. *(Ren Zhengfei: Meeting Minutes, 1996)*

We need to cultivate business people, not professors. We don't encourage our employees to publish academic papers. We need to adjust our value assessment system. We should give pay raises to those who create profits, not to those who author academic papers. *(Ren Zhengfei: Speech at the Huawei Telecommunications Work Meeting, 1997)*

We assess employees based on their contributions rather than on their ambitions. *(Ren Zhengfei: Remaining United to Help Huawei Scale New Heights, 1999)*

We pay our employees based on their contributions and their ability to contribute continuously, not on their academic degrees, length of employment, titles, or interpersonal relationships. Cognitive abilities are not a C&Q criterion. Instead, we value dedication, contributions, and potential. *(Source: EMT Meeting Minutes No. [2005] 054)*

There are two ways for employees to change their destiny at Huawei. One is working hard and the other is making outstanding contributions. Contributions can be implicit or explicit, can be long-term or short-term, and can even be unknown or misunderstood. Cognitive abilities are not considered in our value assessments. At Huawei, we don't recognize dumplings in the teapot – employees who fail to contribute to the company even though they are highly capable. Therefore, our employees should work hard and create value for the company. Only then will they be able to receive good results during assessments. *(Ren Zhengfei: Speech at a Meeting with Huawei University and the Strategic Reserve Pool, 2005)*

Acquiring knowledge is the process of preparing oneself for work. So this is a part of employees' own responsibility, and they therefore must invest in this area. *(Ren Zhengfei: Speech at the Regular Meeting of the Reserve Pool, June 24, 2009)*

2.3.2 Valuing hard work that creates no value

Many people like to talk about how hard they work when presenting their work reports. I don't like that. I don't care how hard you work. What I care is how much you have accomplished. If you don't accomplish anything, then all your work is meaningless. So you should emphasize your performance in your work reports, because good performance is the basis of survival and development. *(Ren Zhengfei: Speeches During the Early Years of Huawei, 1996)*

In a market economy, we must be market-oriented. This is a direction we should always follow. Everything we do should be directed by the market. For instance, it is meaningless to work really hard to scrub coal and make it white because it creates no value. Meeting market needs will always be our goal. *(Ren Zhengfei: Having a Sense of Service and Branding, and Showing Team Spirit, 1996)*

We need to improve management efficiency and must not work overtime for its own sake. *(Ren Zhengfei: Comments at the Meeting with New Employees of the 22nd Session of 2000)*

We need to improve efficiency and we don't encourage working overtime. Instead, we should be clear about what to do and what not to do. This will save us a lot of money. Think about the functions our R&D engineers have developed. Less than 22% have actually been used. The ratio is much smaller – less than 1% – in the case of telephones. But the problem is that our engineers are obsessed with advanced technologies because they lead to promotions and pay raises. As a result, no one is willing to research simple but commonly used technologies. If we cut 20% of the useless work, we can save a lot of money and won't need to work overtime as much. *(Ren Zhengfei: Timely, Accurate, High Quality, and Low Cost Delivery Calls for Professional Process-compliant CFOs, 2009)*

2.3.3 Being too technology-oriented in R&D

When researching new products, we need to prioritize commercial value and benefits over creativity and uniqueness. In other words, we should emphasize the practical benefits that our products offer to customers rather than how novel or cutting-edge they are. We need to establish a customer-oriented R&D system. *(Ren Zhengfei: Speech at the Meeting Regarding the Report of the R&D and Marketing & Sales Departments, 1996)*

For a long time, our R&D department has focused on technology and research, and has neglected management and culture. If the department does not assess value the same way as the company, how can we achieve synergy? We have to remain united to compete in the international market. Only when all our departments share one common culture can we create synergy. For instance, we can't simply develop new products while ignoring problems faced by existing customers, or optimize existing products while neglecting the problems with those already deployed in customer networks. Such behavior is a result of an incorrect orientation in our value assessment system. *(Ren Zhengfei: Articles During the Early Years of Huawei, 1997)*

Huawei aims to cultivate business people who have a deep understanding of products and customers. Our aim is not to turn out professors. Those who are obsessed with new, cutting-edge technologies but don't pay attention to customer needs can never become successful business people. *(Ren Zhengfei: Speech Before the Appointment of New R&D Managers, 1997)*

We must focus on customer needs – quality comes first, followed by functions and then technology. Customers view good products as having high quality, stable functions, and relatively advanced technologies. We should determine salaries and bonuses based on employee contributions, rather than on technologies. *(Ren Zhengfei: Speech at the Meeting with the R&D Managers of Huawei Technologies and Avansys, 2001)*

We can't afford to be fanatical about technology. I once analyzed the possible factors that may lead to the fall of Huawei and Lucent, and my conclusion was that we needed to be customer-oriented rather than technology-oriented. So last year we started restructuring Huawei, which turned out to be the correct decision. Several years ago, we invested a lot of money in promoting our cutting-edge products. However, about seven or eight months later, our competitors launched similar products and their prices were 10% lower. This 10% was actually equal to the cost we spent promoting these advanced products. This case indicates that our advanced products didn't bring about the benefits we expected, but instead paved the way for our competitors. In a network society, existing technology is spreading rapidly and new technology is emerging all the time. However, our new technology is not translated into customer needs, but instead benefits our competitors. So we shouldn't overemphasize technology, but instead focus on customer needs. *(Ren Zhengfei: Comments at a Meeting with Staff of Avansys, 2001)*

Technology is important. There is no doubt about it. But meeting customer needs is more important, which involves many processes and technologies. It's not easy to develop products that are simple and sell well. Everyone should understand that although technology is very important, we can't afford to overemphasize it. *(Ren Zhengfei: Corporate Development Should Focus on Meeting the Current Needs of Customers, 2002)*

We should remain business-oriented rather than technology-oriented in our restructuring. The same is true of our assessment system. *(Ren Zhengfei: Speech at the Meeting of the R&D Management Committee and the Q3 Meeting of Marketing & Sales, 2002)*

When developing products and assessing value, we can't solely focus on technology. If someone is really good at high tech but can't develop products that meet customer needs, then he or she is not contributing to the company. So we can't assess employees based solely on technology, or the company will collapse. *(Ren Zhengfei: Still Waters Run Deep: Continuously Improving Ourselves Based on Customer Needs, 2002)*

During value assessments, we shouldn't think that only those who can develop cutting-edge technologies can receive high salaries. Instead, those who can develop simple products that sell well should receive high salaries and be promoted to managerial positions. For example, digital cameras produced in Japan seem to contain no cutting-edge technologies, but are the most popular around the world. Why? Do they really involve no technology? Of course not. Technology is neither a theory nor a function. Instead, it is a combination of techniques, materials, and ideas from many different domains. Huawei needs engineers who can develop products that sell well, rather than scientists who simply develop functions that are not needed. *(Ren Zhengfei: Corporate Development Should Focus on Meeting the Current Needs of Customers, 2002)*

A mistake often made by our R&D team is focusing too much on whether someone has strong technical skills. I don't care about technical skills; I only care about the person's contributions. Developing a simple product that sells well is a contribution. *(Ren Zhengfei: Speech at the Meeting Regarding the ISC³ Project Report, 2003)*

2.3.4 Being too manager-oriented

Good managers emphasize facts, stick to principles, and look out for their subordinates. They don't do things simply to please their managers. We need to watch out for those who try their best to please their managers, because they are looking out for their own interests rather than the company's. We've seen this all too often before. *(Ren Zhengfei: Being Mentally Dedicated and Trying Your Best to Successfully Complete Your Work, 1996)*

I think a serious problem we have is that many employees are not customer-oriented. They are guided by their managers' opinions rather than customer needs. They will do anything that their managers request, even if it's wrong. That way, they don't have to assume any responsibility, because their managers will be held accountable if something goes wrong. This is a serious problem. If we don't change this, we will cease being customer-oriented and our company will fail. *(Source: EMT Meeting Minutes No. [2008] 021)*

We need to improve our appraisal criteria and base appraisals on the value employees create for customers, rather than on managers' opinions. *(Source: EMT Meeting Minutes No. [2008] 021)*

2.3.5 Setting job levels based on exam results

You give pay raises to those who do well in exams and ignore those who do their jobs well. This is wrong because the latter will not be motivated to improve their job quality. We should appraise employees based on what they can do rather than what they know. You never promote those who walk the walk, but often give pay raises to those who talk the talk. If we don't correct this, Huawei will end up being nothing more than a lark – only good at singing. *(Ren Zhengfei: Speech to the Training Center Heads Regarding Huawei Telecommunications, 1998)*

Employees are expected to contribute to the company and we need to compensate and reward them based on their results and responsibilities. We should never appraise employees based solely on their exam results. Employees should develop their competences and skills during their spare time at their own expense. When they possess certain competences and skills, they will be able to make contributions and then they will be paid accordingly. *(Ren Zhengfei: Speech About Employee Skills Exams, 2009)*

Huawei is a results-driven company, so we expect our employees to create value. It is wrong to promote someone who merely gets a good result in an exam but makes no contribution to the company. How can an employee who does well in an exam prove that he or she deserves a higher salary and bonus? *(Ren Zhengfei: Speech at the Regular Meeting of the Reserve Pool, June 24, 2009)*

---

3 ISC stands for Integrated Supply Chain. It is a set of models, concepts, and methodologies for managing the supply chain.

FAIRLY DISTRIBUTING VALUE

Huawei's value distribution system has been developed on the basis that labor, knowledge, entrepreneurship, and capital create a company's total value. Productivity determines the relations of production[1]. The contribution made by each element of value creation defines the structure of value distribution. The key is to balance labor-based and capital-based value distributions. Huawei considers organizational authority a distributable value, and prioritizes development opportunities and organizational authority in its value distribution system.

Huawei's value distribution system is oriented towards dedicated employees and high-performing teams. In addition, Huawei values the contributions of dedicated employees and rewards them accordingly. If employees work hard and are paid based on their contributions, they will believe in this system, and their values will become part of Huawei's corporate culture.

Compensation management, a primary method of distributing value, needs to address four major issues: what, how, how much, and affordability. "What" concerns the orientation of the company's compensation. Huawei compensates employees based on their contributions and does not recognize employees who have knowledge but are unable to use it to create value. "How" defines the roles of different types of compensation, such as salaries and bonuses. A compensation system works effectively only when it has a reasonable structure and clear positioning. "How much" is determined by both external and internal factors. Huawei needs to consider how big a gap should be set in employee rewards. In terms of affordability, Huawei needs to balance what is expected and what is feasible to ensure that compensation policies remain stable. The overriding principle is to make the HR policies fair, reasonable, and sustainable.

Huawei's value distribution system needs to manage various conflicts. These include conflicts between individuals and teams, labor and capital, fairness and efficiency, the short-term and the long-term, previous and current value contributors, and expectations and reality. Resolving and balancing conflicts can drive the company to move forward. According to Ren Zhengfei, Huawei needs to develop strong conflict-resolution capabilities. To maintain vitality, the company should alternately experience stability and instability, and balance and imbalance. This process is dissipative. A company can establish new advantages and a new state of stability and balance only when it dissipates its previous stability, balance, and advantages.

Non-monetary incentives are very important in that they complement monetary ones and satisfy the diverse needs of employees. To make full use of non-monetary incentives, Huawei needs to plan and build a robust system.

Chapter Three describes Huawei's guidelines on value distribution, how Huawei manages the conflicts that can arise, and what policies Huawei has implemented in this area.

---

[1] Relations of production refers to the sum total of social relationships that people must enter into, in order to survive, to produce and reproduce their means of life. Popularized by Karl Marx and Friedrich Engels.

3.1

Guidelines on Value Distribution

3.1.1 Giving more rewards to dedicated employees and value contributors

Huawei's value distribution system is designed to reward employees based on their contributions. We need to let everyone know that we value the contributions of dedicated employees and reward them accordingly. *(Source: Summary of the Speech by a Professor from China Renmin University at a Meeting with Shenzhen Institutional Reform Committee, 1997)*

Our compensation system must not turn our company into a charity for employees. If we have extra money, we can donate it to society. Employees have to earn money through hard work before they retire. If they don't work hard, we will have to ask them to leave no matter how talented they are. *(Ren Zhengfei: Survival Is Fundamental to an Enterprise, 2000)*

Our appraisal and incentive mechanisms must be oriented towards employees who are realistic and conscientious. At present, our company is still in a state of chaos. As the company continues to develop very rapidly, you may become excited, but I find it terrifying because our company may fall apart as a result. Therefore, it is very important for everyone to work hard and fulfill their responsibilities. *(Ren Zhengfei: Speech at the Preparatory Meeting for GSM^2 Production Capacity, 2000)*

A market economy prioritizes efficiency while also considering fairness. If we reverse this, society will become paralyzed, because there will be no engine for growth. To get rich, we must ensure that we have growth engines. To move forward, engines need driving forces, which mean differences in employee compensation and benefits. *(Ren Zhengfei: Speech at a Meeting for Directors of HR Branches, 2006)*

Our value distribution system is oriented towards dedicated employees and values contributors as we aim to fuel our growth engines. We must dare to break away from outdated conventions, and give more rewards to dedicated employees, employees with successful track records, and employees who have made contributions. We will identify employees who possess a sense of mission from among the high performers. If they are highly capable, we will make fast-track promotions available to them. Differences generate driving forces. For instance, differences in temperatures result in wind, and differences in altitude make water flow. We must motivate our best employees. To improve efficiency, we must fuel our engines to motivate them to move forward and remain dedicated. *(Ren Zhengfei: From "Philosophy" to Practice, 2011)*

If you maintain a low profile like Bian Que's[3] eldest brother and are not overly concerned about how much money you're making right now, you will eventually succeed and get what you deserve. *(Ren Zhengfei: Remarks at a Meeting with Staff of the Guangzhou Representative Office, 2013)*

3.1.2 Orientation towards forging ahead

When our HR management system is standardized and our corporate operations are mature, we will move away from the system initiated by Hay Group and begin innovating on our own. We will then bring in talented professionals who aim high but might be poor. They will not accept the status quo, nor will they confine themselves to existing conventions. They will drive a new round of transformation in our HR management system, and stimulate another round of growth for the company. This will not change our current policy. Instead, these new recruits will set an example for veteran employees and stimulate innovation. By injecting new blood into our company, we can motivate our slacking organization. Only then can we build an innovative system where no employees can maintain the status quo. Innovation comes in phases. After talented people join our company, our core values and value assessment system will change, veteran employees will learn from role models, and a stable system will form again. Without a well-organized system, innovation will be chaotic. At Huawei, there are employees who want an easy life, are not enterprising, and eventually become mediocre. The center of gravity is most stable at its lowest point. After stability is achieved, nobody wants change. This recurring cycle is hard to break, but we must free ourselves from the tragic cycle of success followed by failure. *(Ren Zhengfei: Survival Is Fundamental to an Enterprise, 2000)*

Our HR management transformation aims to encourage employees to forge ahead. With the help of Hay Group, we aim to develop a strong team that is courageous, tenacious, and able to achieve success. We won't select a well-coordinated gymnastics team that is full of attractive, strong, graceful, and agile people. Our goal is not to look good, but to succeed. Our positions, responsibilities, compensation, and benefits must be designed to support our business development. *(Ren Zhengfei: Guidelines for Human Resources Management Transformation, 2005)*

I have confidence in Huawei because we have established systems and mechanisms to guard against its collapse. I mainly focus on high performers. As long as these employees are motivated, others will automatically march forward, and the entire team will become increasingly effective. In that case, how can we lose? That's why I say we must forge ahead. The HR system should consider how to keep our teams dedicated. *(Ren Zhengfei: Human Resources Must Be Oriented Towards Forging Ahead and Refrain from Being Dogmatic and Rigid, 2009)*

We must create a mechanism that motivates excellent employees to move to subsidiaries rather than stay at the parent company. This mechanism should also encourage employees to sell their shares in the parent company and buy shares in our subsidiaries. This is the right mechanism for Huawei. *(Ren Zhengfei: Speech at the EMT ST Meeting, 2009)*

Faster salary increases and promotions should be made available to staff from field operating teams, followed by field support staff, and then support staff in back offices. For support staff in the field, we need to first unify bonus and then salary assessments. Then, everyone will go all out to succeed as a team. If a team fails to achieve its goals, no one will get anything. We must not emphasize that there are outstanding employees in a defeated team. Otherwise, some employees may not strive for success. *(Ren Zhengfei: Do Not Expand Blindly and Do Not Assume That We Are Already Strong Enough, 2012)*

In terms of financial resources, human resources, compensation, and bonuses, we need to shift from our current granting system to a Contribute and Share system. *(Ren Zhengfei: Comments at a Meeting with Managers from Finance, 2012)*

3.1.3 Rewarding dedicated employees

As we aim to use material wealth to strengthen our culture, we have adopted a long-term policy of rewarding dedicated employees. Through this, we have encouraged employee dedication and created a new corporate climate where our employees love their nation and company, in addition to their families and friends. *(Ren Zhengfei: Characteristics of Huawei's Development, 1996)*

At Huawei, we are exploring an internal incentive mechanism where value is distributed according to the factors of production. In this way, we can reasonably create and distribute wealth, and generate greater combined driving forces. We value the contributions of dedicated employees and reward them accordingly. Conflicts will arise in the process of value distribution, but we must not allow these conflicts to become unsolvable. Instead, we must transform them into a collaborative force that can drive our development. *(Ren Zhengfei: How Long Can Huawei Survive, 1998)*

We do not advocate that everyone is dedicated, but we continue to reward those who are based on their contributions. This commitment is not only included in our core values, but is also our company's basic policy for value distribution. *(Source: Out of Chaos, 1998)*

We have made it clear that there are only two ways for employees to change their fate at Huawei: dedication and contribution. If employees make contributions selflessly, we should value their contributions and reward them accordingly. *(Ren Zhengfei: Guidelines for Human Resources Management Transformation, 2005)*

"Staying customer-centric, inspiring dedication, and persevering" is a benefit-driven mechanism. To sustain our culture of inspiring dedication, we must reward our dedicated employees. We will not forget those who have a sense of mission and proactively contribute. That might be our corporate culture. We cannot build our culture and make it sustainable with empty talk. Instead, we must incorporate it into our appraisal system. *(Ren Zhengfei: From "Philosophy" to Practice, 2011)*

3.1.4 Receiving income from a single source

We seek to receive income from a single source. Our EMT has made it clear that the income of senior managers and key employees can only come from the salaries, incentives, bonuses, and other schemes offered by Huawei. Income from other sources is not allowed. We have established organizations and systems to prevent anyone at Huawei, from the most senior corporate officers down to the execution level, from destroying our collective interest through conflict-of-interest transactions for personal gain. Over the past two decades, we have mainly received income from a single source, and through this have formed a team of 150,000 employees who are united and dedicated to the company's success. I believe our HR policies will become more scientific if we continue to receive income from a single source. Consequently, our employees will become more passionate about their work. Then, there will be nothing that we can't achieve. *(Ren Zhengfei: Working Together Towards the Same End, Receiving Income from a Single Source, 2012)*

If we can work together towards the same end and receive income from a single source, Huawei will not fail. If we abandon these principles, we will probably fail. History tells us that if large companies begin to decline, few can reverse this trend through restructuring. To avoid this, we must exercise self-restraint, and remain united and dedicated. *(Ren Zhengfei: Working Together Towards the Same End, Receiving Income from a Single Source, 2012)*

3.1.5 Ensuring sustainable development

Prioritizing efficiency while considering fairness and sustainable growth is the basic principle of value distribution. *(Source: The Huawei Charter, 1998)*

At Huawei, we prioritize efficiency while considering fairness. We offer outstanding employees greater rewards, but we do not condone employees who behave improperly, break the law, or fail to exercise self-discipline after they become rich. We must create a culture that fosters moral integrity and encourages employees to comply with corporate regulations and national laws. We will not forgive employees who violate either. *(Ren Zhengfei: Remaining United to Help Huawei Scale New Heights, 1999)*

Our company must continue to survive, yet natural laws determine that all men must die. Even if it is not constrained by natural laws, a legal entity is constrained by social norms. Even if a person is not successful, he or she may still live a long life. An enterprise, however, cannot survive for even a week if it lacks key capabilities. If an enterprise can adapt to both natural laws and social norms, it may survive for centuries. Thus, we advocate seeking the truth based on facts. An enterprise must follow rules, which include natural laws and social norms, and constantly seek the truth during operations and management. We must understand and follow these rules. In the wild, the law of the jungle means that only the fittest survive. In the marketplace, this law also applies. Inside enterprises, survival of the fittest means that managers can be promoted or demoted based on their performance, employees can be recruited or dismissed, and compensation can be increased or decreased. *(Ren Zhengfei: Survival Is Fundamental to an Enterprise, 2000)*

To ensure our company's sustainable development, we must ensure that employee income does not grow faster than our business. *(Ren Zhengfei: Speech at the Meeting Regarding the Hay Pilot Project, 2000)*

We do not offer our managers lifelong tenure. Senior managers can be promoted or demoted based on their performance. When their tenure expires, they should be appraised by both the company and their colleagues through their work reports and C&Q applications for the next phase. Their compensation may be adjusted based on results. Some managers may complain as follows: "I work hard and perform well, and have integrity. Why can't I keep my position?" Standards change with the times, and others may progress more rapidly than you. To enable our company to survive and grow, we may not be able to keep you in your current position. A well-known Chinese story describes that you cannot locate a sword dropped overboard if you simply notch the side of the boat to mark where it happened. As a manager you cannot continue using the same standards when circumstances change. After all, the waves of the Yangtze River are pushed by the waves behind them. Without change, there would be no life. It is necessary to dismiss underperformers. The fixed-term system is a gentle way to dismiss underperformers. *(Ren Zhengfei: Continuously Improving Per Capita Efficiency and Building a High-performance Corporate Culture, 2004)*

For future survival, we must adapt our HR policies to the evolving macro environment. We must enhance our competitiveness to attract talent and our capability to endure business risks. We must be flexible. We need to prepare for crises even when our business is developing smoothly. When formulating policies, we must consider potential risks and not overpromise to our employees so as to avoid creating a heavy burden for the company. It is important to cultivate a sense of crisis within the company, and get everyone mentally prepared for potential crises. We will dismiss underperformers and demote unqualified managers, and we must get employees accustomed to this practice. *(Source: EMT Meeting Minutes No. [2007] 009)*

3.1.6 Promoting balanced development

If we only improve our strong areas, our weak areas will become even weaker and the company will fall apart. This is also true for managing managers. As long as there is an incentive mechanism in place, people will take positions in our weak areas. We must establish an incentive mechanism to select managers and regulate talent mobility. We will allocate certain people to you. If you rate them poorly, they will be demoted. I have no problem with that. However, we must adopt different policies for different positions. If your policies can only retain the same key staff year after year, your departments will eventually disappear. *(Ren Zhengfei: Speech at the Meeting Regarding the Report by the Technical Service Department on Its Organizational Structure, 1997)*

Why must we improve our company's weak areas? Across Huawei, we focus on R&D, marketing, and sales, but not inventory, goods receipt and delivery, teller, order, and other systems. Those untended systems are often our weakest areas. Regardless of how well the front end of the process performs, our efforts will be wasted if goods are not delivered. Therefore, we must establish unified value assessment and performance appraisal systems across our company. Only then can we move people around internally and develop in a balanced way. I'm not against focusing on technology, marketing, and sales. However, we also have to pay attention to other areas, because they also play significant roles in our business. Compared with an R&D engineer, a technical service engineer at the same job level may have stronger overall capabilities. If we do not recognize the importance of the after-sales service system, we will never attract talented people. Therefore, we must focus on balanced development rather than only on a few areas.

For example, shipping incorrect goods is all too common at Huawei, and these shipments have to be returned from overseas. Aren't freight and lost interest included in our costs? We must establish a balanced appraisal system. We can then improve our weaknesses and achieve balanced development – just like a wooden bucket can hold more water if the shortest wood strips are lengthened. In recent years, we have developed many good products that cannot be sold. This is a waste. Our failure to focus on building an appraisal system is a waste. To reduce the number of short wood strips in our bucket, we must establish a balanced value system and strive to enhance our company's overall core competencies. *(Ren Zhengfei: Huawei's Hard Winter, 2001)*

We must continue to strive for balanced development. We must gradually establish a unified, reasonable, and balanced performance appraisal system to ensure we grow in a balanced way. Through continuous improvement, we will boost our vitality and core competencies. Our ultimate goal of striking a balance is to enable our company to develop sustainably. *(Ren Zhengfei: Key Points for Management, 2002)*

Currently, we need to focus more on adjusting salaries for positions that have received little attention thus far. Previously, we focused on salary adjustments in R&D, marketing, and sales, but ignored other departments. As a result, there was a salary imbalance across departments. We must strike a balance between male and female employees, and also between different types of positions. Otherwise, some areas will become isolated and very vulnerable. We have resolved disparities in compensation and benefits for different types of positions. Previously, we compared positions across different departments, and applied discounted compensation and benefits for finance staff, even though they worked just as hard as staff from other departments. We have now adjusted this while allowing some disparities to remain across regions. In short, we must achieve balanced development. *(Ren Zhengfei: Comments at a Meeting with Staff in Venezuela, 2007)*

Huawei has grown into what it is today because of its relatively balanced distribution mechanism. Looking ahead, we must adopt diverse and multi-dimensional benefit distribution mechanisms. Support provided by different appraisal units must be reflected in the way we distribute benefits to ensure that the interests of different stakeholders in our company are balanced and that all units across the company collaborate to achieve business success. We should also identify potential risks involved in planning, budgeting, and accounting of business units to prevent the emergence of cliques with their own agendas. *(Source: EMT Meeting Minutes No. [2008] 014)*

Compensation and benefits should be the same for employees at the same level. However, we do believe that some positions are more important than others. If you think a position is more important when reviewing its responsibilities, you can rate it one level higher. We do not condone favoritism when distributing rewards. Rewards should be based on contributions. If we resort to positional favoritism, an imbalance in the development of our human resources will emerge, and employees will move to the favored positions. *(Ren Zhengfei: Speech at the Regular Meeting of the Reserve Pool, June 24, 2009)*

In the past, we consolidated trunks and weakened branches. Now, we need to change this practice and strengthen the balanced development of our company. What does consolidating trunks mean? Previously, we focused on marketing, sales, and R&D, and neglected the balanced development of our company, which resulted in even weaker branches. We currently prioritize technology over management, while Western companies do the opposite. From now on, we need to make changes. To achieve balanced development, our senior managers should take the lead and set an example. If you do not emphasize balanced development, how will our line managers and junior employees know what to do? We need to think outside of the box and pursue comprehensive development, or we will not be able to compete in the international market. *(Ren Zhengfei: Speech at the Senior Management Seminar, January 4, 2011)*

Value creation is more than just winning contracts. It also involves contract execution and management; services, including platform services; and support. We need to weigh each position during all-around evaluations. We haven't done so yet for field offices, so there are differences in the compensation packages of different employees. We need to change this. One measure is to make faster salary increases and promotions available to staff from field operating teams, followed by field support staff, and then support staff in back offices. This is just a general guideline with no regard to specific job types. *(Ren Zhengfei: Comments at a Meeting with Managers from Finance, 2012)*

3.1.7 Guarding against the threat from excessive benefit packages

After we get rich, we must guard against the potential problems of slowed momentum. Many nations that offer good welfare are suffering a heavy brain drain due to excessive taxation to fund the welfare system. We have to learn from them and develop sustainably. *(Ren Zhengfei: Spring of Northern Country, 2001)*

We must control our overall level of compensation, and guard against the threat to our company posed by high basic salaries and excessive benefit packages. *(Ren Zhengfei: Huawei-3COM's Report on Manager Development, Organizational Building, and Human Resource Policies, 2005)*

We must study why feudal dynasties in China were overthrown. Right after a new emperor overthrew the previous one, the cost of running the empire was very low because the new emperor did not yet have many children or grandchildren. In contrast, the cost of running the previous empire was high because the children of the former emperor formed a huge parasitic clan, which dragged the empire down. However, the new emperor would have dozens of children, each of whom would have a princely residence and was fed by the dynasty. Many generations later, his parasitic clan would become too large to bear. Civilians would not accept it, and they would overthrow the dynasty. So each dynasty shared the fate of the previous one. If Huawei follows this same path, it will go bankrupt in a few years. *(Ren Zhengfei: Guidelines for Human Resources Management Transformation, 2005)*

No customer is willing to pay higher prices to support greater rewards for our employees. We have to earn everything we want through hard work. Do not expect things to simply fall into your laps. If a company runs reward plans it cannot afford in the long run, it is like quenching thirst with poison. *(Ren Zhengfei: Digging In and Widening Out, 2009)*

---

[2]   GSM: Global System for Mobile Communications. This is a second-generation mobile networking standard that offers subscribers global roaming.

[3]   According to legend, Bian Que was the earliest Chinese physician. His eldest brother possessed great skill, and could identify symptoms as they appeared. Because of this, the brother did not become well-known. In contrast, Bian Que mainly cured patients who were visibly suffering, and thus became well-known. A rough Western equivalent is the idea that prevention is better than cure.

3.2 Handling Value Distribution Conflicts Appropriately

3.2.1 Unity and dissipation

Teamwork and collective dedication are the two perpetual driving forces behind Huawei's development. Department directors must take the lead in serving other departments, achieving unity, and promoting collective decision making. Unity is essential between new and veteran managers, between departments, and – in particular – in each department. We must unite as many people as possible. Those unwilling to collaborate with their teammates will be dismissed. *(Ren Zhengfei: Speech at the Inauguration Ceremony of Finance and Procurement Managers, 1996)*

Maintaining unity in our company depends on our common values and identity. We must use an economic lever to drive our company's growth, and use our value assessment principles to guide our employees in identifying with our corporate culture. *(Source: Minutes of the CEO's Staff Team Meeting, 1997)*

There are certainly conflicts between different segments. When tectonic plates collide, earthquakes and volcanic eruptions occur, and new continents emerge. Conflicts definitely exist between different segments at Huawei. How can we resolve them? The answer is a dissipative structure. Without this type of structure, some state-owned enterprises have devolved into chaos when control became lax, or grown too rigid when control became tight. Cohesiveness must be renewed. However, I do not think renewed cohesiveness can necessarily ensure the survival and development of an enterprise. Cohesiveness must dissipate. Otherwise, no energy will be generated.

We must identify the conflicts within our enterprise and study them further. *(Source: Out of Chaos, 1998)*

A company must have a dissipative structure in one sense or another. To maintain the company's vitality, we need to allow it to alternately experience stability and instability, and balance and imbalance. *(Ren Zhengfei: Speech at the Mobilization and Training Meeting Regarding Recruitment of New Graduates of 2001, 2000)*

A company has a dissipative structure. This means the company dissipates its energy between balance and imbalance, and between stability and instability. Huawei is currently doing well, so we must boldly dissipate what we have accumulated, and expose our faults so that we will be relaxed when others are in trouble. Success is possible if we are confident enough to reveal our mistakes to the outside world. *(Ren Zhengfei: Developing Managers Based on the Selection Mechanism, Reviewing and Streamlining Organizations Based on Processes, and Promoting the Open and Balanced Development of Organizations, 2011)*

So what is a dissipative structure? Jogging every day is dissipative. Why? Because you dissipate energy, turn it into muscle, and improve blood flow. If you dissipate all latent energy, you can avoid diabetes and obesity and instead remain slim and attractive. This is the simplest concept of a dissipative structure. Why does Huawei need a dissipative structure? Employees are committed to the company mostly because the company pays them too much, which is unsustainable. Therefore, we must first dissipate the commitment that arises from excessive pay, and establish this commitment by inspiring dedication and optimizing processes. There is a difference between the idea of working hard before being rewarded and the idea of making contributions after being rewarded. The first idea is better than the second. We must reward dedicated employees fairly and dissipate our latent energy to convert it into new momentum. *(Ren Zhengfei: E-mail No. [2011] 004 Success Is Not a Reliable Guide to Future Development)*

Those who cannot figure out the relationship between short-term investment and long-term returns cannot be generals. A general should have strategic awareness. How can someone be a general if he or she doesn't possess strategic awareness? This is my first point. Second, I want to revisit the concept of a dissipative structure. Huawei is doing quite well right now, but we must increase investment to dissipate our current advantages to create new ones. The world is declining, and the global economy may undergo a cyclical downturn. Statistics show that our growth is slowing, but we're still doing better than other companies. Our net profits this year are expected to reach US$2 billion to US$3 billion. We cannot hesitate when investing in the future. Not daring to invest in the future is a sign that we lack leaders, generals, and long-term strategies. *(Source: E-mail No. [2012] 35 Minutes of the Meeting Between Mr. Ren Zhengfei and Staff from the 2012 Laboratories)*

I previously introduced the second law of thermodynamics from physics into social science. The intention is to widen the compensation gap so that we will have a nucleus of several thousand people to lead the rest of us forward. We must always keep our team active to avoid an entropic death. We will never allow a black hole to exist in our organization. Slacking off is that black hole. We must not let it suck away our light, heat, and vitality. *(Ren Zhengfei: Applying the Spirit of the Tortoise to Catch up with the Dragon Spacecraft, 2013)*

3.2.2 The company and its stakeholders

Our organizational goal is to keep our company stable and secure by following the principle of interest sharing. Cooperation between people is actually based on interest distribution. If our initial aim were to get rich alone, we would have fewer partners, our organization would be less effective, and our profits would be lower. In that case, we would have a higher distributable percentage out of a smaller sum. When these two factors are multiplied, the outcome would be small. Our aim is to make the overall pie bigger and decrease our own slice of the pie. This adheres to the principle of interest sharing. *(Ren Zhengfei: Speech Regarding Corporate Organizational Goals and System Blueprints for the Future, 1994)*

If we have common interests, and if we properly resolve problems relating to interest sharing and unity, things will become a lot easier. *(Ren Zhengfei: Comments at a Meeting with Visiting Experts of the 863 Program[4], 1995)*

Huawei aims to create a community united by common interests. This community includes not only all our employees, but also our suppliers and customers. *(Ren Zhengfei: Comments to Staff of the Beijing Research Center, 1996)*

We translate labor, knowledge, and the entrepreneur's management contributions and risks taken into capital to reflect and reward the contributions made by each factor. We use shares to develop the nucleus of our company, effectively control our company, and achieve sustainable growth. We must explore how to transform knowledge into capital and how to develop a dynamic stock ownership system that can adapt well to technological and social changes. At Huawei, we have established an employee stock ownership plan. Model employees who identify with our corporate culture will benefit from the plan. As a result, we will create a group with vested interests within the company. We will gradually select the most talented and responsible employees to be part of this nucleus. *(Source: The Huawei Charter, 1998)*

The concept of a community united by common interests is reflected not only in our core values but also in our overall strategy. We must truly understand the meanings of employees, customers, and partners. Employees also include our investors. The people and organizations to whom we supply products and services are our customers. Suppliers, contracted companies, research institutes, financial institutions, HR services providers, agents, the media, government agencies, communities, and even some of our competitors are all our partners. We can motivate our organization when we have both a community united by common interests and a benefit-driven mechanism in place. Having a community united by common interests is key to Huawei's global success. *(Source: Out of Chaos, 1998)*

We should be kind to our suppliers. Managers at our headquarters should learn from the spirit and poise with which account managers deal with customers. Both customers and suppliers are our strategic partners. Future competition will be between supply chains. To become even stronger, we must establish a strategic supply chain. This does not mean that conflicts won't occur between strategic partners. It will be important to resolve these conflicts. We want reasonable prices and timely supplies, but we cannot achieve this by treating our suppliers with indifference or even hostility. Partnership does not mean concessions. Respect and humility are not signs of weakness. Our purpose is to achieve win-win results. We need strategies, poise, and principles, but at the same time we must be flexible. *(Ren Zhengfei: Speech at the Farewell Meeting for R&D Staff and Managers Sent to Field Offices, 2001)*

We must not be hostile to our competitors. They are important teachers for us. I made this clear at the Egypt Representative Office. We must recognize the importance of our competitors and be thankful to them rather than hostile. Their existence enables our company to continuously develop and progress, in the same way as hyenas maintain their vitality by hunting their prey and competing with other predators such as lions. If all lions died out, hyenas might become the prey of less competitive animals. When their environment is relaxed and easy, with no competition or crises, hyenas may become listless, slack, dispirited, and possibly extinct. Huawei has become what it is today because of the pressures of competition from rivals both inside and outside of China, who have chased us every step of the way. These pressures have driven us to relentlessly improve. Were it not for these pressures, Huawei might have become less vigilant, slacked off, and fallen apart. Therefore, we must be kind to our competitors. But if they aim to snatch our food, how can we be kind to them? To live through a cold winter, they also need food. If we don't spare some food for them, how can they survive? Helping them survive also helps ourselves, because they are the ones compelling us to make progress in the future. *(Ren Zhengfei: Speech at the Farewell Meeting for R&D Staff and Managers Sent to Field Offices, 2001)*

We must be adept at making allies. In today's world of cut-throat competition, we'd rather suffer a loss than let our allies suffer. We can afford a loss but our allies can't – it might mean their death. As long as our allies do not compete with us or harm our interests, we will protect their interests. As prices continue to fall, our agents' interests may decrease. We need to know how to protect our allies, because we need them. Once spring comes, they will be sufficiently energized to win purchase orders. Accordingly, we will be able to recover our losses. *(Ren Zhengfei: Acting According to Universal Laws, Giving Full Play to Core Teams, Constantly Improving Per Capita Efficiency, and Working Together to Survive Hard Times, 2002)*

To achieve growth, an enterprise must focus on creating multiple wins for its customers, capital providers, and employees. An enterprise must satisfy its customers, as this is the basis for its survival. It must also satisfy its shareholders, as this is the purpose of their investment. The enterprise must satisfy its value contributors, value the contributions of dedicated employees, and reward them accordingly, as this is the driving force behind its sustainable growth. *(Ren Zhengfei: Guidelines for Human Resources Management Transformation, 2005)*

Competition in modern times is no longer between individual enterprises. It's between supply chains. The supply chain of an enterprise is actually a business ecosystem that ties together customers, partners, suppliers, and manufacturers. An enterprise can survive over the long term only when it strengthens cooperation with others, focuses on the interests of its customers and partners, and pursues success for all. *(Source: Huawei's Core Values, 2007)*

We must seek common development with our peers – both our competitors and partners – to create a favorable business ecosystem and share the benefits of the value chain. We call our competitors "peers". We cooperate with them, and complement one another. To achieve rapid growth, Huawei will have to grab market share from its peers. This will directly endanger their survival and development, make us enemies, and perhaps encourage alliances against us. So, we must keep a low profile. We should give up some markets and interests to cooperate with our peers, become their partners, jointly create a favorable business ecosystem, and share the benefits of the value chain. We have established partnerships with our peers in many fields. Through our efforts over the last five to six years, people are more willing to accept us. Today, many large global companies consider us to be more like a partner and hold frequent talks with us on cooperation. Thus, we have achieved harmony in the midst of diversity. Harmony promotes co-existence and common prosperity and diversity fosters mutual support. This is time-honored Eastern wisdom. Huawei will create an extensive group with vested interests to nurture long-term cooperation, interdependency, and joint development. *(Source: Huawei's Core Values, 2007)*

When we expand overseas, we stress that we do not disrupt the market. We must earn our customers' recognition by providing high-quality products and excellent services. We must not harm the profits of the entire industry for a few small sales, and we must never break market rules. *(Source: Huawei's Core Values, 2007)*

3.2.3 Individuals and the team

We must always put our company's interests and efficiency first and individual interests second. The efforts of individuals must be aligned with the efforts of teams. *(Source: Huawei Business Conduct Guidelines, Before 1996)*

Our value assessment system, which manages managers and employees, should prioritize corporate interests over individual interests. Employees should be rewarded as long as they improve their work efficiency and quality. *(Ren Zhengfei: Speech at the Meeting Regarding the Project Report on the Value Assessment System for Junior Employees, 1998)*

There are conflicts between enhancing competitiveness and ensuring the current performance of our company. There are also conflicts between ordinary employees and managers. These conflicts are the driving forces for the company's growth. However, they may also become forces that hinder growth. Therefore, we must strike a balance between all conflicts and encourage collaboration for the company's growth. What is the essence of conflicts between managers and ordinary employees? They are conflicts between corporate goals and personal goals. A company is most concerned about its long-term interests and how to constantly boost its long-term competitiveness. Employees are most concerned about their short-term interests, because they do not know whether they will continue to work for Huawei in the future. To resolve these conflicts, we must strike a balance between long-term and short-term interests. We have adopted an employee stock ownership plan – employees earn their salaries, bonuses, pensions, and medical insurance from the recent business returns of the company, and receive dividends from their corporate shares for long-term investments. With the employee stock ownership plan, we avoid employee short-termism. *(Ren Zhengfei: How Long Can Huawei Survive, 1998)*

We have only one dream, which is our company's vision. Our employees should fully utilize their talent to realize our company's vision, and in doing so realize their own dreams. To enhance our core competencies, we need talented employees. However, they must follow the overall direction of our company. If employees only concern themselves with their own beliefs and career paths, it will be very hard for them to remain at Huawei. If you accept Huawei's vision and realize your own dreams while realizing this vision, I think you are very wise. *(Ren Zhengfei: Speech at the Meeting Regarding the Work Report of the Training Center, 2000)*

Our company is transforming. Managers at all levels should not worry too much about personal gains or losses. To transform means to change the principles of benefit distribution. Our employees must not worry too much about personal gains, but instead be open-minded about our transformation. Since its inception, Huawei has attached great importance to employee benefits and the interests of its partners. The combination of these two factors has led to Huawei's success. We will continue to adopt such practices, and we hope all of our employees can understand and support this. Why is there resistance to transformation? Because it often involves changes in benefit distribution. *(Ren Zhengfei: Speeches During the Early Years of Huawei, 2001)*

What is transformation? Transformation is the process of redistributing benefits, which is a significant issue. A powerful management organization is necessary to support benefit redistribution and transformation. During transformation, we will gradually move away from the previous balance of benefit distribution to a new one. This cyclic process of balancing is necessary for an enterprise to enhance its core competencies and increase efficiency. However, there will never be a perfect balance when it comes to benefit distribution. As we transform our positions, we will face challenges in benefit redistribution. Regardless of your rank, you need to adopt a correct attitude towards transformation, or it will be unable to take root or succeed. *(Ren Zhengfei: Huawei's Hard Winter, 2001)*

Our incentive mechanism must help to fully implement our company's core competency strategy and enhance our current core competencies. Only in this way can our employees have the opportunity to realize their own personal value. *(Ren Zhengfei: Key Points for Management, 2002)*

To survive, a company must have its own interests, because they are the basis for ensuring the interests of its shareholders and employees. *(Ren Zhengfei: Guidelines for Human Resources Management Transformation, 2005)*

Our company has only one goal: realizing corporate value. The value of employees can be assessed only through their dedication and contribution to creating value for the company. *(Ren Zhengfei: Speech at the EMT ST Meeting, 2009)*

3.2.4 Short-term and long-term interests

We must enable our employees to fully recognize the relationship between short-term and long-term interests, and the significance of long-term investment. We must avoid short-termism, because this is like killing the goose that lays golden eggs. Our company entered the communications industry out of naivety, not realizing that our competitors were global leaders. Driven by a sense of urgency, we have invested heavily in R&D, market expansion, and talent development every year, even though 95% of our employees didn't own their own homes at that time. Thanks to this huge pressure, we became strongly united as a company. The spirit of remaining dedicated and prioritizing work over life was internalized by all Huawei employees. Therefore, many are willing to dedicate their youth to Huawei's development and to their country's prosperity. *(Source: Characteristics of Huawei's Development, 1996)*

We will not maximize the short-term interests of our employees at the cost of Huawei's long-term interests. However, Huawei ensures that the average annual income of employees is higher than the industry's highest level when the economy is booming and when Huawei's business is strong. *(Source: The Huawei Charter, 1998)*

We must oppose short-termism, peer comparisons, and the idea that all employees deserve an equal share in our value assessment and distribution systems. *(Source: The Huawei Charter, 1998)*

In the future, we will motivate employees by decreasing long-term rewards while increasing short-term rewards, and decreasing dividends while increasing bonuses. *(Source: EMT Meeting Minutes No. [2005] 016)*

The ratio of short-term to long-term employee rewards must be constantly adjusted according to business development and management requirements. We must gradually decrease long-term rewards and increase short-term rewards, especially bonuses. We may also increase short-term benefits and rewards that help keep our employees healthy and dedicated. *(Source: EMT Meeting Minutes No. [2007] 009)*

Our overall orientation is to increase short-term incentives and keep long-term incentives at a proper level, so that our employees will have a sense of hunger. Through this, we can ensure that our employees will remain motivated and dedicated. *(Source: EMT Meeting Minutes No. [2008] 011)*

Short-term incentives encourage our employees to forge ahead, while long-term incentives keep our company stable. These incentives have different objectives. We must design short-term compensation incentives and long-term share incentives separately. The design of short-term incentives must not be distorted or affected by long-term ones. During implementation, we may consider the shares of specific groups and adjust the standards for short-term incentives accordingly. *(Source: EMT Meeting Minutes No. [2008] 011)*

To encourage continuous dedication, we must reward dedicated employees fairly and keep them healthy over the long term. However, if we increase the interests of dedicated employees excessively, the cost of internal operations will soar. Consequently, our customers will abandon us, leaving us defeated and our dedicated employees jobless. Love that does not last long is not true love. Our HR policies should be reasonable, moderate, and sustainable over the long term. At home, my mother was reluctant to put an extra bowl of rice in the pot, ignoring the anxious eyes of her hungry children. She considered the hard times when there could be a shortage of rice, and when her children might starve. She was a good mother. In contrast, some mothers were generous when there was a good harvest, but unable to keep their children alive when there was a famine. These mothers were not skilled at survival. Our HR policies must follow the first example. *(Ren Zhengfei: Deepening our Understanding of the Corporate Culture of Staying Customer-centric and Inspiring Dedication, 2008)*

Network equipment will become increasingly simple in the future. All systems including sales and services will also become simpler. Managers of future networks will be about 35 years old with around ten years of work experience. How much will they be paid? You are Huawei's founders, so how can these managers possibly be paid more than you? They will be given higher bonuses if they perform well. This is why we have implemented the capped share distribution system based on job levels. This way we have changed the ratio of long-term to short-term compensation. As our team becomes younger, relatively experienced managers should move to our subsidiaries where they can seek wealth. We must create a mechanism that motivates excellent employees to move to subsidiaries rather than stay at the parent company. This mechanism should also encourage employees to sell their shares of the parent company and buy the shares of our subsidiaries. This is the right mechanism for Huawei. *(Ren Zhengfei: Speech at the EMT ST Meeting, 2009)*

We must remain prudent with regard to our long-term HR policies. If we are overly generous in good times, we will find it hard to keep going in bad times. Falling soon after peaking has been repeated throughout history. We must continue to advocate a spirit of dedication and maintain a simple working style. The transformation of our HR policy must not be overly radical. As long as we can surpass our competitors and are not destroyed by their value systems, we must not be too radical. In addition, we must not be blindly optimistic about our HR policies. Personally, I don't want to have lasting fame. We must restrain our desire for success and our hunger for the spotlight, because both will distort our value system. The spotlight is temporary and short-lived. *(Ren Zhengfei: Speech at the HRC Meeting, 2009)*

Huawei must implement a Contribute and Share system, and its business departments and regional offices must have a system of self-control in place. Through these systems, our costs will not become unbearably high because budgets will be in the hands of field teams. Field teams will starve if they cannot make money. This is a principle we will stick to in the future. *(Ren Zhengfei: Speech at the EMT ST Meeting on March 29, 2013)*

3.2.5 Inflexibility and flexibility

We must establish a flexible mechanism where employee rewards are linked to the business performance of the company and department. Currently, we should do some research on linking employee rewards to the company's business performance. We can only maintain control at critical moments with a well-established HR policy. *(Source: EMT Meeting Minutes No. [2007] 009)*

We must further strengthen the effects of short-term incentives. The flexible part of short-term incentives must be increased, while the inflexible part must be decreased. We will adhere to our existing principle of people-job matching, and continue to assess the value of each position. In addition, we must channel our extra money towards the flexible part of incentives. *(Ren Zhengfei: Speech at the HRC Meeting, 2009)*

This year, our employee base will become smaller while our sales will grow. We must adjust any improper positioning of jobs. Considering this, we will moderately lower the inflexible part of compensation packages. Within the next few years, the total compensation of Huawei Technologies will be capped at 18% of our sales revenue, with appropriate percentages fixed for Huawei Device and Huawei Software. The inflexible part of compensation will be 10% to 12%, whereas the flexible part will be 6% to 8%. By doing this, we can better motivate our employees. The inflexible part can only be raised through promotions and increases in C&Q levels. You will be rewarded with higher bonuses if your performance is excellent, but this does not mean you will be promoted. We should further increase the flexibility of bonuses. I do not readily agree to an overall reduction in salaries. *(Source: EMT Meeting Minutes No. [2009] 022)*

I mentioned previously that in the future, the inflexible part of compensation will be 10% to 12% of our sales revenue and the flexible part will be 6% to 8%. If we use these baselines, we need to change our calculation methods for financial data. Each year, we review our business plan, budgets, and execution. For example, the plan for this year's sales is US$30 billion. We may think it is impossible to meet the plan's target, so we base our compensation and bonus packages on sales revenue of US$27 billion. At the end of the year, however, if our sales revenue actually reaches US$30 billion, we will then add the extra US$3 billion to the bonus packages and allocate it to employees. By doing things like this, we make our bonus packages more flexible. In a table of compensation, positions, and job levels, we may raise or lower job levels each year. This is how we manage inflexible costs. By removing bonuses from this table, we increase the flexibility of bonuses. The most important task for HR is to manage the responsibilities defined for each position. HR is not supposed to intervene in the specific approaches adopted for bonus distribution. In the future, bonuses will be distributed mainly by ATs[5]. *(Ren Zhengfei: Speech at the HRC Meeting, 2009)*

Our compensation structure must be motivational. As long as the size and growth of our compensation packages are linked to our operational baseline, and as long as we are not too inflexible, there won't be much risk. Compensation packages can be increased only when our business performance improves. We must decisively link our compensation packages to business performance. *(Ren Zhengfei: Speech at the HRC Meeting, 2009)*

3.2.6 Striking a balance and disrupting the balance

Will each department implement separate accounting, with value distribution based on departmental performance? Possibly. Our current value distribution is based on overall profits, but we will gradually establish a new distribution mechanism. *(Ren Zhengfei: Being Down-to-earth and Adapting to Your Position to Embrace the Corporate Transformation, 1996)*

Huawei lacks growth engines. We must implement a long-term preferential policy for Marketing & Sales and R&D personnel. We must ensure that people who do the most challenging work benefit the most. *(Ren Zhengfei: Speeches During the Early Years of Huawei, 1996)*

A key reason to transform the compensation system is to optimize management. We must give more rewards to staff who endure the greatest pressures and do the most difficult and creative work. There is no way to ensure fairness and justice in all situations. Egalitarianism will erase the enormous differences in the pressures that employees endure. As a result, we might overlook the contributions of employees who create the most value for our company. This, in turn, is unfair. *(Ren Zhengfei: Speeches During the Early Years of Huawei, 1996)*

By continuously disrupting and restoring balance, the entire company will be able to take large steps forward. *(Ren Zhengfei: Resolutely Implementing ISO9000, 1997)*

Department heads who cannot identify good managers are not qualified to hold managerial positions, because they lack management capabilities. We would rather they step down and take non-managerial jobs. Top experts can also receive high pay, sometimes even higher than some department presidents. As long as managers are in managerial positions, they should show no favoritism. Rather, they must adhere to our company's principles and completely implement the value assessment system while keeping the company's interests at heart. *(Ren Zhengfei: Speech at the CEO's Staff Team Meeting, 1998)*

Our company is stable because our organizational structure is stable. But excessive stability may hamper creativity, which in turn will lead us nowhere. In terms of manager deployment, we will not rely on appraisals, but instead use a C&Q management system. This system may not work very well at present. That's why we need to work with Hay, a US company, to develop our compensation system. Hay's compensation system is very innovative. By combining standard management practices from the UK with innovations from the US, Huawei will surely maintain its vitality. *(Ren Zhengfei: Remarks at a Meeting with Veteran Experts, 1999)*

In terms of rewards, we must prioritize our best employees. *(Source: The Huawei Charter, 1998)*

Differences are essential for life; without them, life would be stagnant. Without differences in potential energy, electricity could not be generated and hydropower would not exist. Without temperature differences, there would be no wind. At Huawei, differences in employee rewards will motivate them to work hard and bridge gaps. It is exactly this type of difference that will drive organizational improvements. *(Ren Zhengfei: Comments to Senior Executives of Huawei Electric, 2000)*

In the past, our HR policies were unbalanced. Many of our senior executives were promoted from R&D and Marketing & Sales, so they had no experience as branch office directors. As a result, our value assessment system determines compensation based on sales, products, or the success of a technology. Supporting segments often remain unrecognized for their contributions.

Many segments such as Finance, Supply Chain, and IT have been marginalized. Like an isolated force cut off from resupply or the Marine Corps deep in the middle of a desert, our company faces great operational risks. *(Ren Zhengfei: Speech at the Meeting Regarding the IFS[6] Project Report, 2007)*

By resolving internal imbalances over the past two decades, we have reached a state of balance and established a well-rounded management system. Our employees can move around within our organization as we forge ahead, united as a team. This can largely be attributed to our previous system, which was focused on balance. Of course, this system is not optimal, and must be further refined. During our early years of development we didn't have enough to eat, but we are now self-sufficient. If we continue to implement the same balanced long-term policy, our employees may start to slack off. Over the next two decades, our HR policies must appropriately disrupt the balance and keep our people motivated. *(Source: EMT Meeting Minutes No. [2009] 022)*

In our HR policies, we must be proactive when disrupting the balance. We must not reactively seek balance when things get out of control. If we are forced to react out of panic, we will not be able to correctly recognize the value of our employees. In 2002, we did not know what policies we should adopt, how much money we should pay, or what positions we should offer to retain people. As a result, our positions and salaries were in a state of disarray. In response to this, Huawei has expended much effort on trying to strike a balance. If we do not disrupt the balance while the decision is ours, we will be too passive when change is forced upon us. *(Ren Zhengfei: Speech at the EMT ST Meeting, 2009)*

I don't think a salary cut will help improve employee efficiency. Taking this action may be interpreted as accepting poor performers. I believe our bonus and incentive mechanism should favor high performers. Differences generate driving forces. If there were no differences in temperature, there would be no wind. If there were no differences in water levels, there would be no water flow. What is fairness? If the Tibetan Plateau and the Himalayas were leveled as low as the North China Plain, there would be no water flow and stagnant water would be scattered everywhere. I agree that we can dismiss poor performers and replace them with excellent new hires. Of course, if our business performance is not good, we will have to decrease salaries. We have changed our appraisal system this year – by adjusting our existing five-level appraisal system. Employees that get a "D" will receive no bonus and those that get a "C" may receive little or no bonus. I also agree that we must motivate excellent employees. We will transform our bonus distribution system beginning in the second half of this year. When implementing people-job matching and basing the salary on the job levels, we must abandon the practice of giving an equal share to everyone regardless of what work they do, and we must change our method of distributing bonuses. To improve efficiency, we must fuel our engines – top-performing employees – to give full play to their strengths and reinforce their dedication. *(Ren Zhengfei: Speech at the Regular Meeting of the Reserve Pool on March 25, 2009)*

(Regarding incentives and reward distribution) I think we should raise the C&Q level of employees with strong capabilities, and increase bonuses for employees who make an outstanding contribution. Raising an employee's C&Q level requires that he or she can contribute continuously. In this sense, internal balance and unity will be ensured. Horse racing – an internal competition mechanism – may easily lead to conflicts, but if it is well managed, it can enhance unity. The result completely depends on how it is managed. We must disrupt the balance to further stimulate development. But, during this process, we need a reasonable approach to strike a balance. *(Ren Zhengfei: Speech at a Report Meeting of the Eastern and Southern Africa Multi-country Management Department, November 15, 2012)*

In the past, our compensation system emphasized balance, which caused an exodus of smart people. But how then has Huawei managed to achieve success? It is because our 150,000 employees have remained united, just like water that flows out of a single hole to generate immense amounts of power. This power is so strong that it has helped us win customers and seize opportunities. Our current transformation aims to unlock the potential of outstanding employees and widen the gap in employee benefits. Normally, water flows from high to low places. To unlock the full potential of our water – our employees – we must reverse the flow from low to high, and then use pumps to get the water even higher where it will play a larger role. We must transform our appraisal mechanism immediately, and widen the gap in bonuses, especially for employees in field offices and entry-level organizations. It is difficult to change our salary system and any blind change may have serious consequences, so we need to start by transforming our bonus system. Through transformation, we must let employees clearly know that high performers will get higher bonuses. As a result, these employees will not want to leave, and we will have a larger pool of outstanding employees.

(Ren Zhengfei: Remarks at a Meeting with Staff of the Guangzhou Represent-ative Office, 2013)

We must widen the gaps in employee compensation based on the value that each employee contributes. We must fuel engines in the organization to the maximum so that they can pull the train to run faster and deliver more. To live our core values, we must have a group of people who set the example. Employees' compensation is not based on their scope of management; it has to be based first on contributions, results, and responsibilities, and second on dedication. *(Ren Zhengfei: Speech at the Huawei Annual Management Conference, 2013)*

3.2.7 Labor and capital

Our company will run out of cash if we don't open up our capital system. A cash-strapped company will lose its vitality and be unable to share its interests. If we open up our capital system, we can receive funding from shareholders. Through this process, we must properly handle the relationship between labor-based and capital-based distributions, and deal with the conflict between the company's vitality and shareholders' desire for higher returns. If we can't effectively manage this conflict, we will be unable to ensure fair distribution, and the company will lose its vitality and enter a vicious circle. *(Ren Zhengfei: Speech Regarding Corporate Organizational Goals and System Blueprints for the Future, 1994)*

Since its inception, Huawei has adopted a labor-oriented ownership structure that unites as many employees as possible into a group with vested interests. As Huawei continues to expand, we have struck a balance between labor-based and capital-based distributions. This balance has created a new environment where both new and veteran employees are dedicated. Using this distribution model, we ensure that veterans will not slack off and new employees will feel fairly rewarded. As a result, talented professionals will continue to join us. Some 80% of our employees hold company shares. This increases our company's resistance to corruption. We also use high salaries to keep people incorruptible. Through this, our company has created a dynamic operating control mechanism with strong constraints. For a high-tech company that is not heavily reliant on resources, an employee shareholding mechanism is significant as it helps stabilize the company and avoids the loss of information assets. *(Ren Zhengfei: Characteristics of Huawei's Development, 1996)*

Labor and capital create our total value. How we assess the role of venture capital in creating value is an important issue. We must not overemphasize the interests of our founders. Instead, we must unite as many people as possible. *(Source: Out of Chaos, 1998)*

Huawei's Board of Directors represents investors and employees – currently all our board members must be Huawei employees. Although we have achieved success and balanced development over the past 25 years, this doesn't necessarily mean there won't be any other better policies for our balanced development over the next two decades. Over the next three to five years, we will push forward administrative transformation. After that, we will transform our governance structure and operational model. Superfast transformation is likely to tear up the management system in which we have invested so much, and any gap will impede our future efforts. Remember that haste makes waste. A huge influx of capital may force Huawei to diversify its business blindly, causing us to spin out of control. *(Ren Zhengfei: Speech at a Meeting of Representatives of Shareholding Employees, March 30, 2013)*

3.2.8 Regular employees and dedicated employees

The word "dedication" has many connotations. We value dedicated employees and reward them accordingly. Those who are dedicated include not only employees, but also investors. These investors put their money into our company, and share the risks and liabilities. They are also dedicated. These are two types of dedication, and they share the same goal – to make money. *(Ren Zhengfei: Comments to Staff of the Kenya Representative Office, 2008)*

In the future, we will emphasize the differences in compensation between dedicated and regular employees. We will treat the latter according to applicable laws, for example, offering paid leave and long maternity leave. However, their salaries will be based on industry standards, not Huawei's standards, and their bonuses will be fixed. In contrast, dedicated employees must give up some rights, such as overtime pay. However, they will receive a capped number of shares based on their job levels, as well as a portion of our annual business returns. The income of dedicated employees is directly tied to Huawei's business performance. When business is good, their income will be very high. When it's not, their income may be lower than that of regular employees. However, dedicated employees will be rewarded for their contributions over the long run. *(Ren Zhengfei: Speech at a Meeting with the IFS Project Team and Staff from Finance, 2009)*

3.2.9 Previous and current value contributors

As our company continues to develop rapidly, conflicts between labor-based and capital-based distributions have become increasingly evident. Effectively motivating new hires to maintain vitality is a matter of life and death for our company. We must constantly reinvent ourselves. Our founders must possess a spirit of sacrifice to support Huawei's rebirth. *(Ren Zhengfei: Reinventing Ourselves to Achieve Greater Success, 1994)*

Previous value contributors are not necessarily in senior positions, but they can enjoy certain benefits. Our bonuses and positions must be offered to those who take responsibility and make contributions. Huawei does not advocate lifelong employment, which is different from working all one's life for Huawei. *(Ren Zhengfei: Freeing Your Mind and Embracing Market Challenges in 1996, 1995)*

Huawei faces a real dilemma in assessing previous value contributors. At critical moments, these value contributors fought bravely to find a way for the company to develop. In today's Huawei, do we recognize them or not? We recognize them, but we do not necessarily place them in senior positions. These two approaches are interwoven and make assessments complicated. However, this issue is easier to tackle at Huawei than at any other enterprise in China's mainland, because we view knowledge as a type of capital and an implicit contribution. We compensate previous value contributors with shares. A demotion does not necessarily impact their personal income as we link dividends to previous contributions, and salaries and bonuses to capabilities and current contributions. Using this approach, we can resolve some problems, but not all. We should constantly train our veteran employees and offer them new opportunities to move to other positions. *(Ren Zhengfei: The Secretarial System Is an Information Bridge, 1996)*

We should acknowledge and care for previous value contributors and help them improve their management skills. *(Ren Zhengfei: Speech at the Marketing Work Meeting, 1996)*

Eight years of guerrilla-type market operations have created numerous heroes at Huawei. There would be no Huawei today if not for these heroes' dedication all over the world. They have fought far and wide, in the mountains of Yunnan, the deserts of Northwest China, the blizzards of the Greater Khingan Mountains, and throughout Europe and Africa. They made many sacrifices in leaving behind the comfort of home and their loved ones to undertake such arduous work. They dedicated themselves to our company's development, ignoring the temptations of this chaotic world. Without them, Huawei might not have become what it is today. We should not forget those who dug the well from which we drink. We must not forget these heroes. The experience they have accumulated over the past eight years in identifying talent is invaluable, and the noble character they have demonstrated is worthy of our respect. They are the best talent that we can develop. To develop talent is relatively easy, but to cultivate a virtuous character is quite difficult. These employees are great treasures and the nucleus of our company. Managers at all levels should help them grow and offer them more opportunities. *(Ren Zhengfei: Do Not Forget Heroes, 1997)*

Stock ownership is a way to manage the relationship between the company's founders, veterans, and new employees. By allocating shares to new employees, the company encourages them to identify with and contribute to the company as if it were their own. In this way, the company can constantly attract new hires. At the same time, the shares of veteran employees are adjusted dynamically. In other words, the shares of previous value contributors who no longer create value for the company are diluted. In theory, stock ownership is the answer to the question of who creates surplus value for Huawei. *(Source: Summary of the Speech by a Professor from China Renmin University at a Meeting with Shenzhen Institutional Reform Committee, 1997)*

Employees who once contributed to our corporate development must be able to adapt to new demands, which include their emotional adaptability. Competition makes it certain that Huawei will not always win, and so Huawei cannot protect employees who do not help enhance its competitiveness. Departments at all levels should help and develop these employees and provide them with appropriate guidance. However, the mindset of these employees is more important. *(Ren Zhengfei: It's Not Always Easy to Enjoy the Shade Under a Big Tree, 1999)*

I think any nation, company, or organization will come to a halt if the old are not replaced by the new. Where there is life, there are conflicts, disputes, and agony. If we pay too much attention to every previous value contributor, we will ruin this company. *(Ren Zhengfei: Speech at the Honor Awards Ceremony for the Fourth Anniversary of the Group Resignation of Marketing & Sales Staff, 2000)*

If certain employees cannot keep pace with the times, they must be assigned to new positions. Otherwise, our company will lose its competitive edge. Even if these employees agree to change positions, their compensation must be aligned with their new contributions. Otherwise, our company will operate at a high cost, lose its competitive edge, and gradually perish. Considering the previous contributions of these employees, their number of shares may remain unchanged so that they can enjoy dividends from their investment. If our company collapses, these employees will receive no returns from their investment. Since its inception, Huawei has maintained this practice, which has enabled us to overcome many of the common difficulties found in large enterprises. *(Ren Zhengfei: Guidelines for Human Resources Management Transformation, 2005)*

I hope you realize that self-reflection can help you correct your mistakes and open your mind so you can endure criticism from others. We have made this somewhat easier for you, but I still think 10% of managers should fail this time. They may have to be transferred to other positions, but we won't reduce the shares they hold. At Huawei, managers should remain committed regardless of the roles assigned to them. Although your salary may decrease, the shares you hold will remain unchanged, and you will still have sufficient income. We simply help you correct the mistakes in your thinking. *(Ren Zhengfei: Speech at the Communication Meeting with the Steering Committee on Self-reflection, 2006)*

Talent emerges all the time and must constantly improve. We cannot ensure that all our managers will continuously rise up the corporate ladder. It's common for the old to be replaced by the new. Therefore, we have established a mechanism that adjusts your position if you fail to keep pace or have a health problem; however, your shares will remain unchanged. We must promote new managers, especially those in hardship regions. If no new managers are promoted, our business model will be unable to endure. *(Source: EMT Meeting Minutes No. [2008] 028)*

Newly issued shares should favor high performers so that we can gradually make the distribution of our long-term interests balanced and reasonable among our previous, current, and future value contributors. *(Source: EMT Meeting Minutes No. [2009] 040)*

Stock ownership may someday be a disaster for Huawei. It is possible that one day many of our employees will suddenly become too rich when our company goes public. As a result, our effectiveness will be weakened. That's why we will bring in talented individuals who aim high but are not yet rich. As they are both hungry and talented, they will know how to operate under a modern business model after two to three years of molding at Huawei. I believe that people in their thirties will be able to lead our company after they are molded, cultivated, and motivated. We will keep our employees dedicated by rewarding them according to their contributions, and our parent company will continue to supply talent to our subsidiaries. *(Ren Zhengfei: Speech at the EMT ST Meeting, 2009)*

The employee stock ownership plan adopted at the company's inception and the capped share distribution system based on job levels have resolved the main conflicts our management faced in certain periods. However, these systems largely reflect factors such as seniority and job levels. The future growth of our company will depend more on new key employees. If we do not distribute benefits fairly among employees who are currently contributing to the company, imbalances in internal interests will emerge. This will reduce our effectiveness. By optimizing the capped share distribution system based on job levels, we have developed a performance-based stock ownership plan, which will make the distribution of our business returns more balanced and reasonable. *(Source: EMT Meeting Minutes No. [2009] 040)*

3.2.10 Fairness and efficiency

Prioritizing efficiency while considering fairness and sustainable growth is the basic principle for our value distribution. *(Source: The Huawei Charter, 1998)*

At Huawei, we prioritize efficiency while considering fairness. We offer outstanding employees greater rewards, but we do not condone employees who behave improperly, break the law, or do not exercise self-discipline after they become rich. We must create a culture that fosters moral integrity and encourages employees to comply with corporate regulations and national laws. We will not forgive employees who violate either. *(Ren Zhengfei: Remaining United to Help Huawei Scale New Heights, 1999)*

3.2.11 Relative fairness and absolute fairness

From a materialistic perspective, unfairness is absolute while fairness is temporary. If decisions are made through group appraisals, the individual employees concerned should accept the decisions even if they are not satisfied. We cannot ascertain the smallest details, but we must continue carrying our transformation forward. Any effort to seek absolute fairness for a small minority will mean unfairness to the remaining 99% of people. We hope that you will work hard and use all of your abilities and wisdom to overcome whatever unfairness you may face. Don't give up. Our managers grow through trial and error and need more experience in modern enterprise management. You are expected to give us time to try and gain experience so we can standardize our operations. *(Ren Zhengfei: Do Not Profess To Love What You Actually Fear, 1996)*

Do not overly promote fairness or justice, because neither truly exists. We can only improve gradually and try as hard as we can to bring about fairness and justice to a certain extent. *(Ren Zhengfei: Minutes of the CEO's Staff Team Meetings, 1996)*

To new graduates, we must promote hardship. We should never tell them how fair things are at Huawei, as this might cause serious problems in the future. Someday, they may become discontented and ask for fairness and justice, and then release their anger like an explosion if they feel they haven't received it. Different people interpret fairness and justice differently. But absolute fairness does not exist in this world. Only dutiful and content employees will have good career prospects. During Huawei's transformation, we must recruit dedicated people who are content and willing to shoulder a heavy burden. To avoid making management more difficult, we should not recruit those who are easily discontented. You work here to earn a living, and your compensation is mainly based on your contribution. How much others earn has nothing to do with you. Comparing your salary with that of your peers will ultimately result in Huawei's failure. Young people may have many illusions; however, we must not leave any room for illusions and we must avoid pampering talent. We have a very relaxed environment at Huawei, but over-emphasizing democracy will give employees too many illusions, which in turn will destroy our relaxed environment. Things will always move in the opposite direction when they become extreme. *(Ren Zhengfei: Speech at the Meeting Regarding the Report by the Human Resource Management Department on Recruitment of New Graduates, 1996)*

There is no absolute fairness, and errors in judgment are inevitable. However, unbridgeable divides or calling right wrong will not occur. You must tolerate unfairness, even if you have worked well. If you lack endurance, how will you be able to shoulder responsibilities in the future? Our company strives to offer equal opportunities. However, opportunities favor those who are down-to-earth. *(Source: Out of Chaos, 1998)*

There is no absolute fairness, so don't expect too much in this regard. However, we offer equal opportunities to those who apply themselves. Your manager will know if you consistently achieve results. You must tolerate unfairness, even if you have done your work well. "From the ashes the phoenix is reborn" – This is how Huaweiers act when they are wronged or feel frustrated. It is also the principle Huawei uses to select managers. If you lack endurance, how will you be able to shoulder greater responsibilities in the future? You are the master of your own destiny. Inevitably, there will be errors in judgment. However, unbridgeable divides or calling right wrong will not occur. You can place your confidence in Huawei. The sun is sure to rise, even if it currently remains below the horizon. *(Source: Welcome Letter to New Employees, 2005)*

An enterprise is not a supernatural being that ensures things are always fair. There is no absolute fairness. As long as our leaders are truly dedicated to our company's goals, you may be treated unfairly once, but the next time they may correct their mistake. You may experience several unfair situations, but eventually things will balance out. If you are made of gold, you will shine sooner or later. *(Ren Zhengfei: Guidelines for Human Resources Management Transformation, 2005)*

By implementing our HR policy and establishing a fair and reasonable reward system, we instill employees with a mindset where good performance naturally leads to high rewards. This allows our employees to focus their attention on their work rather than on benefit distribution. *(Source: EMT Meeting Minutes No. [2007] 009)*

3.2.12 Expectations and reality

Huawei has improved over the years, and has constantly unlocked employee potential. However, conflict also exists. We must resolve unresolved issues one by one and avoid acting rashly. It is impossible for our company to grow all the time. We may experience downturns from time to time. At such times, salaries may be decreased and downsizing may be inevitable. We currently give generous benefits to our employees; this has increased the expectations of some. They just want more, believing they are not getting enough. When we transform our benefit distribution system, we need constraints and patience. We hope that our employees can objectively assess and position themselves and have reasonable expectations. Managers at all levels must strengthen management and internal control, communicate more, and listen attentively to employees. Otherwise, our company will perish. We must correctly understand democracy as it applies in a corporate setting. Democracy does not mean that control is not needed – it means that we need to communicate more with our employees and exchange views. When conflicts arise, we should provide facts and think things through. When drafting documents, we may ask for opinions. Do not count on corporate democracy to create better results; rather, it can make people unrealistic and unable to seek the truth from facts or accurately assess themselves – it increases people's expectations. Therefore, democracy at Huawei must be appropriately controlled. *(Ren Zhengfei: Being Committed and Trying Your Best to Successfully Complete Your Work, 1996)*

Our company cannot increase employee income without limit, nor does it have the capacity to make promises. Good prospects require joint efforts. You can only expect to have good prospects at Huawei by applying yourself and helping your colleagues improve. *(Ren Zhengfei: Key Points for Management, 1999)*

To ensure the sustainable development of our company, we must ensure that employee income does not grow faster than our business. *(Ren Zhengfei: Speech at the Meeting Regarding the Hay Pilot Project, 2000)*

We must manage employee expectations and refrain from making rash promises. We definitely cannot meet every employee requirement. I believe next year will be a very challenging year, maybe not for Huawei, but for other companies. Many conflicts will erupt all at once and, at this critical moment, we must ensure that we steer clear of internal conflict.

Our Human Resources Management Department and our Committee of Ethics and Compliance must not make too many promises to employees, nor stir the pot. Criticism from employees must be discussed and analyzed only among our decision makers. Once decisions are made, we must communicate them to our employees. To avoid conflict, we must not change our decisions without proper justification; we must not open up our resolutions for discussion either. *(Ren Zhengfei: Speech at the HRC Meeting, 2009)*

We should not discuss corporate policies with employees, which may whet their appetites. We only need to explain policies to them. Listen to them. Do not interrupt them. We must ensure that our corporate policies are not changed arbitrarily. *(Ren Zhengfei: Speech at the EMT ST Meeting, 2009)*

An employee's income depends on individual, departmental, and company performance. Good performance in any of these respects may lead to higher personal income. Poor performance may reduce personal income or decrease the bonus (as a variable part of income) to zero. *(Source: AT Member's Statement, 2010)*

As an AT member, I should control my own expectations and, more importantly, manage the expectations of my subordinates. My duty not only includes motivating employees; more importantly, I must also manage them on behalf of the company, especially when it comes to their expectations of compensation and benefits. This makes it possible for employees to adopt a positive attitude towards fluctuations in income, and ensures that they do not complain or cause trouble, but remain dedicated to their work. If, due to the improper management of employee expectations, my subordinates complain extensively or cause trouble, I will accept responsibility, and resign from my current managerial position, and be disqualified from managerial positions for the next three years. *(Source: AT Member's Statement, 2010)*

---

4 The 863 Program is funded and administered by the Chinese government, and aims to stimulate the development of advanced technologies in various fields.

5 At Huawei, an administrative team (AT) is an organization responsible for making decisions on people management.

6 IFS: Integrated Financial Services. This is Huawei's transformation program in the finance domain.

3.3 Value Distribution Policies

3.3.1 Balancing labor-based and capital-based value distributions

Traditional economic theory holds that labor, land, and capital are the basic factors of production. Adam Smith believed that these three factors create all wealth. Workers receive wages for their work; land owners receive rent from the land they own; and those with capital can receive returns on investment. This concept was first proposed in the 18th century. In the 19th century, the French economist Jean-Baptiste Say proposed that capitalists need to be further classified into two categories: those who lend money for interest, and those who use others' capital. The latter are entrepreneurs. It should be the same for income distribution: Workers should get paid for their work; land owners should receive rent from land ownership; and capitalists should earn interest from lending. Only entrepreneurs deserve profits. *(Ren Zhengfei: Seizing Opportunities, Adjusting Management Systems, and Meeting Challenges, 1997)*

In value distribution, we must consider both the role of labor and the role of venture capital. We must convert labor, knowledge, and the contributions of these two factors into capital through stock ownership. *(Source: Out of Chaos, 1998)*

Huawei accumulates capital through the work of its employees, so assessing their work is critical. Many private companies overemphasize the interests of their founders while ignoring those of new employees. I am against this, as it will prevent founders from rallying people around them.

I am also against providing excessive benefits, because doing so may produce lazy employees. *(Source: Out of Chaos, 1998)*

Some companies focus more on creating profits for their founders; Huawei emphasizes the interests of all its dedicated employees. If we insist that all our capital belongs to our initial investors, we will deny the rights of those who contribute their labor and intellect (or knowledge) to own the surplus value they create. If so, it will be hard for us to attract and retain leading technical and managerial talent, and it will be detrimental to our survival and development. We should find out how high-tech companies like Huawei can translate labor, knowledge, and the entrepreneur's management contributions and risks taken into capital, in compliance with the law. *(Source: Out of Chaos, 1998)*

In today's highly developed information society, knowledge assets dwarf financial assets. In labor-based value distribution, we consider the knowledge required to do your work. Capital-based distribution is now transforming into knowledge-capital-based distribution. *(Source: Out of Chaos, 1998)*

We translate labor, knowledge, and the entrepreneur's management contributions and risks taken into capital to reflect and reward the contributions made by each factor. *(Source: The Huawei Charter, 1998)*

Labor and capital create our total value. How we assess the role of venture capital in creating value is an important issue. We must not overemphasize the interests of our founders. Instead, we must unite as many people as possible. *(Source: Out of Chaos, 1998)*

While emphasizing the importance of contributions, we also need to work out a reasonable ratio between gains from labor and gains from capital. *(Ren Zhengfei: Guidelines for Human Resources Management Transformation, 2005)*

To achieve growth, an enterprise must focus on creating multiple wins for its customers, investors, and employees. An enterprise must satisfy its customers, as this is the basis for its survival. It must also satisfy its shareholders, as this is the purpose of their investment. The enterprise must satisfy its value contributors, value the contributions of dedicated employees, and reward them accordingly, as they are the driving force behind sustainable growth. *(Ren Zhengfei: Guidelines for Human Resources Management Transformation, 2005)*

3.3.2 Providing dedicated employees and successful teams with more opportunities

Compensation is more than just money. It also involves opportunities, status, authority, and responsibilities. While transforming our management systems and organizations at our growth stage, we should consider how to redistribute authority. *(Ren Zhengfei: Resolutely Implementing ISO9000, 1997)*

In *The Huawei Charter*, authority is placed before economic interests. This indicates that our company prioritizes organizational authority. Among the factors considered in value distribution, responsibility comes second. At Huawei, we often say that being a manager means making greater contributions and taking more responsibilities. According to *The Huawei Charter*, "We value the contributions of dedicated employees and reward them accordingly." *(Source: Second Coaching Report on Huawei's Charter, 1998)*

Huawei considers development opportunities as a primary distributable resource. On the one hand, Huawei continuously creates new businesses and provides employees with opportunities for growth and development. On the other hand, Huawei allocates opportunities through a fair competition mechanism and creates a favorable environment for the growth of talented employees. *(Source: Second Coaching Report on Huawei's Charter, 1998)*

Employees have equal opportunities to be promoted if they work hard and continuously improve at work. Accordingly, we must maintain a fair competition mechanism – those who are not competent will be removed from their positions and replaced by more competent employees. Huawei gives its employees opportunities in the areas where they are most likely to excel. Based on fair and objective performance appraisals, we will establish a process-based ownership system, assigning the most responsible and capable employees to the most important positions. During this process, we will not consider factors such as seniority or job levels; instead, we will fast-track those who display outstanding talents and make exceptional contributions according to our selection procedure. In this way, we can achieve our goals and seize more business opportunities. However, we should take a step-by-step approach in this regard. *(Ren Zhengfei: How Long Can Huawei Survive, 1998)*

We need to give more opportunities to field employees when it comes to pay raises and promotions, because unexpected situations occur frequently in field offices and require very experienced employees. We can't simply appraise managers in terms of skills, because managers working in the desert are definitely at a disadvantage compared with those working at the HQ who receive frequent training. We should properly appraise, select, and cultivate managers. If we don't focus more on employees who fight on the frontlines or give them more opportunities, we will bring ruin upon ourselves. Therefore, we must give more opportunities to field employees. *(Ren Zhengfei: Speech at the Mobilization Meeting for a Final Sprint in the Marketplace, 2000)*

While implementing a performance-based appraisal system, we also need to track key events. We must identify and cultivate managers at all levels based on successful decisions, particularly those made in the process of achieving goals. We should also summarize project failures, and identify good managers via these projects. We should avoid using results as the sole basis for appraisals. *(Ren Zhengfei: Key Points for Management, 2002)*

We must accelerate the promotion of new managers and provide them with opportunities. This is in fact a strategic policy of our company. As our company develops, we are lacking in managers. If we can't cultivate competent managers, we may lose our markets and eventually fail. *(Source: EMT Meeting Minutes No. [2008] 028)*

The least valuable thing in the world is gold and the most valuable thing is a better future and opportunities. *(Ren Zhengfei: Remarks at a Meeting with Staff of the Guangzhou Representative Office, 2013)*

3.3.3 The distribution of economic interests should reflect the positioning of each type of compensation

The goal of our next transformation is to pay employees based on their competency, provide employees with equal pay for equal work, and give them bonuses based on their performance. In doing so, we can develop a virtuous cycle and cultivate a group of energized employees. *(Ren Zhengfei: Speech at the Terminal Business Unit's Work Meeting, 1997)*

Contributions can be short-term or long-term. The two are different: The former are rewarded with bonuses and the latter are rewarded with promotions.

(Ren Zhengfei: Speech at a Meeting with Hay Group Experts at the Competency and Qualification Assessment Meeting Regarding Research, 1997)

Huawei's value distribution system has several layers, including opportunities, authority, salaries, benefits, bonuses, and shares. According to the two-factor theory, such factors can be divided into hygiene factors and motivators. Many companies' value distribution systems are largely fixed. The reason for this is that many factors that are meant to be motivators end up becoming hygiene factors. As a result, only new factors can be added and existing ones are hard to adjust. At Huawei, however, as the value of employees is dynamically assessed, our value distribution system can thus be flexibly adjusted. This will in turn translate hygiene factors into motivators. *(Source: Summary of the Speech by a Professor from China Renmin University at a Meeting with Shenzhen Institutional Reform Committee, 1997)*

In labor-based value distribution, factors considered include competency, responsibilities, contributions, and work attitudes. We must widen the gap in the value distributed to different employees and maintain a continuous distribution curve. When distributing shares, we need to give priority to key employees, and keep the shareholding structure dynamic and reasonable. We must work out a reasonable ratio between gains from labor and gains from capital. Changes in the distribution amount and ratio should ensure our company's sustainable growth. *(Source: The Huawei Charter, 1998)*

We must establish a value distribution system where the income of each employee is linked to the company's overall performance. When the company performs well, we must dare to expand and share risks together. When the company is in difficulty, we need to get through the hard times together. In this way, we can share the pressure with all segments and all employees. *(Ren Zhengfei: Key Points for Management, 1999)*

We don't pay employees based on their knowledge. Instead, we pay them based on the contributions they make with their knowledge. When we select managers, we should consider their responsibilities, competency, and contributions, rather than their knowledge or academic degrees. *(Ren Zhengfei: Minutes of the Meeting with Employees Who Are in Adversity, 2002)*

When designing compensation packages for different regions, we must follow market rules and consider factors such as performance, contributions, cost, and the pay levels and structures of local markets. When designing our compensation structure – including monthly salaries, benefits, and bonuses – we consider both our management principles and the characteristics of Western countries to ensure that our fixed compensation is attractive. In places where we have less brand recognition, our compensation must be more competitive. *(Source: EMT Meeting Minutes No. [2005] 028)*

The transformation of our compensation system will focus on monetary income, such as monthly salaries and bonuses, not on the gains from shares, which are considered extra income. In the future, we will gradually separate shareholders from business operators. *(Source: EMT Meeting Minutes No. [2005] 028)*

Salaries will be based on individual contributions and the ability to contribute continuously, while bonuses will be based on short-term contributions. *(Ren Zhengfei: Guidelines for Human Resources Management Transformation, 2005)*

Our salaries need to be competitive in the international market to help us attract global high-end talent. To make this happen, we need to separate salaries from shares. In the future, we may hire people to fill the managerial positions of the company or a department but offer them few or no shares. *(Source: EMT Meeting Minutes No. [2006] 012)*

To ensure that our employees can live and work safely around the world, starting in 2005, we have transformed our insurance and benefits system and enacted a series of policies on employee insurance, medical insurance, medical aid, and personal insurance. In addition to compulsory social and medical insurance, we also purchase commercial insurance for our employees, including personal accident, life, critical illness, and business travel insurance. If, for example, an employee dies of injuries at work, his or her family will receive a payout from both policies. If an employee suffers from a critical illness, he or she will receive compensation from the critical illness insurance policy. If he or she dies of a critical illness, the family will also receive a payout. For employees assigned to countries with poor public medical systems, we purchase commercial medical insurance for them and their families. We have also established close relationships with global medical service organizations (e.g. ISOS) to ensure that our employees assigned overseas and their families can receive prompt medical care. *(Source: Notification on the Status of Human Resources Management Transformation, 2007)*

We have to ask ourselves three questions before making an investment: First, how can we maintain a certain level of hunger among junior employees? Second, how can we maintain a sense of crisis among mid-level employees? Third, how can we maintain a sense of mission among senior managers? If we can't do any of these things, we'd better not invest. If employees slack off once they get rich, what's the point of earning so much money? I have noticed this problem in our company over the past two years, so I began to transform the bonus system. This year, 5% of employees will not get a bonus, meaning that junior managers will not be equally dividing bonuses between all employees regardless of performance. In addition, the highest performers will get about four to six times as much as the average bonus. So, junior managers will find it hard to please everyone. Also, we now allow junior employees to work overtime and earn more. To maintain a sense of crisis among middle managers, we will demote those whose performance is in the bottom 10%. To maintain a sense of mission among senior managers, we have a system in place to select them from among the best performers, not based on appraisals alone. *(Ren Zhengfei: Speech at the Meeting with Staff of the Huawei People & Improvement Editorial Office & Employee Relations Department, 2009)*

The purpose of giving bonuses is to motivate employees, especially those who perform well. Poor performers will gradually be dismissed. We should continue to downsize. We have many expectations of our employees, but these must not be all linked to bonus assessments. Bonus assessments, unlike position assessments, should be simple; otherwise, we will become lost in the complexity. If an employee does a great job on a project, we will give him or her a bonus, but we will not promise a promotion. If we don't provide a bonus simply because he or she is unlikely to become a manager, I would think our incentive system has problems. *(Ren Zhengfei: Speech at the HRC Meeting, 2009)*

The most important thing for people-job matching is to see whether an employee is competent enough to do a job and able to contribute. Bonuses are given to employees who have made contributions. Then what is the purpose of distributing shares? The purpose, focus, characteristic, and method of each type of assessment varies case by case. *(Ren Zhengfei: Speech at the HRC Meeting, 2009)*

The key to people-job matching, position-based salary setting, and compensation management is to clearly describe job responsibilities and contributions. The weight of a job will change based on time, place, and position. If an employee is a good fit for a position and his or her performance meets expectations, then he or she should be paid according to relevant criteria. This shows that our compensation is consistent with our corporate policies. As we now have limited time and resources, we should focus first on bonuses and incentives. Currently, bonuses account for 6% of our total revenue and salaries account for 12%. As efficiency improves, we may increase the floating portion of compensation. *(Ren Zhengfei: Speech at the EMT ST Meeting, 2009)*

The purpose of transforming our compensation system is to establish a globally competitive system that will help us attract and retain global talent to improve our management and competitiveness. *(Source: EMT Meeting Minutes No. [2009] 005)*

Value creation is more than simply signing contracts. Activities such as contract execution, scientific management, and services and support also create value. Services provided by functional departments are also a part of our value chain. We should consider all of them and evaluate each job. Currently, as we haven't centralized the management of functional departments, compensation gaps exist between field employees. We will adjust this. Faster salary increases and promotions should be made available to staff from field operating teams, followed by field support staff, and then support staff in back offices. This is just a general policy with no regard to specific job types. *(Ren Zhengfei: Comments to Staff from Finance, 2011)*

3.3.4 Salary distribution

We base salaries on employees' contributions and responsibilities, rather than their academic degrees. In other words, employees who have the same job and responsibilities will receive the same pay. In the same position, if an employee with a bachelor's degree or lower makes the same contribution as an employee with a master's degree, they will be paid equally. But a senior employee will receive a bit more than a junior one in the same position. Right now, we are recruiting talent nationwide on a large scale and it is unrealistic to negotiate salaries with every one of them. So we have set starting salaries based on academic degrees and made adjustments as the recruits gain more experience. As salaries increase, the appraisal criteria should also be raised. There is no such a thing as a free lunch, so those who perform poorly should expect a pay decrease or dismissal. *(Ren Zhengfei: Speech Regarding the Project Report on the Value Assessment System for Junior Employees, 1998)*

We should make it clear that salaries may fluctuate. If we expect salaries to always increase, the company will be doomed to fail. *(Ren Zhengfei: Speech at the Farewell Meeting for R&D Staff and Managers Sent to Field Offices, 2001)*

To maintain internal operation costs at a low level, we need to set job levels based on positions and salaries based on job levels, match employees with jobs, and adjust salaries when positions change. *(Ren Zhengfei: Guidelines for Human Resources Management Transformation, 2005)*

When determining the salaries of different positions, we need to consider salary levels in the job market, and the value each position creates with regard to the company's strategic execution and business operations. We need to balance salaries for different types of positions. *(Source: EMT Meeting Minutes No. [2005] 054)*

We should not raise the starting salaries for new graduates too quickly. We can frequently increase their salaries after they join Huawei but within a controlled range. This will not only prevent a negative impact on the compensation structure for senior employees, but also ensure we actually motivate people who make real contributions. *(Source: EMT Meeting Minutes No. [2005] 047)*

The same salary standards should be adopted for the same jobs in different business units. Otherwise, if the support departments are weak, delivery cannot be guaranteed after orders are secured. *(Source: EMT Meeting Minutes No. [2005] 028)*

We will adopt the following practices in HQ departments: determining positions including position names, purposes, responsibilities, and reporting lines, and then the number of employees required to fill these positions. *(Source: EMT E-mail No. [2006] 36)*

Employees' salaries should be based on their job responsibilities, actual contributions, and ability to contribute continuously. Elements such as academic degrees, length of employment, and title should not be considered. *(Source: Regulations on Employee Salaries, 2006)*

We should determine the salaries of positions at different levels based on the company's business performance and affordability. Salary management should be standardized to help create a high-performing team and maintain our market competitiveness while keeping labor costs at a reasonable level. We must manage our salaries in compliance with the compulsory requirements of laws and regulations in the countries and regions where we operate. *(Source: Regulations on Employee Salaries, 2006)*

The salaries of junior employees in business, technical, and managerial positions should be benchmarked against salary levels in local markets for the same profession in the same industry. Mid-level employees can be paid a little more than local market levels. The salaries of senior employees should be determined according to specific company requirements and salary levels in global markets. *(Source: Regulations on Employee Salaries, 2006)*

Currently, there is still room to improve in terms of setting job levels and matching people and jobs. When it comes to people-job matching, we need to be flexible and patient, and move forward step by step while not deviating from our direction. In terms of execution, we need to be practical and consider things on a case-by-case basis. It is also important to hold discussions with management teams, stick to our company's principles, and compromise when necessary. *(Source: EMT Resolutions No. [2007] 005)*

Salaries will float based on performance. We need to determine the corporate coefficient for floating salaries based on our company's overall business performance, and the departmental coefficient based on departmental performance. The actual salary that each employee receives will be determined based on his or her performance. We will never implement salary adjustments for all employees at the same pace. We should ensure that the baseline salary for each job level remains stable and ensure that the actual salary curve changes with the company's business performance. *(Source: EMT Meeting Minutes No. [2007] 009)*

We need to understand that employees in primary leadership positions face both internal and external pressures. Therefore, they should be paid much more than those in deputy positions. *(Source: EMT Meeting Minutes No. [2007] 009)*

After a manager is appointed, his or her compensation should be adjusted accordingly. If he or she proves to be competent in a new position after half a year, the job level should be adjusted accordingly. *(Source: EMT Meeting Minutes No. [2007] 009)*

The goal of our HR transformation is to standardize position management and people-job matching, thus enabling each department to define its own positions and the number of employees it requires based on fixed compensation packages. If the compensation package of a department exceeds the pre-set limit, the department director will need to explain why additional employees or efforts are required and obtain approval from the respective business executive. Every department should make full use of its existing resources and avoid recruiting more employees. *(Source: EMT Meeting Minutes No. [2007] 022)*

Do not be afraid of negative reactions from those who receive a pay cut. Decreasing pay or adjusting positions is also an opportunity to test our managers. If a manager stays positive and works hard after being demoted or receiving a pay cut, he or she may still have the opportunity to be promoted again in the future. *(Source: EMT Meeting Minutes No. [2008] 002)*

We need to evaluate each position to understand its weight, and ensure that each position can create value. Also, the weight of each position may change over time. When a job is not clearly defined, a lower-level position may require a higher-level employee. However, if the job is defined clearly, the position may no longer need a higher-level employee. The Human Resource Management Department can set up a department to create rules in this regard. This department can then evaluate the weight of each position from time to time. After the weight of each position has been clarified, we will understand how many employees we need for each level. *(Ren Zhengfei: Human Resources Must Be Oriented Towards Forging Ahead and Refrain from Being Dogmatic and Rigid, 2009)*

We have made it clear that the Staffing Sub-committee under the Human Resources Committee determines the number of positions we need and the weight of each position. Managers and HR management departments determine how to evaluate each job and whether an employee is suitable for a certain position. If a position only requires one manager, but you have two, then you should demote one or transfer the extra manager to another department. In the past, job evaluations were based on the number of employees instead of position requirements. Now we need to change that. *(Ren Zhengfei: Human Resources Must Be Oriented Towards Forging Ahead and Refrain from Being Dogmatic and Rigid, 2009)*

When considering pay raises for junior employees, we focus on their contributions to the company and the value they have created for customers. We must avoid being too rigid regarding job levels. We adjust salaries based on the absolute appraisals of these employees, which is simpler, more transparent, and easier to quantify. This also encourages junior employees. *(Ren Zhengfei: Speech at the Meeting Regarding the Report on the Pilot Program for Absolute Appraisal of Junior Employees in Operational Positions, 2012)*

3.3.5 Favoring high-performing employees in bonus distribution

We need to work out transparent bonus plans for business departments, stabilize bonus-related policies, and create a sustainable development mechanism through which employees motivate and constrain themselves. *(Ren Zhengfei: Work Report to the Board of Directors Regarding the Completion of the 2003 Business and Budget Goals, 2004)*

The UK Representative Office has raised a very good proposal for appraising local employees. Under this proposal, short-term bonuses and PBC[7]-based appraisals and promotions are effectively managed, and bonuses for local employees are transparent. Employees can calculate and manage their own bonuses. This practice avoids the old practice of ranking people for bonus distribution. I think we can review the appraisal system proposed by the UK Representative Office, send it to our Human Resource Management Department for archiving, and initially deploy the proposal in the UK. *(Ren Zhengfei: Speech at the Meeting Regarding the Report by the BT Account Department and the UK Representative Office, 2007)*

We need to improve our bonus system to motivate employees throughout our organization. Senior management will determine the principles behind bonus distribution, and delegate authority to subordinate teams to formulate diverse distribution plans. These plans should be well-targeted, prompt, and aligned with business needs and management requirements so that employees will be effectively motivated. *(Source: EMT Meeting Minutes No. [2007] 009)*

When assessing managers' bonuses, we need to consider their overall performance during the bonus assessment cycle, rather than recent key events. Their bonuses should be determined based on individual, departmental, and, most importantly, company performance. *(Source: EMT Meeting Minutes No. [2007] 009)*

We need to find ways to shorten the bonus distribution cycle. For instance, we can divide our annual bonus packages into quarterly bonuses. The first three can be smaller, for example, 20% of the annual total for each, leaving the last bigger one for the last quarter. Responsible departments should devise viable plans for achieving this. *(Source: EMT Meeting Minutes No. [2007] 009)*

We must be systematic and serious about bonus assessments. We can implement a bonus point scheme. For instance, each month, each representative office can score each employee based on their performance. At the end of the year, we can add up all the points for each employee and make the total the basis for distributing bonuses. *(Source: EMT Meeting Minutes No. [2008] 028)*

We need to continue improving our bonus distribution system, and widen the gaps between regions, between departments within each region, and between employees. If we still see employees receiving equal bonuses somewhere, the responsible manager will need to be replaced, because distributing bonus like this will only drive away high-performing employees. This year, we have set down a policy that 5% of employees will receive no bonus. If the head of any large department fails to select this 5%, no one in that department will receive a bonus until the decision has been made. This policy mainly applies to large departments; we can be more flexible in smaller departments. However, when it comes to C&Q assessment and people-job matching, we need to strike a balance between different regions, because employees might transfer from one place to another. *(Source: EMT Meeting Minutes No. [2009] 022)*

Our bonus distribution system needs to favor high-performing employees. This is necessary to motivate these employees to achieve even better performance, and allow bonuses to play a motivational role. *(Source: EMT Meeting Minutes No. [2009] 008)*

We need to establish a bonus distribution system within each business unit to motivate the unit to meet or exceed its targets. We will widen the gap for bonuses between high performers and ordinary employees to encourage all employees to perform better. For key projects, we need to reward project members as soon as targets are achieved. *(Source: EMT Meeting Minutes No. [2009] 024)*

We should simplify bonus assessment procedures and give employees bonuses once they have made a decent contribution. Don't mix different things together, because it will make things too complicated to be fair. *(Ren Zhengfei: Speech at the HRC Meeting, 2009)*

We are now wondering if it is possible to establish baselines (including bonuses and excluding salaries) when assessing well-established business units like network equipment. In that case, we will have a baseline for each representative office after it works out its plan. We can then compare the performance of each representative office with the baseline to produce a rating. We can have more than one baseline, for instance, one for sales and one for profits. The weights of the two baselines may vary from time to time or from region to region. But once the weights are established, we should avoid changing them frequently. *(Ren Zhengfei: Speech at the HRC Meeting, 2009)*

The bonus distribution system should promote the company's continued growth and ensure that it can maintain a certain level of profitability. Our bonus packages should be based on both revenue and profits. Using only profit-based appraisals will prevent the company from growing. Using only revenue-based appraisals will result in blind expansion without regard for profits. Striking a balance between the two is a challenge for managers at all levels. *(Source: EMT Meeting Minutes No. [2009] 024)*

Huawei must implement a Contribute and Share system, and our business departments and regional offices must have a system of self-control in place. Through these systems, our costs will not become unbearably high because budgets will be in the hands of field teams. Field teams will starve if they cannot make money. This is a principle we will stick to in the future. *(Ren Zhengfei: Speech at the EMT ST Meeting, March 29, 2013)*

3.3.6 Avoiding the threat from excessive benefit packages

The purpose of increasing benefits is for us to work better together, be more effective, and move forward faster. That will make for better work and a happier life. But we have to do this ourselves – it won't fall into our laps. The money in your pocket comes from your own work. If you don't work, your pockets will be empty. So we have to keep improving efficiency to ensure our company develops sustainably. *(Ren Zhengfei: Being Mentally Dedicated and Trying Your Best to Successfully Complete Your Work, 1996)*

All our benefits will be monetized, because the distribution of other types of incentives will create a lot of trouble. Huawei does not utilize non-transparent distribution as it complicates the distribution process, causes asset losses, and creates extra expenditures. Senior executives are in a position to benefit most from non-transparent distribution, and I don't want to see that happen. *(Ren Zhengfei: Comments to Employees with a PhD, 1997)*

I am also against providing excessive benefits, because doing so may produce lazy employees. *(Source: Out of Chaos, 1998)*

We need to help employees get used to paying for the services they use. In the future, we will charge employees for any service we provide. We pay employees for their work and they have to pay for the services we provide to them. *(Ren Zhengfei: Remarks at a Meeting with Employees, 2000)*

Our compensation system should not turn into a welfare system. *(Ren Zhengfei: Survival Is Fundamental to an Enterprise, 2000)*

We need to be wary of the potential problem of slowing momentum that may arise after we get rich, and must take preventive measures in advance. Currently, many countries that offer large amounts of welfare have high taxation and a brain drain. We must learn lessons from these countries to maintain our company's sustainable growth. *(Ren Zhengfei: Spring of Northern Country, 2001)*

We must control the overall level of compensation, and guard against the threat to our company posed by high basic salaries and excessive benefit packages. *(Ren Zhengfei: Speech at Huawei-3COM's Report on Manager Development, Organizational Building, and Human Resources Policies, 2005)*

Life is precious. With regard to critical illnesses and accidents, both the company and employees should fulfill their responsibilities. In this case, the company purchases commercial insurance for employees. *(Source: Huawei Regulations on Employees' Personal Insurance, 2008)*

We will try to construct more high-end apartments with kitchens, and rent them out to single employees to help them cope with the current real-estate bubble. I previously thought that we should let employees take care of their own housing. Now I am not against building some apartments, but these apartments should not be sold. That could cause a lot of internal conflicts that we would find difficult to resolve. *(Ren Zhengfei: Speech at the EMT ST Meeting, 2009)*

No customer is willing to pay higher prices to support greater rewards for our employees. We have to earn everything we want through hard work. Do not expect things to simply fall into your laps. If a company runs reward plans it cannot afford in the long run, it is like quenching thirst with poison. *(Ren Zhengfei: Digging In and Widening Out, 2009)*

We provide free plane tickets every year for employees who work overseas so that they can be reunited with their families. This helps ensure that families stay together and maintain healthy relationships. *(Source: Regulations on Home-Visit Plane Tickets for International Assignees from China, 2010)*

The Administrative Service Department should avoid using employee satisfaction as a yardstick in assessments, because it is directly related to costs. We have to understand that a comfortable life does not last long.

Only through hard work can we have a good life. So the company will only satisfy employees' basic needs. If they want a better life with, say, designer clothes, they have to pay for them out of their own pockets. Our responsibilities to our employees are limited. We cannot afford to give them everything they want. *(Ren Zhengfei: Minutes of the 2010 Annual Awards and Experience Sharing Meeting with the Global Administrative Staff, 2010)*

3.3.7 Systematically planning non-monetary incentives

We must make it clear that our care for our employees is based on results and responsibilities. If an employee performs very well at work, why cannot he or she go to the café or exercise during work time? But if he or she works really hard, trying to scrub the coal to make it white, we will not recognize him or her, because the work doesn't create any value. *(Ren Zhengfei: Speech at the EMT ST Meeting, March 29, 2013)*

Non-monetary incentives should be planned systematically. It won't work by just giving employees medals. I think the Russian army sets a good example. There is always a veteran unit in its parades. This is both impressive and motivating. So can we copy their example? *(Ren Zhengfei: Speech at the EMT ST Meeting, March 29, 2013)*

We should establish an honor accumulation system so that heroes can benefit over the long term. For instance, what benefits do employees working in hardship regions enjoy in terms of healthcare? We need to design a benefit plan for this. The money for this benefit system will come from the total compensation package. If someone gets more benefits, others will get less; the compensation package will not increase. It is not enough to just reward heroes with a certificate of merit. We have to provide them with some tangible benefits as well. As long as they create value for customers, we will recognize them, no matter what motivates them. *(Ren Zhengfei: Speech at the EMT ST Meeting, March 29, 2013)*

---

[7]   PBC: Personal Business Commitment. This refers to the commitment made by an employee for his or her performance objectives and measurement standards concerning a specific assessment period.

PART TWO

ON MANAGERS

Staying customer-centric, inspiring dedication, persevering, and growing by reflection: These are the core values that we have established over the past two decades. They are the essence of our corporate culture.

Achieving sustainable growth is the biggest challenge that all companies face. To overcome it, we need to identify the major driving forces behind Huawei's development, and figure out how to sustain and improve these forces. Now, people are beginning to understand that a company's core values power the joint efforts of all employees. We need to ensure that our successors identify with our core values, and are able to grow by reflection. We need to mold our successors through our core values. This is necessary to ensure the sustainable growth of our company.

— Ren Zhengfei

CHAPTER 4

MANAGERS' MISSIONS AND RESPONSIBILITIES

The goal of an enterprise is to create value for its customers and achieve business success. Competition in the business world is in essence about company management. The missions and responsibilities of managers at all levels are to live and pass on the corporate culture and core values; take the corporate culture and core values as their central focus; manage value creation, assessments, and distribution; and lead their teams to continuously create value for customers, thereby achieving business success and long-term survival for the company.

The basic responsibilities of managers include improving productivity, giving employees a sense of accomplishment, and creating a promising future for the company by working actively and responsibly based on corporate requirements. How well a manager fulfills these three responsibilities will determine to what extent he or she is accepted by subordinates.

Managers' top priority is to set the correct direction. They must focus on the most important issue and the key factors that influence it, and properly control the pace and flexibility required to achieve goals. Strategic thinking in a manager means having a global view that allows a clear understanding of short-term and long-term interests. CEO Ren Zhengfei once said that the job of the first-in-command is alignment, deployment, and customer engagement. Alignment refers to building organizations. Deployment refers to effectively resolving issues in manager selection, appointment, appraisal, incentives, and replacement. Customer engagement means fully understanding customer needs and future trends through frequent exchanges.

Huawei describes managers' behavior as the wolf spirit. To expand, Huawei believes an enterprise must develop a wolf pack. Wolves have three key characteristics: a keen sense of smell; a pack mentality; and tenacity. In addition, senior managers must boost employee confidence through great passion and firm beliefs.

An important responsibility of a manager is to identify, recommend, develop, appraise, and supervise talent. Managers must assume joint responsibility for the moral character of the talent they recommend. When identifying talent, managers need to focus on their strengths and respect their individuality. While the Chinese tradition of sticking to the middle of the road contributes to stability, it has certain negative impacts on developing talent – it makes talent hesitant to express itself and unable to influence or contribute to social development.

This chapter mainly describes the missions and responsibilities expected of managers at Huawei. The next chapter primarily focuses on how managers at Huawei are expected to behave.

4.1

Managers Should Live and Pass on the Corporate Culture and Core Values

4.1.1 Staying customer-centric, inspiring dedication, persevering, and growing by reflection

An enterprise must make profits to survive. Profits can only come from customers. Huawei's survival depends on meeting customer needs, providing products and services that customers want, and receiving reasonable rewards. We need to pay our employees and investors, and only our customers pay us. If we do not serve our customers, who do we serve? Huawei only exists to serve its customers because they determine the company's destiny. *(Source: Huawei's Core Values, 2007)*

Huawei does not have any external resources to depend upon. What we have is the diligence and perseverance of our employees. We must eliminate anything that undermines our internal vitality and innovation. This is critical for us to survive fierce global competition. The road ahead is not easy and is full of uncertainties. We cannot guarantee that our company will survive over the long term. Therefore, we cannot promise our staff that we will offer them lifelong employment. We will not tolerate lazy employees, either. If we do, it is unfair to those who work hard and make real contributions. Nothing is free. We have to earn a happy life through hard work. *(Source: Notification on the Status of the Human Resources Management Transformation, 2007)*

We must stay customer-centric and inspire dedication; it is not appropriate to only inspire dedication. If dedicated employees work very hard but do not create value for customers, their efforts are meaningless. *(Ren Zhengfei: Speech at the PSST Managers' Meeting, 2008)*

While the company's management is scaling new heights, what should we use to determine the future direction of our organizations, processes, and managers? How should we appraise performance? I think providing effective customer services is what we should focus on at work. It is also the yardstick we use to assess both direct and indirect value. *(Ren Zhengfei: Deepening our Understanding of the Corporate Culture of Staying Customer-centric and Inspiring Dedication, 2008)*

More than two decades of practice has taught us how important self-reflection is to the company's development. If we hadn't adhered to this principle, Huawei wouldn't have become what it is today. Without self-reflection, we wouldn't have listened to our customers so attentively or understood their needs so well. We also wouldn't have noticed the merits of our peers or learned from them. In short, we would have become egocentric, and wouldn't have survived in this volatile and competitive market. Without self-reflection, we wouldn't have been able to introspect, motivate ourselves, and boost team morale in the face of crises. Without self-reflection, we would have isolated ourselves from the outside world, ignored our weaknesses as an inexperienced local company, and missed out on the new ideas that have been essential for us to become a world-class company. Without self-reflection, we would have been blinded by pride in our achievements and easily fallen into the abyss. Without self-reflection, we wouldn't have streamlined our organization or processes, improved our management system, or reduced our operating costs. Without self-reflection, our managers wouldn't have spoken the truth, listened to critical voices, studied the best ideas, or made progress. As a result, they wouldn't have formulated and implemented the right decisions. In other words, only people who reflect on themselves can be truly open-minded, and only companies that reflect on themselves will enjoy a bright future. Self-reflection has helped us get where we are today. How far we can go in the future will depend on our ability to maintain our tradition of growing by reflection. *(Ren Zhengfei: Anyone who climbed out of the pit of setbacks is a saint, 2008)*

I think the most important goal of a CFO is to ensure that we promptly deliver the right, high-quality products and services to customers at low costs. To stay customer-centric, we must meet these four requirements at the same time. Staying customer-centric means minimizing costs to help customers succeed, which will in turn help us succeed. If we stay customer-centric, we will definitely achieve sustainable and profitable growth.

(Ren Zhengfei: Timely, Accurate, High Quality, and Low Cost Delivery Calls for Professional Process-compliant CFOs, 2009)

The key to Huawei's success lies in staying customer-centric, inspiring dedication, and persevering. At Huawei, we focus on customers rather than bosses. Customer-centricity will lead Huawei to success. What is the essence of inspiring dedication? It is actually customer-centricity. Why do dedicated employees work hard? They work hard to satisfy customers' needs. There are slackers at Huawei. If they want customers to pay for their laziness, there is no way that will happen. Why would a customer be so selfless? To win customers, we must persevere. No matter how much money we earn, we still need to remain dedicated. By dedication, I mean a committed heart and soul, not the general notion of working hard. If we stop working hard, our company will gradually wind up in dangerous straits and ultimately collapse. *(Source: Simple Interpretations of "Three Success Principles", 2010)*

Self-reflection is essential to the survival of an enterprise. This concept has existed in our company since we first embraced the Chinese proverbs "from the ashes the phoenix is reborn" and "those who climbed out of the pit of setbacks are saints". Such self-correction has enabled us to maintain steady growth over the years. *(Ren Zhengfei: Speech at the Huawei Annual Management Conference, 2013)*

4.1.2 Successors must identify with our core values and grow by reflection

What types of employees will be promoted as managers at Huawei? Those who identify with our corporate culture and create value for the company. If you don't identify with our core values, we won't promote you. This cultural identification is very important. It is a kind of exchange. Employees have the right to slack off, but we have the right to not promote them or give them pay raises or incentives. This way, they have no choice but work hard and make progress. *(Ren Zhengfei: Seizing Opportunities, Adjusting Management Systems, and Meeting Challenges, 1997)*

Whether or not Huawei will collapse depends on whether we can improve our management. This in turn will depend on whether our managers identify with our core values and whether they grow by reflection. *(Ren Zhengfei: How Long Can Huawei Survive, 1998)*

We only appoint managers who identify with our core values and have contributed more than other employees. Managers must be the first to endure hardships and the last to enjoy relaxation and comfort, just like a general must be the first to charge forward and the last to withdraw. Managers must place strict requirements on themselves and set a good example for their subordinates. *(Ren Zhengfei: Adapting the Appraisal System for Managers to Challenges Facing the Transforming Industry, 2006)*

Achieving sustainable growth is the biggest challenge that all companies face. To overcome it, we need to identify the major driving forces behind Huawei's development, and figure out how to sustain and improve these forces. Now, people are beginning to understand that a company's core values power the joint efforts of all employees. We need to ensure that our successors identify with our core values, and are able to grow by reflection. We need to mold our successors through our core values. This is necessary to ensure the sustainable growth of our company. To me, the word "successor" has a broad meaning. It does not mean that, when a senior executive steps down, a successor will appear automatically. Succession is an ongoing process, and occurs in every activity, every position, and every process. It is a process of continuous improvement. We need to ensure that we have successors for every position and that all of our successors identify with our core values. *(Ren Zhengfei: Managers Should Live and Pass on Huawei's Core Values, 2010)*

Managers should pass on our core values, know rules and abide by them, and be down-to-earth. Toadying is prohibited. All managers must pass on our core values. To do this, they must first understand them. I hope that our HR management, business management, and finance management philosophies can be discussed and brainstormed across the company over a period of three to five years. The longer this process goes on, the better quality they will be. We should allow dissenting opinions within the company. If we can keep the same pace and move forward in spite of differences, we will walk no other path but success. It will be very risky if employees are forced to agree on everything. *(Ren Zhengfei: Developing Managers Based on the Selection Mechanism, Reviewing and Streamlining Organizations Based on Processes, and Promoting the Open and Balanced Development of Organizations, 2011)*

4.1.3 The major talent of leaders lies in their ability to shape culture

Passing our corporate culture down to subordinates is the responsibility of managers at all levels. If our managers can't understand our culture, it will be impossible for them to pass it to others. People won't be promoted to managerial positions if they don't understand or identify with our corporate culture. (*Ren Zhengfei: Having a Sense of Service and Branding, and Showing Team Spirit, 1996*)

If you don't identify with our corporate culture, you will feel very uncomfortable as a manager and often be criticized. Then you will not find meaning at work. In fact, it is unlikely that people who don't identify with our corporate culture will serve as managers. Everyone at Huawei must follow our business conduct guidelines. Managers need to carry on and shape our corporate culture. (*Ren Zhengfei: Speech at the Group Resignation Ceremony for All Marketing & Sales Staff in Primary Leadership Positions, 1996*)

The major talent of any corporate leader lies in his or her ability to shape culture. People are driven by material needs. However, if people are only driven by material needs, they will argue over little things, be unwilling to cooperate, and have no ambitions. The role of culture is to help people move beyond their basic material needs, pursue higher-level needs such as the need to fulfill themselves, and unleash their full potential. During this process, people cooperate with each other, and earn respect and recognition. These needs are the foundation of effective team operations. (*Ren Zhengfei: Seizing Opportunities, Adjusting Management Systems, and Meeting Challenges, 1997*)

Huawei must strike an overall balance. To achieve this, we need to rely on our corporate culture. If there is no consensus on corporate culture across an organization, there will be no overall balance. The Chinese philosopher Confucius once said, "Follow your heart without breaking rules." We are not restraining you, but requesting that you strike an overall balance: to correct yourself, adjust yourself, and make progress. Self-adjustment is not realized by the leader. The leader is like the head of a wolf pack, and his main job is to secure opportunities. Then the wolf pack automatically strikes an overall balance. This is a culture-based integrated propulsion system that develops on its own. (*Ren Zhengfei: Speech at the Meeting for the Fourth Revision of The Huawei Charter, 1997*)

Maintaining unity in our company depends on our common values and identity. We must use an economic lever to drive our company's growth, and use our value assessment principles to guide our employees in identifying with our corporate culture. *(Source: Minutes of the CEO's Staff Team Meeting, 1997)*

Managers at all levels need to face reality, accept it, and love it. The basis of our beliefs should be consistent with reality. Otherwise, we will meet with conflict. When faced with transformation, some employees might feel unsatisfied. To stabilize the situation, managers should set strict requirements for themselves, and lead by example to help employees understand and identify with corporate policies. Managers need to help the company understand its employees; more importantly, they need to help employees understand the company. *(Ren Zhengfei: Building Finance into an Invincible Organization That Adapts Quickly to Our Business Development, 2005)*

Huawei's corporate culture embodies its core values. This makes it possible for us to break down our customer-centric strategy, and integrate it into our daily work. By emphasizing that "Huawei only exists to serve its customers," we can improve service awareness and reinforce this concept in the minds of our employees. We ensure that all of our goals are driven by customer needs through a result- and responsibility-oriented value assessment system and a sound incentive mechanism. We ensure that customer needs are satisfied through process-based organizations and standard operating procedures. As a result, we have developed a customer-centric corporate culture that is oriented towards high performance. *(Source: Huawei's Core Values, 2007)*

4.2 Identifying Customer Needs, Seizing Business Opportunities, and Pursuing Business Growth

4.2.1 Managers need to remain close to customers, listen to them attentively, and understand their needs

How have our senior managers made progress? The answer is by spending a lot of time with customers. Customer engagement enlightened our senior managers, and laid a solid foundation for their future development. *(Ren Zhengfei: Corporate Development Should Focus on Meeting the Current Needs of Customers, 2002)*

We should establish a policy that requires all VPs in R&D to meet with customers several times a week. If we often communicate with our customers and listen to what they say, we will know more about their thoughts. We owe our progress to our customers. By constantly communicating with customers, we are inviting them to help us move forward. If an R&D manager claims to be thinking about products and markets every day, but doesn't remember the names or phone numbers of customers and marketing & sales people, what is the point of his claim? Huawei exists to serve its customers, so whatever we do at the company needs to center on them. Customers, not one or two corporate leaders, are the soul of Huawei. Our core values should be built on customers. If we stay customer-centric, we will gradually become process-based and institutionalized. Then governance without intervention will become a reality at Huawei. *(Ren Zhengfei: Acting According to Universal Laws, Giving Full Play to Core Teams, Constantly Improving Per Capita Efficiency, and Working Together to Survive Hard Times, 2002)*

We have defined the three responsibilities of the first-in-command as alignment, deployment, and customer engagement. Alignment refers to developing organizations and organizational behavior. Deployment refers to effectively resolving issues in manager selection, appointment, appraisal, and replacement. Customer engagement means fully understanding the needs of both internal and external customers. *(Ren Zhengfei: Seeing the Situation Clearly and Accelerating Organizational and Reserve Pool Development to Embrace Huawei's New Development, 2005)*

We should stay customer-centric. In this way, we can cultivate a large number of generals. When trying to win customers, we need to think hard and try hard because customers only choose the best. In this process, many heroes and generals will emerge. *(Ren Zhengfei: Simple Interpretations of "Three Success Principles", 2010)*

We should maintain good relationships with our customers at both the corporate and BG levels. Corporate senior executives need to stay on good terms with customers' key decision-makers at both the organizational and personal levels, and build an effective mechanism to maintain customer relationships. Even when transferred to another BG or region, these executives need to maintain their previously established personal relationships with customers. *(Source: EMT Resolution No. [2011] 047)*

We need to stay customer-centric when communicating our strategies. To do so, we need to clearly understand our customers' pain points and how we can help them solve their problems. During the Mobile World Congress in Barcelona this year, I visited Ericsson's booth. I found that their consultants had done their homework in advance about topics to discuss with their customers – they focused only on their customers' pain points. Customers could stay longer and look around if they wanted to find out more. However, when we receive customers at our booths or exhibition halls, we present everything to them as if they were primary school students. Our role is more of a presenter than a consultant. So we need to directly focus on the pain points of our customers, and then show them our solutions. *(Ren Zhengfei: Speech at the Retreat for Huawei's Branding Strategy and Communication – Staying Customer-centric and Communicating Huawei at the Strategic Level, 2012)*

We need to present our future rather than our history to customers. They already know a lot about us through daily communication. What is the point of repeating what they already know? What they don't know is the future. We don't know it, either. Before the iPhone was launched, nobody ever thought that the mobile internet would far surpass the fixed version. So, we need to know what our customers care about when they approach us. As we now realize, they come to us to study what the future will look like. *(Ren Zhengfei: Speech at the Communication Meeting Regarding the Reconstruction of the F1 Exhibition Hall – Being Future-oriented, Focusing on Customers' Pain Points, and Demonstrating Huawei from a Global Perspective, 2012)*

The enterprise market certainly has a bright future, but it will take time for it to mature. Currently we are only familiar with the needs of telecom carriers and we know little about the needs of other customers. It's risky to expand our business into fields that are largely unknown to us, such as finance and insurance. We don't understand how things work in these fields. How can we develop solutions for them? It will be better for us to focus on a small number of customers and projects. Gradually, we will be able to make breakthroughs in these fields. *(Ren Zhengfei: Remarks at a Meeting with Staff of the Guangzhou Representative Office, 2013)*

In the future, traffic will not be confined to carriers' pipes. We need to redefine our understanding of pipes, and consider things from the customer perspective. So who are our customers? Both carriers and individual consumers. *(Ren Zhengfei: The Best Defense Is a Good Offense, 2013)*

4.2.2 Increasing per capita efficiency through sustainable and profitable growth

When I last spoke at our UK Representative Office, I emphasized fine-grained management. By that, I meant we must create order in the midst of chaos. But I didn't mention the need to seek to create chaos out of order, or disrupt balance to fuel further growth. Doing business is not like painting or embroidery, and it requires much more than just fine-grained management. We must have clear goals, and focus on the most important issue in the market and the key factors that influence the issue. If we only emphasize fine-grained management, we will shrink. The purpose of fine-grained management is to prevent chaos during growth, not to close our doors tight. Fine-grained management doesn't mean we stop growing. We must stand up to face the competition, and have the courage to win. This is necessary to become skilled at achieving success. Fine-grained management and growth don't conflict with each other; we must effectively combine them. *(Ren Zhengfei: Speech at the UK Representative Office, 2007)*

During our current organizational restructuring, we should prioritize market opportunities over per capita efficiency. It doesn't make much sense if we only emphasize the latter. The reason is this: Based on our business performance this year, per capita efficiency will increase as long as we don't recruit new people. But in this case, we may not achieve much business growth. The measures we take to increase per capita efficiency must also support sustainable growth. So we need to think strategically and focus on business growth rather than merely on per capita efficiency. Otherwise, we will be doomed to fail. *(Ren Zhengfei: Speech at the Regular Meeting of the Reserve Pool, March 25, 2009)*

Sustainable and profitable business growth is a major way to increase per capita efficiency. Measures taken to increase per capita efficiency must support business development. We need to constantly improve organizational efficiency and mobilize existing human resources, instead of simply laying off employees. *(Source: EMT Resolution No. [2009] 002)*

Huawei cannot afford to collapse. We must remain dedicated, and improve ourselves while moving forward. It will be too risky if we stop just to improve ourselves. Our emphasis on positive cash flows and profits has already constrained our employees, and we can't impose more controls on them. These appraisals have changed our previous growth model into one that ensures sustainable and profitable growth. *(Ren Zhengfei: Speech at a Meeting with the IFS Project Team and Staff from Finance, 2009)*

Our profits now come from our growth rather than management. If the company stops growing, we will have negative profits and cash flows. So we need to increase internal efficiency before we stop growing. For example, operating departments must continue to improve themselves. If they require more staff, they can recruit more, but they also need to generate more profits. *(Ren Zhengfei: Speeches at the EMT ST Meeting on May 25 and the HRC Meeting on May 26, 2009)*

We will use appraisals to demote managers who don't achieve business growth goals, and place those who are ambitious and able to achieve our goals in key business management positions. *(Source: EMT Meeting Minutes No. [2011] 002)*

What is scale? We must focus on profits and must not expand blindly. In the enterprise business, there are no critical markets that we have to fight for, and there is no need to talk about the market landscape. We simply have to find a suitable market to make a breakthrough, and then gradually expand our market presence. The device market does not involve market landscape issues either, and we need to develop steadily while ensuring profitability. In these two markets, we need to avoid price wars. Previously, we tried to compete on price. We need to stop doing that, or we will destroy order in the marketplace. We need to win customers through high-quality products and services rather than through low prices. *(Ren Zhengfei: Remarks at a Meeting with Staff of the Guangzhou Representative Office, 2013)*

4.2.3 Having the courage to win is necessary to become skilled at achieving success

As modern technology becomes more complex and develops more rapidly, high-tech companies will fall behind or even perish if they make the slightest mistake. From the start, we lagged far behind our peers in developed countries, where tens of thousands of professionals can work on a single piece of software. If we don't work hard as a team, we will be doomed to fail. When we promoted collective dedication, we met barriers and many key employees left, which often left us in crisis. But by working hard as a team and focusing our limited resources on a very specific area to make breakthroughs, we managed to take the lead in certain fields and overcome the difficulties of our startup phase. Looking back, I still tremble with fear. I believe no company does R&D like us, adopting so many new technologies at the same time and starting from scratch, without any examples to learn from. Luckily, we succeeded. I can't imagine what would have happened if we'd failed. So sometimes, we need to think big in order to accomplish something. *(Ren Zhengfei: Current Situation and Next Steps, 1995)*

As long as there is a market need, we must seize opportunities. Because we don't know what will happen in the marketplace in the future, we need to compete on a wider front and must not give up easily. When things become clear, we should immediately shift our investment to key areas. Therefore, I advocate orienting towards business and products. Profitability is also important, but we can't be completely profit-oriented. What we need are future opportunities. For instance, by approaching marketing and service personnel, you R&D engineers are taking the first step towards understanding customers' needs and serving the market. We need to develop talent with comprehensive knowledge. We need to take this seriously. It is especially important for senior engineers to acquire knowledge and become all-around experts. In doing so, we are developing future opportunities. *(Ren Zhengfei: Meeting Minutes of the R&D Management Committee, 2001)*

Having the courage to win is necessary for us to become skilled at achieving success. In the past, our chairwoman courageously led our efforts to win large customers such as BT, Vodafone, and Telefonica. If we'd not been brave enough back then, we would not be where we are today. Our chairwoman is a role model that all managers need to learn from. Management departments at all levels must continuously improve their work and effectively increase efficiency from end to end to support the company's growth. *(Ren Zhengfei: Speech at the UK Representative Office, 2007)*

I think we need to strengthen fine-grained management in all regions and product lines where the sales growth rate is lower than the company average. I don't want to force these regions and product lines to eliminate redundancies, but I require that you share experience with and dispatch managers to regions that are growing faster. It is a wonder that you have managed to achieve your current growth rate. You simply grew too fast in the past. So you don't need to compare yourself with others. The goal of our entire operations is to grow rapidly. We are facing an opportunity that only occurs once in a blue moon. We witnessed a similar opportunity about seven or eight years ago. However, back then we were still small and didn't have the ability to seize it. Now that we're capable of seizing the current opportunity, we must have the courage to win – that is necessary for us to become skilled at achieving success. We need to adhere to our managerial and organizational principles, and stick together to exploit this opportunity for which we've waited two decades. *(Source: EMT Meeting Minutes No. [2008] 009)*

When working to seize the opportunity arising from the current transformation, listed companies may not be as passionate as us because they need to control financial costs. We must learn from the hard work of the Koreans. Many employees in our company work as hard as they do, like Richard Yu. He fights hard to achieve every goal possible. Following 20 years of development, we have stable products and mature organizations, which support our ordered growth. We will select managers from among those who work as hard as the Koreans, and this will help us achieve our growth goals. *(Ren Zhengfei: Speech at the EMT ST Meeting on January 20 – Increasing Investment to Seize Strategic Opportunities, 2011)*

We need more hardworking and persistent managers like Richard Yu in our strategic businesses and strategic markets. We are eager to promote them and see them fighting in the field. These managers are prepared for sacrifice in the field. In this case, what can prevent them from winning? But if we don't have the courage to fight in the field, we won't have the opportunity to succeed, no matter how good our plan is. So I think we must encourage outstanding young people to go and fight in strategic markets. Senior managers must fight in the field. Going to the field does not mean you have to sell products or provide services to customers. At least you should get to know whether our products meet customer needs, and systematically think about the value of our products from different perspectives, such as ease of installation and maintenance, rather than simply from a technological perspective. *(Ren Zhengfei: Working Together Towards the Same End, Concentrating Advantageous Resources on Strategic Businesses, and Having the Courage to Seek Greater Opportunities and Further Widen the Gap, 2011)*

4.3

Leading the Team in Achieving Organizational Goals

4.3.1 Professional managers should be responsible for achieving organizational goals

The social responsibility – in a narrow sense – and historic mission of a professional manager are to help an organization achieve its goals with the minimum amount of resources, including time. These are the professional ethics and sense of accomplishment required in a manager. *(Ren Zhengfei: Mission and Responsibilities of Professional Managers, 2000)*

The primary responsibility of managers at all levels is to lead their teams in achieving key goals rather than focusing on specific tasks with little consideration for team management and development. *(Source: EMT Resolution No. [2006] 016)*

4.3.2 Achieving synergy within departments responsible for growth

We target the strongest competitors in the world, and gradually catch up with and overtake them. Only in this way can we survive. Therefore, in the R&D and marketing and sales fields, we must establish an organization and mechanism that facilitates the survival and development of "wolves" – aggressive managers. We need to attract and develop a large number of aggressive managers who are eager for success and growth, and motivate them to develop a sense of smell as keen as that of wolves. They must remain united and do whatever it takes to seize opportunities, sell products, and increase market share. *(Ren Zhengfei: Establishing an Organization and Mechanism That Facilitates Enterprise Survival and Development, 1997)*

We have never proposed a wolf culture. Instead, we proposed a *Wolf-Bei* program, which summarized the behaviors of these two animals to help us establish our branch office organizations. As we know, wolves have a keen sense of smell, a pack mentality, and tenacity. A Bei, on the other hand, is very smart and pays attention to detail. However, a Bei is unable to fight on its own because of its short forelegs. As a result, they have to work together with wolves, and help wolves run in the right direction. We expect our sales support team to work like Bei and help those fighting in the field with regard to bidding, network planning, administrative services, and other services. Salespeople must have a clear sense of direction like the keen sense of smell of wolves, work together closely like a wolf pack, and never yield in the face of difficulties. Nothing is easy; otherwise, there would be lots of Ciscos rather than just one. Our culture is not a wolf culture. It is misleading to simply talk about the wolf spirit. The cooperation between the wolf and Bei is the real point. Also, such cooperation does not mean becoming workaholics. We work hard, but we also work smart. *(Ren Zhengfei: Deepening our Understanding of the Corporate Culture of Staying Customer-centric and Inspiring Dedication, 2008)*

4.3.3 Creating a favorable environment to inspire employee dedication

When motivating subordinates, managers at all levels need to show them how bright the future is. More importantly, they need to tell their subordinates that they can only get there by improving every day. Managers tend to assess employees based on their own values and code of conduct. But they need to understand that no one is perfect. It is demoralizing if managers only focus on employees' weaknesses, misunderstand them, or fail to objectively appraise their performance. *(Ren Zhengfei: Speech at the CEO's Staff Team Meeting, 1998)*

Every leader needs to learn how to lead and create a favorable environment to inspire employee dedication. Managers need to understand that their subordinates' success will be their biggest accomplishment. *(Ren Zhengfei: Living with Peace of Mind, 2003)*

The role of managers is to face and address problems with the right attitude. During daily work, they need to stick to principles, focus on efficiency, and appreciate and support each other. We need to create a harmonious and effective management team to help us overcome any difficulty. *(Ren Zhengfei: Living with Peace of Mind, 2003)*

Managers need to think about how to motivate their teams and also set learning and development goals for their teams. *(Ren Zhengfei: Speech at the Annual Meeting of the Market Finance Department, 2005)*

Some managers like to take credit for everything, so they do everything themselves and leave dozens of subordinates with little to do. At the same time, they complain about it and accuse others of doing nothing. We should remove such people from managerial positions and send them back to operational positions. We believe there are no incapable employees, only incapable managers. Employees don't work hard because their managers are incapable. Good managers need to focus on the most important issue and the key factors that influence it, make proper work arrangements, and unleash everyone's potential. *(Ren Zhengfei: Speech at the PSST Managers' Meeting, 2008)*

4.3.4 Managers need to be strict as well as caring

Some junior managers have very poor management skills. I am not saying that they are not good at their jobs, but they really need to learn how to manage effectively. We need to be strict with employees, but at the same time, we need to implement effective approaches to minimize conflict. Managers could be strict and caring at the same time. *(Ren Zhengfei: Speech Regarding Recent Publicity Requirements, 1997)*

Our managers should be tough but not arrogant. We need to be strict with our employees with regard to appraisals, but at the same time, we need to be caring and support our peripheral departments. Throughout history, the leaders of many invincible teams cared for their team members. In addition, we need to carry on our fine tradition of "toasting those who succeed and offering a helping hand to those who fail". It is important to coordinate effectively between different people and between different departments to improve overall efficiency. *(Ren Zhengfei: Guidelines for Human Resources Management Transformation, 2005)*

There is a military slogan: "With me joining the first battle, we will definitely win." An unbeatable army develops after many battles. The generals of unbeatable armies are extremely strict with their soldiers, but they also care for them deeply. As late as two or three o'clock in the morning, they will inspect sentries to check whether soldiers are slacking or sleeping on duty, but they will also visit the barracks to replace a blanket that has fallen off a sleeping soldier. They are not only managing soldiers, but also caring for them. Managers need to be strict with their employees, and cannot allow personal feelings to intrude on work-related issues. However, managers can show care and concern when it comes to problems outside work. We should strengthen our understanding in this regard and work together for the common cause of the company. Some of our junior managers are not good at uniting their subordinates and are cold towards them. If managers are cold-hearted, why would their subordinates devote themselves to the team? *(Ren Zhengfei: Speech at the Meeting Regarding the Work Report of the Asia Pacific Region, 2006)*

An unbeatable army develops after many battles, and high-performing soldiers are cared for by their generals. Since ancient times, the leaders of all effective teams have cared for their team members. There are no exceptions. A Chinese saying holds that, "A man is ready to die a loyal death for those who know his worth." Our corporate culture does not welcome tough and ferocious managers. It instead provides employees with a soul, a centripetal force for cooperation, and values for interpersonal relationships. According to these values, managers must be able to solicit admiration and conviction among employees. When organizing hands-on practice sessions for employees, managers at all levels must set a good example through word and deed, because "he who cannot command himself is unfit to command others". Managers must care for their employees and pay attention to their capability development and the difficulties they encounter in their daily work. They should also show proper care for their employees outside work. If managers do not treat their subordinates well, how will they work for them in return? *(Ren Zhengfei: Deepening our Understanding of the Corporate Culture of Staying Customer-centric and Inspiring Dedication, 2008)*

In China, there is a place called Jiuquan, which literally means the spring of liquor, and there is a story related to the name. Over 2,000 years ago, there was a general named Huo Qubing[1]. One day, the emperor rewarded him dozens of bottles of liquor. To share it with tens of thousands of soldiers, he poured it into a stream so that everyone could partake. This story reflects how much he cared for his soldiers, and that is why he was such a great general. *(Ren Zhengfei: Speech at the PSST Managers' Meeting, 2008)*

We need to care about those who suffer poor health after working extremely hard, especially those who have just finished a project on a tight schedule. We can give them two or three days off so that they can relax and rest. Invincible teams are developed through constant care by their leaders. We expect employees to work hard but, at the same time, we also need to care about them. *(Ren Zhengfei: Remarks After Watching the Battle of Moscow, 2008)*

Everyone present here today is a senior manager. You need to pay attention to your health, because you are the company's future leaders and our most valuable treasure. You need to learn how to delegate authority, reduce stress, take more exercise, and invest in your own health. The company's development depends on every employee, rather than just a few. You will eventually be leading the company. If you are in poor health, how can you lead the company forward? *(Ren Zhengfei: Speech at the EMT ST Meeting, June 30, 2011)*

I think the best way to protect the health of our senior managers is to work less overtime, have fewer meetings, take fewer business trips, and take more time off. If a job is too much to handle, it's better to create more deputy-level positions. I previously said that we should not have too many deputy-level positions, but that doesn't mean we shouldn't have any. We need them if they're necessary. Otherwise, holders of primary leadership positions will be exhausted. I can accept full-time deputy-level managers. But we should not create an unnecessary deputy-level position for someone simply because of his or her past contributions. I previously asked managers at level 18 and above to clock in and out. This is not for supervisory purposes, but for their own good. For instance, if a manager always works overtime on weekdays as well as weekends, the number of extra hours worked can be recorded so that he or she can take some time off and relax when necessary. *(Ren Zhengfei: Speech at the EMT ST Meeting, June 30, 2011)*

4.3.5 Boosting employee confidence through great passion and firm beliefs

Some departments (especially those handling routine affairs) must not expand randomly. Neither should they lay off employees randomly, as it will weaken their competitiveness. Over the past two years, we've been beating the gongs and drums, and charging forward. Despite the dangers ahead, we have remained courageous and never faltered, so our competitors have lost heart. In two or three years' time when a market opportunity emerges, our managers will be ready, our organizations and systems will be more efficient, our processes will be optimized, and our IT systems will be in place. As long as our operating teams are effective, we will be able to make breakthroughs, achieve scale, and leave our competitors behind. *(Ren Zhengfei: Speech at the 2000 New Graduate Recruitment Work Meeting, 1999)*

What is the role of our senior managers? Each senior manager should behave like Danko, a character from the Russian folktale. Danko tears out his heart and sets it alight to illuminate the road for his people. Similarly, senior managers should guide their teams, especially in the midst of endless darkness. The more difficult the environment, the more light the senior managers should provide to dispel the darkness. They must take the initiative to ignite the entire team's faith in success and guide the team towards success. *(Ren Zhengfei: Acting According to Universal Laws, Giving Full Play to Core Teams, Constantly Improving Per Capita Efficiency, and Working Together to Survive Hard Times, 2002)*

I think senior managers must boost employee confidence through great passion and firm beliefs. This is the historic mission that they are supposed to undertake. *(Ren Zhengfei: We Must Ignite Our Faith in Success through Great Passion and Firm Beliefs, 2002)*

Managers at all levels need to regularly communicate with their employees, share the vision and goals of the department, and motivate them to look ahead. *(Ren Zhengfei: Speech at the PSST Managers' Meeting, 2008)*

Managers at all levels should be able to meet challenges, and have the courage to assume responsibilities and lead their teams through difficulties. If a manager spreads rumors, loses confidence in the company, panics in the face of challenges, or complains constantly, it means he or she is unable to fulfill his or her job, and we must replace them with someone more suitable. *(Ren Zhengfei: Critical Moments Are a Touchstone for Managers at All Levels, 2012)*

---

[1]   Huo Qubing (140 BC–117 BC), born in Linfen, China's Shanxi province, was a distinguished military general of the Western Han dynasty during the reign of Emperor Wu.

4.4 Managers Need to Set the Correct Direction and Focus on the Most Important Issue

4.4.1 Managers' top priority is to set the correct direction

Leaders are not necessarily tech-savvy, but they must move beyond technical thinking, think strategically, and set the correct direction and business goals. *(Ren Zhengfei: Speech at the Shanghai Research Center, 2007)*

Many of our managers are always busy with issues that do not create value. As I mentioned at the UK Representative Office, good leaders must focus on the most important issue and the key factors that influence it, and then figure out where to go. They must identify the correct direction and look before they leap. We have many managers promoted from among employees who like to leap before they look. This results in wasted energy, which has a negative impact on our employees. *(Ren Zhengfei: Speech at the PSST Managers' Meeting, 2008)*

Senior managers must be forward-looking, think strategically, and seize more opportunities to socialize at events such as the World Economic Forum in Davos. The aim is to help them broaden their horizons and absorb new ideas. They cannot remain satisfied just because they are already generals. Instead, they must strive to become a marshal. *(Source: EMT Meeting Minutes No. [2012] 028)*

Senior managers must focus on strategy more. I have forwarded several articles on aircraft carrier experts to our EMT members. When discussing what the US would fight for, these experts mentioned things like currency and finance. Similarly, we should have managers who act like marshals. Starting from our strategy research institute, many of our managers and experts should focus on long-term strategies and have the courage to exchange ideas, and shouldn't be concerned with day-to-day operations. Why do we encourage our senior executives to attend the World Economic Forum in Davos? It's because these sessions discuss social structures that are likely to emerge in two or three decades, and our executives may be inspired and identify the correct path. Sometimes, a thought leader is much like a good book or an interesting article. We have a large group of strategists and thousands of generals, and thought leaders will certainly emerge from among them. Some asked how I would develop thought leaders. My answer was to free them from their daily work and invest heavily in improving their strategic thinking capabilities. *(Ren Zhengfei: Speech at the EMT ST Meeting, October 30, 2012)*

Currently, many of our managers still like to have complete control; otherwise they feel uneasy. They don't think much about strategy. How can such managers lead? They must broaden their horizons. *(Ren Zhengfei: Speech at the EMT ST Meeting, October 30, 2012)*

We will try to approve the appointments of Huawei fellows before the Chinese New Year. In the future, our senior managers will either pursue fellowships or assume administrative management positions. They need to choose one path, not both. In terms of vision, I think we are doing much better than before. We are able to listen to different voices, as opposed to doing things completely on our own. This is a strength that we must maintain. However, we still lack the capacity to leverage the most important global value chain. Nowadays, wherever we go, we are still competing on price, just like 20 years ago. *(Ren Zhengfei: Speech at the EMT ST Meeting, October 30, 2012)*

During the current period of transition, we are calling on more employees with strategic awareness to take up managerial positions. We need to look into the future. We are now taking a gamble to test our strategic viewpoints. We are betting that the pipe will be as wide as the Pacific Ocean. *(Source: E-mail No. [2012] 35 Minutes of the Meeting between Mr. Ren Zhengfei and Staff from the 2012 Laboratories)*

We were once criticized and told we would be unable to succeed as we were involved in both fixed and wireless networks. At the time, Ericsson, for example, only focused on wireless. My answer was that both fixed and wireless networks would be used to transmit information. I had no idea then that information technology would change so dramatically. However, based on such an understanding, we persisted and survived. Looking ahead, we can see that fixed and wireless networks will converge. This convergence can be compared to an estuary. If we go further, we will see another estuary. While the makeup of an estuary may change, the rivers supporting it will always be the same. Employees who do not realize this will assume that the company's strategy is always changing. Therefore, we must ensure all managers and employees understand the big picture. Today, we have tens of thousands of employees. We must be clear about where our own river is flowing, so that all our employees will understand the assumptions behind our branding strategy and our direction, and we can then move forward together towards a common goal. *(Ren Zhengfei: Speech at the Retreat for Huawei's Branding Strategy and Communication – Staying Customer-centric and Communicating Huawei at the Strategic Level, 2012)*

The role of a leader is to set a clear direction and let others follow. *(Ren Zhengfei: Speech at the EMT ST Meeting, March 29, 2013)*

4.4.2 Focusing on the most important issue and the key factors that influence it

I recently saw presentations from several representative offices. Their Pow-erPoint slides seemed to cover every possible aspect, with meticulous atten-tion to detail. However, the slides lacked a core, or soul. Simply put, they did not focus on the most important issue and the key factors that influ-enced it. Fortune favors those with the intelligence to recognize and seize opportunities. *(Ren Zhengfei: Speech at the UK Representative Office, 2007)*

For fast-growing markets and products, our main objective is to win strategic projects, win more customers, and win more market share. At the same time, we should carry out fine-grained management to prevent chaos caused by blind expansion. When assessing growth, we need to take sales revenue into account, but also look at sales growth potential and break-throughs with tier-1 carriers. When I say we should win more customers, I do not only mean geographically, but also from product and carrier per-spectives. Doing that is like shaping the market landscape. *(Source: EMT Meeting Minutes No. [2008] 014)*

We are progressing towards an unknown future filled with risks. Con-fronted with uncertainties, managers at all levels must focus on the most important issue and the factors that influence it, set the correct direction, properly control the pace, and apply *huidu²* to achieve goals. *(Ren Zhengfei: Who Calls for Artillery and How Do We Provide Timely Artillery Support, 2009)*

Throughout history, many reforms have failed because they were executed hastily, stretched too thin, and were too rigid. Over the past two decades, Huawei has been improving step by step, making only one or two radical changes. During our transformation, we need to focus on the most important issue and the factors that influence it, set the correct direction, and look before we leap. We should choose feasible plans that are urgently needed even though they are not perfect. We must not pursue perfection or act hastily to take credit for the success of others. Perfectionism is not feasible for Huawei. What we really need is pragmatism. To achieve our great mission, we must have a clear mind, and set the correct direction. We must take solid steps and stay focused on our core business, which will allow us to surf the wave of this new era, progress, and reap the harvest of our transformation. *(Ren Zhengfei: Who Calls for Artillery and How Do We Provide Timely Artillery Support, 2009)*

In this era, it doesn't matter if we cannot influence market demand. Rather, we must be able to adapt to changes. Many of our existing assets are a legacy of the voice era. Our success over the past two decades will not ensure our future success. We need to put our past success behind us and move forward. I don't think we should consider technology to be a threshold, because competitors will catch up with us sooner or later. Customers might not remain loyal to us all the time, because we might not treat them with the same passion as time goes by. What actually matters, in my opinion, is the business model. Why do I insist on earning small money, instead of big money? It's because of our business model. We have managed to catch up with other vendors because many of them decreased their investment in areas that generated lower profits. If we continue to earn small money after we become the industry leader, it will be impossible for other players to earn big money in the industry. Will they remain dedicated if they can only earn small money? If not, we will remain the industry leader. If we can stay hungry for a long time and do not seek to earn big money, we can keep earning small money and survive. If we give employees decent pay, they will stay and we can keep the company running. If we only focus on short-term interests and seek to earn big money, we will dig our own grave. Although a company's survival depends on many different factors,

I think that maintaining sustainable and profitable growth and providing quality services are the most important. *(Ren Zhengfei: Speech and Comments at the Carrier Network BG's Strategy Retreat in Huizhou, 2012)*

4.4.3 Moving forward via continuous improvements

I am in favor of gradual management improvements instead of radical changes. We should resolve problems one by one as they emerge, and not expect to address them all at once after they have piled up. One cannot implement radical changes simply to achieve a good reputation, even if not doing so may allow others to say you are an incapable manager. *(Ren Zhengfei: Survival Is Fundamental to an Enterprise, 2000)*

I am also against having someone without a holistic view lead a transformation, because the changes they implement will only make our processes less effective. Therefore, when we select managers to lead a transformation, we need to first see whether they have a holistic view. Transformation managers who arbitrarily overthrow existing processes and make radical changes must be demoted immediately to avoid chaos in management and high costs. *(Ren Zhengfei: Adapting the Appraisal System for Managers to Challenges Facing the Transforming Industry, 2006)*

Managers must avoid going to extremes. These lead to arguments and conflicts, and may disrupt mature processes. We need moderate approaches, not radical ones, to improve processes. When building our systems, we must build upon the past, instead of starting from scratch. *(Ren Zhengfei: Huawei University Must Become the Cradle of Generals, 2007)*

Our entire organization is oriented towards being pragmatic. We are dedicated to making improvements but object to drastic and hasty changes. This is because slight shifts may affect the overall situation, and arbitrary improvements can be costly. We advocate gradual improvements, the replication and promotion of successful practices, and devotion to improvement. Any new manager must not drastically overturn the management system established by his or her predecessor. If a manager's transformation goes beyond a certain scope, he or she should be replaced. We must effectively manage corporate innovations, continue to improve per capita efficiency, and build a high-performance corporate culture. *(Source: Huawei's Core Values, 2007)*

Transformation itself is impossible to stop, but it won't last forever, either. What we should emphasize is a relatively stable state, rather than continuous destruction. Seeking perfection is not feasible, because we will never know what is perfect. What we really need is pragmatism. To put it philosophically, any balance can be disrupted, which gives birth to new life. Through this process, the world moves forward. Similarly, after one generation dies, another rises. This is balance being disrupted. *(Ren Zhengfei: Speech at a Meeting with the IFS Project Team and Staff from Finance, 2009)*

I think structures and processes are important, and suggest that we appoint a management team to handle them. The team will also participate in the design of structures and processes, which should not be designed only by a small number of experts. Our future transformation will involve both management and professionals. We will not allow professionals to shut themselves away and discuss transformation on their own. Reforms often fail because of a lack of consultation. To achieve a successful transformation, we must allow our managers to negotiate with us regarding benefits. This negotiation is a process of compromise. *(Ren Zhengfei: Speech at the EMT ST Meeting, November 30, 2011)*

I am not worried about integration at the executive level, but I am worried about entry-level integration. It takes a lot of effort to integrate. If a manager can effectively integrate into an organization, that's good. If not, we can let those who are adept at integration take over the whole business department. Experience tells us there have been very few cases of successful integration. Ineffective integration will cause an organization to fall apart. During the integration of different cultures, compromise is necessary. We should not put too much emphasis on commendable qualities such as integrity and the ability to take a global view during integration. Adaptability is the key and focus. Managers who cannot adapt to a new environment will be transferred, though they are not necessarily incompetent managers. Of course, if two parties can work closely and complement each other, we don't need to intervene. *(Ren Zhengfei: Speech at the EMT ST Meeting, March 30, 2012)*

---

[2] *Huidu* is a Chinese term used to describe the shades of grey that exist between black and white, and implies flexibility and balance without losing sight of direction.

Improving Business Processes from End to End Based on a Holistic View

4.5.1 Building a process-based organization is the goal of enterprise management

We have to make it clear that our company's development relies on our customer-centric management system where survival is our bottom line, rather than on the decisions of an entrepreneur. When such a system is in place, the soul of an enterprise is no longer an entrepreneur; it is customer needs. Customers are always there, so the soul of the enterprise will also be there. For Huawei, our product development will always be directed by customer needs, and our enterprise management goal is to develop a process-based organization. In addition, we should always remember that Huawei only exists to serve its customers. *(Ren Zhengfei: Living with Peace of Mind, 2003)*

Why do we need to build a process-based organization? IPD, ISC, CMM, C&Q Assessment systems and performance appraisal systems are all methodologies. While they don't seem to be alive, they can still endure over the long term. Why do we implement them? They can help us remove unnecessary layers, and streamline our processes from end to end, thus making our company less reliant on individuals. This is the most cost-effective and efficient approach. *(Ren Zhengfei: Living with Peace of Mind, 2003)*

The purpose of our management is to streamline our processes from end to end in the most simple and effective way possible. We start by identifying customer needs and end by accurately and promptly satisfying these needs. This is our lifeline. As long as we understand the importance of serving customers, Huawei will survive and endure. Internal management activities serve to accurately and promptly satisfy customer needs. This is the principle that we must follow in our internal management transformations. Any other management activities that do not serve this purpose would be bureaucratic. *(Ren Zhengfei: Key Points for Management, 2003–2005)*

I am against partial optimization without overall efficiency improvements. If an intended change won't contribute to productivity, it would be better not to implement it at all; any change will involve additional work and coordination with other departments and thus lead to extra costs. Therefore, when we select managers to lead a transformation, we need to first see whether they have a holistic view. *(Ren Zhengfei: Adapting the Appraisal System for Managers to Challenges Facing the Transforming Industry, 2006)*

Global Technical Service (GTS) and Manufacturing, as downstream departments, need to interact more with R&D to make our products easier to install, maintain, and manufacture. While trying to respond to customer needs as quickly as possible, our product departments need to come up with rules on version management to minimize the number of versions, make it easier and cheaper to maintain future versions, and reduce potential quality issues. We may consider appointing a dedicated VP for each product line who will focus on the ease of product installation, maintenance, and manufacturing. *(Source: EMT Meeting Minutes No. [2008] 013)*

When it comes to mature markets where we are growing steadily but have limited potential for growth, and products in the final stage of their life cycles, we need to focus on lean management while exploring new opportunities. We need to transfer outstanding employees from those markets and products to work in our weaker areas such as planning, financing, and government relations. In this way, we can improve the quality of our operations and achieve balanced development. We have a clear assessment criterion regarding mature markets and products: generating cash flow and profits for the company. *(Source: EMT Meeting Minutes No. [2008] 014)*

We should first address unbalanced workloads between departments and remove departmental silos that hinder the flow of employees across departments. We should increase efficiency by improving management, instead of simply asking employees to work overtime. *(Source: EMT Resolution No. [2006] 023)*

We are now developing a process-based and professional management system. It is time for us to begin building a CFO management system. We expect that the CFOs, once they come on board, will help cut down on waste and costs while maintaining rapid business growth, and avoid partial optimization without overall efficiency improvements. We should always keep the big picture in mind. *(Ren Zhengfei: Timely, Accurate, High Quality, and Low Cost Delivery Calls for Professional Process-compliant CFOs, 2009)*

Have you ever watched the mini-series *Band of Brothers*? One US army company was deployed to the Asia Pacific region as soon as they finished fighting in Europe. You should lead your own Marine Corps to make market breakthroughs. A general should be able to win a carrier customer with a team in the field. Product line presidents should have a holistic view of our processes and should work in the areas where we are weakest rather than just working in the R&D section. *(Ren Zhengfei: Building the Competitiveness of Back-end Access Products with High Quality and Low Costs, 2009)*

Only when department heads are held responsible for achieving strategic goals can we prevent them from becoming conservative and putting the interests of their own departments first when allocating resources. Only department heads with a strategic view can carry out transformations that are in the best interests of the company. *(Source: EMT Meeting Minutes No. [2011] 005)*

A process is developed for three purposes: One, to ensure correct and timely delivery; two, to earn money; and three, to ensure no corruption exists. As long as these three purposes are achieved, the simpler the processes, the better. *(Ren Zhengfei: Speech and Comments at the Business Process & IT Strategy Retreat, 2012)*

Process owners are the heads of business departments, rather than people from the Business Process & IT Management Department (BP&IT). BP&IT is a support department that provides services to help business managers build, optimize, and utilize processes and IT tools. *(Ren Zhengfei: Speech and Comments at the Business Process & IT Strategy Retreat, 2012)*

As technology continues to improve, prices will continue to fall. Our company doesn't pursue high profits or impressive financial indicators. Instead, we try to improve the quality of our internal management. *(Ren Zhengfei: Speech at the Retreat for Huawei's Branding Strategy and Communication – Staying Customer-centric and Communicating Huawei at the Strategic Level, 2012)*

We will establish a system under which administrative management is properly separated from business process management. Process owners will be responsible for developing processes, including business decision-making mechanisms, and process risk control and accountability systems that align with business rules. Managers will be responsible for managing people to align with business goals, including organization building, manager appraisals, and resource allocation. One major reason for poor process management is that department heads attach little importance to processes. As such, they should act as Global Process Owners (GPOs) to increase the importance and influence of processes and ensure that processes are executed effectively. *(Ren Zhengfei: Minutes of the Report Regarding Huawei's Control Posture, 2013)*

We must take a holistic view to advance our overall management system, whose development should be systematic, constructive, and simple. To prevent silos caused by isolated transformations, we should build a coordinated management system and integrate processes from end to end. We must respect facts and ensure consistency of inventory accounts and goods. We must allow no lies. Whenever possible, we should try to skip steps in the handover of internal operations data, as long as the necessary separation of duties is observed, so as to increase operational efficiency. *(Ren Zhengfei: Speech at the Huawei Annual Management Conference, 2013)*

4.5.2 Competition in the business world is in essence about company management

Our managers must focus on the big picture, jointly maintain company stability, and accelerate its development. This should be your goal. *(Ren Zhengfei: Comments to Staff of Huawei Electric, 2001)*

IPD[3] and ISC are two major processes in our company. All other methodologies support them. Why have we always prioritized management? It's because it's the only thing that will endure in a company. Without effective management, the company will leave us nothing but debts. We need to learn how to develop our management system, and change our code of conduct so that the system endures. A management system can't work on its own. We rely on our employees to implement and improve it. *(Ren Zhengfei: Living with Peace of Mind, 2003)*

When competing with large companies like Ericsson, we are competing in terms of efficiency and cost to see who can survive longer. Improving management is an ongoing process and there is no point in being radical. If we can keep improving by just 0.1% every year, we will improve by 10% in 100 years. That would be great. *(Ren Zhengfei: Speech at the Meeting Regarding the Report by the BT Account Department and the UK Representative Office, 2007)*

Improving management efficiency is the only way for an enterprise to succeed. Normally, it is easier to improve technology than to improve management, because any changes in management could potentially harm the interests of certain groups. Competition in the business world is in essence about company management. If our competitors are constantly improving their management and we are not, we are destined to decline. *(Ren Zhengfei: Deepening our Understanding of the Corporate Culture of Staying Customer-centric and Inspiring Dedication, 2008)*

No company can keep developing at a high speed forever. In our mature markets where our sales revenue has reached a certain level, revenue may grow slowly or even decrease. If this happens, identifying new opportunities in our existing markets and earning profits would be the goal of our future business management. *(Source: EMT Meeting Minutes No. [2009] 006)*

Only two assets will endure in our company: our management architecture and management system supported by processes and IT systems; and employee management and incentive systems. Not everyone remains at Huawei their whole career; but these systems will endure as long as the company exists. Thus, they will allow our company to thrive over the long term. After being continuously improved by our managers, how much will our management system be worth? As long as we can survive, this system will support our company's development. If we go public one day, the worth of the company will completely depend on the value of these two assets. We must thus give a high priority to processes. *(Ren Zhengfei: Speech and Comments at the Business Process & IT Strategy Retreat, 2012)*

4.5.3 Providing big rewards for small improvements, but only encouragement for "big" suggestions

We provide big rewards for those who make small improvements. This is a principle that we have always followed. We need to evaluate these improvements to see if they align with the company's major processes, and if they can integrate with relevant processes. We need to first simplify and optimize the suggested changes before incorporating them into processes. Whether a process is advanced or not depends on the value it contributes to the company. This is also the criterion we are using to evaluate transformation projects carried out this year. It's very complicated and challenging to achieve rapid growth while implementing management transformations. Managers thus need to have a strong sense of mission and responsibility, and need controlled passion that allows them to work hard and methodically. According to a Taoist saying: "Ruling a big country is like frying a small fish." Similarly, we need to remain cautious when taking action to avoid any damage to our processes and the mistakes that may follow. *(Ren Zhengfei: Huawei's Hard Winter, 2001)*

Anything that has been institutionalized requires constant innovation. Our organization is no exception. Organizational innovation is not individual behavior; instead, it is innovation which follows testing, assessment, and review within the organization. Anyone who simply aims to gain recognition by contributing the most to process development will certainly become an obstacle within our processes. We must remove these obstacles to make governance without intervention a reality. *(Ren Zhengfei: Speech to Executives on the Exam on Writing an Essay on "Governance Without Intervention", 2000)*

Blind innovation would be catastrophic. We are opposed to the practice of replacing all key officials when a new government is formed. And we thus don't allow new managers to change whatever their predecessors accomplished as soon as they assume their positions. We encourage them to carry on existing management practices that work well – maybe as much as 99%. If they replace everything, the relationships built with other departments will be destroyed and processes won't flow smoothly. So it is unnecessary to innovate blindly and change practices that work effectively. If changes are deemed necessary after careful consideration, we will do whatever we can to make them happen, and it's worth paying a price to address unpredictable difficulties. We need to do a thorough review and listen to different opinions before we make any changes, no matter how small they are. Even if the changes are good for your department, they may be harmful to other departments, thus driving down the efficiency of the whole company. Such innovation is harmful. *(Ren Zhengfei: Continuously*

Improving Per Capita Efficiency and Building a High-performance Corporate Culture, 2004)

I am firmly against blind innovation. Sometimes, we may recklessly adopt innovations which cause our system to stagnate due to a lack of testing and verification. We should not approve work reports that talk a lot about innovation. Neither should we give pay raises to those that present them. Unnecessary innovations will only lead to higher management costs. Of course, we welcome improvements that are adopted after repeated testing and verification by the transformation committee, but we don't need to label such improvements as innovations. What is the point of using such a trendy term? We must remain practical when implementing management transformations. To improve management, we must advocate seven NOs: NO perfectionism; NO red tape; NO blind innovation; NO partial optimization without overall efficiency improvements; NO transformative leadership without a panoramic outlook; NO transformations involving employees with no business experience; and NO deployments of premature or untested processes. *(Ren Zhengfei: Adapting the Appraisal System for Managers to Challenges Facing the Transforming Industry, 2006)*

4.5.4 Increasing management professionalism to reduce internal operational costs

In a professionally managed company where employees are paid based on their C&Q and performance appraisal results, professional managers receive the compensation they deserve for the contributions they have made to the company. Therefore, they should not ask for additional compensation on the pretext that they are the company's heroes. Professional managers should contribute to the company as needed. *(Ren Zhengfei: Mission and Responsibilities of Professional Managers, 2000)*

Using templates at work can help employees make rapid management improvements, and is also the key to standardized management. We should therefore develop standardized templates for use in our everyday work. Three months is sufficient for new recruits to understand the templates, as they are all well-educated. Being able to use templates at work means they are global and professional. Our templates embody the many years of experience of early Huawei employees. There is no need for new recruits to reinvent the wheel. All process-management departments should encourage employees to develop templates for all types of work which have been optimized and proven to be effective. Templates must be created for clearly defined and repeated processes. Management improves only when less time and resources are spent on the same task, and the same level of performance is achieved. We believe that only when we create templates and integrate them with processes can IT systems achieve their intended purposes. Therefore, we should pay more attention to template development. *(Ren Zhengfei: Huawei's Hard Winter, 2001)*

Ten years ago, management barely existed at Huawei. Although there is still a lot to improve in terms of management, the company is getting institutionalized. Thus our employees need to receive more training to improve their professionalism. Some people think dismissing employees who have worked in the company for a long time or transferring them to other positions may affect employee loyalty. What is loyalty? It involves high costs, so loyalty won't last long, but during difficult times we need employee loyalty to help the company survive. However, when everything is institutionalized, we need to strengthen professionalism. Only with professionalism can we reduce costs. *(Ren Zhengfei: Speech at the Regular Meeting of the Reserve Pool, March 25, 2009)*

What is professionalism? It is doing the same thing under the same conditions, but at a lower cost. In a competitive market, if our competitors improve but we don't, we will simply wither and die. Currently, we lag far behind Cisco in terms of innovation and Ericsson in terms of management. To close this gap, we must continue to improve our own management, because our customers will abandon us if we don't. The financial crisis that we're facing makes management optimization a top priority. Nonetheless, it's important that we remain calm and have a clear goal. We must not take any action because of short-term emergencies or short-term gains that we will regret in the long term. There's no point in extinguishing a fire today only to dig our own grave. In terms of management transformation, we must remain practical. *(Ren Zhengfei: Digging In and Widening Out, 2009)*

Western professionalism is the result of over 100 years of market reforms and is the most efficient way of doing things. Wearing a suit and a tie is not just about looking good. When studying Western professionalism, we must not copy it rigidly. After all, what's wrong with a Mao suit? Over the past 20 years or so, we have had our own successes. We need to get better at looking at why we have succeeded and how to stay successful. Then we must use Western methods to regulate, standardize, and create baselines for these management ideas; communicate them efficiently; master them; use them to train all levels of managers; and apply them in our work. Only in this way can we move past being a rigid copy of a Western company, and emerge as a living, breathing, and effective company with a soul. *(Ren Zhengfei: Digging In and Widening Out, 2009)*

We live in an age of professional managers; the age of founders and heroes has passed. If we don't adapt to this trend, we will fall behind the times. During the transition process, we need to work together closely as a team and cooperate with one another to achieve synergy, as nobody is good at everything. Those who never seek help are inefficient, and those who only seek individual success are destined to fail. *(Ren Zhengfei: Timely, Accurate, High Quality, and Low Cost Delivery Calls for Professional Process-compliant CFOs, 2009)*

---

[3] IPD stands for Integrated Product Development. It is a set of product development models, concepts, and methodologies, and an R&D management system that covers end-to-end business operations from the research of innovative technologies to product development and lifecycle management.

4.6 Building the Organization and Helping Subordinates Grow

4.6.1 A leader's job is to serve employees

The basic responsibilities of managers include improving productivity, giving employees a sense of accomplishment, and creating a promising future for the company by working actively and responsibly based on corporate requirements. How well a manager fulfills these three responsibilities will determine to what extent he or she is accepted by his or her subordinates. *(Source: The Huawei Charter, 1998)*

Managers need to understand that their job is to serve their subordinates and help them become heroes. Through this, their subordinates can help achieve the company's goals. Thus, subordinates will become heroes, but what about managers? Managers should be leaders, and their job is to serve their subordinates. *(Ren Zhengfei: How Long Can Huawei Survive, 1998)*

Managers need to be broad-minded and willing to help dedicated employees succeed. Don't worry that your subordinates will surpass you. Our relationships and communication are more important. As long as you work hard and fully apply your talents, you will have no regrets in your life. There is no need to aim for a higher position. Don't compare yourself with others. *(Ren Zhengfei: Speech at the PSST Managers' Meeting, 2008)*

4.6.2 Identifying and developing talent

Each manager needs to focus on cultivating successors; otherwise, the company may not be able to sustain itself over the long term. We will only promote managers who perform exceptionally, while at the same time doing a good job in developing successors. Otherwise, if managers leave their positions or the company, not everything will continue working. Here, I mean that we need to be broad-minded in developing our successors. Only those who are selfless and fair will attach great importance to the development of successors. Only when we have plenty of successors will we be able to enjoy sustainable development. These successors should include those who have made mistakes in going against their managers. Without such a broad mind, how can we manage our company? If we can't even manage our company, how can we develop globally? *(Ren Zhengfei: Step Forward or Step Down, 1995)*

Senior managers must be mentors for their successors and help them develop mentally. Otherwise, they are not fulfilling their obligations. Senior managers must play the role of mentors. *(Ren Zhengfei: Thought and Culture Are of Utmost Importance to Corporate Management, 1997)*

Tens of thousands of employees will become the successors for different positions at all levels, which will guarantee the company's sustainable development. *(Ren Zhengfei: Big Rewards for Small Improvements, 1998)*

One of the most important C&Q criteria for middle and senior managers is whether they can recommend and develop qualified successors. Those who fail in this should resign from their positions at the end of the current term. It is not enough for managers to be exceptional themselves. Great managers must help their successors become even more exceptional. *(Source: The Huawei Charter, 1998)*

An important responsibility of a manager is to identify, recommend, develop, appraise, and supervise talent whenever and wherever possible. Managers must assume joint responsibility for the moral character of the talent they recommend. *(Source: EMT Resolution No. [2006] 030)*

Regional managers are focusing more on projects than on developing managers. This year, we will work out regulations regarding the authorization, execution, and accountability of our managers at all levels. By implementing these regulations, we hope to resolve the problem of middle managers not making decisions. Regions are always complaining about the lack of competent managers. To solve this problem, they need to develop more managers on their own. *(Ren Zhengfei: Speech at the Meeting Regarding the Work Report of the Asia Pacific Region, 2006)*

The most important responsibility of a manager is to develop successors. The failure to develop successors is the biggest neglect of duty in a company. A successor does not refer to a particular person, but an entire team. Nevertheless, the formation of cliques must be avoided. *(Source: Financial Transformation Is About Huawei Rather Than Only the Finance System, 2007)*

I think when senior managers go to the field, it is more important for them to identify managerial candidates and communicate with them, than to provide specific guidance regarding business operations. Senior managers need to directly engage with managerial candidates. Otherwise, how can those young people get promoted? *(Ren Zhengfei: Speech at the EMT ST Meeting, May 31, 2011)*

Any Joint Committee of Regions (JCR) executive can initiate removal procedures if he or she finds that a manager does not possess the necessary capabilities for his or her job. But the executive doesn't have the authority to directly demote the manager. Similarly, if the executive identifies a good manager, he or she can also initiate procedures to recommend the manager for a promotion. In either case, JCR executives can only initiate the procedure as opposed to making a final decision on their own. In addition, if we need to communicate with certain managers, a JCR executive can fly to their location and talk with them first face-to-face, in a coffee shop, for example. Of course, the flight costs money, but it is worthwhile, as human beings need to communicate face-to-face. Teleconferences are useful for business communication, but face-to-face interactions allow people to connect personally. *(Ren Zhengfei: Speech at the EMT ST Meeting, June 30, 2011)*

While the Chinese tradition of sticking to the middle of the road contributes to stability, it has certain negative impacts on developing talent – it makes talent hesitant to be themselves and unable to influence or contribute to social development. As a developing country, China is in special need of heroes to keep its engines running, which provides the opportunity for everyone to grow. As Huawei aims to become a leading global company, and there is still a long way to go, it is especially in need of heroes who are hardworking, dedicated, and willing to make sacrifices. *(Ren Zhengfei: From "Philosophy" to Practice, 2011)*

Succession means the succession of culture and systems. When it comes to succession, Huawei emphasizes culture, systems, and processes, and not just one particular person. Similar to Western companies, we will not change our corporate core values no matter who is in charge. A single person cannot be that valuable or important. As a matter of fact, our succession plans have been moving forward for several years. Over the years, we have been implementing Western management philosophies. We have been promoting those who are passionate about work, have high integrity, and are adept at learning and practice. In fact, our succession plans have been moving forward all along. You simply did not realize it because we did not make an official announcement. *(Ren Zhengfei: Success Is Not a Reliable Guide to Future Development, 2011)*

Talent is a company's greatest asset. We must strengthen the development of finance organizations, as well as that of managers, experts, and employee teams, to improve our financial capabilities. *(Ren Zhengfei: Comments at a Meeting with Managers from Finance, 2012)*

To improve the management system, we need to think critically, enhance organizational development, identify gaps in this regard, and set the correct direction. We need to promote talent with successful field experience to expert or managerial positions, and select highly success-oriented individuals to join the CFO team. We need to develop talented professionals via a large number of projects and shape them into people who can manage elite teams. In addition, it is important to develop effective back offices that can efficiently provide quality services and allow professional managers to share the joys of success. We need to avoid perfectionism and care about employees; experts and senior managers need to be responsible for training, coaching, and mentoring younger generations to encourage them to assume more responsibilities and bring out their best. *(Ren Zhengfei: Comments at a Meeting with Managers from Finance, 2012)*

4.6.3 Adopting a balanced approach to organization building and focusing on weak segments

Huawei has an unbalanced organizational structure that operates with low efficiency. The weakest segment of an organization is a bottleneck. For example, in our company's early days, we experienced many difficulties with product and market development, and were eager to win contracts. So we adopted a strategy that focused on R&D, marketing, and sales. It was the correct strategy, because at that time survival was more important than scientific management. However, this strategy was not adjusted after our early years. Our senior managers were mainly promoted from R&D

and Marketing & Sales. Their subconscious favoritism for their original departments prevented them from making the best decisions and developing the right value assessment system. As a result, strong departments grew stronger and weak departments grew weaker, and bottlenecks were created. Some senior managers often complain about poor planning and budgeting, no cost accounting or cost control for projects, poor accounting by product/level/region/project, poor cash flow performance, etc. However, if our value assessment system does not support a balanced organization, weak departments will not be able to attract outstanding managers, which will prevent them from keeping up with other departments. Remember, our consolidated financial statement is determined by our weakest department, not by our strongest. If we don't overcome favoritism, Huawei will be unable to develop. *(Ren Zhengfei: Spring of Northern Country, 2001)*

We need to emphasize organization building. Without an effective organization and strong management, department heads will be very busy while their subordinates will be unable to perform to the best of their abilities because their strengths have not been fully leveraged. Many of our managers only care about business performance and do not pay much attention to the development of their organization or their employees. If we don't change this, it will be difficult for our company to achieve further development. *(Ren Zhengfei: Speech at the PSST Managers' Meeting, 2008)*

Managers at all levels should focus on organization building and manager management, which are the key links. Managers should build organizations and manage managers by adhering to the company's principles of staying customer-centric and inspiring dedication. Only when the key links are grasped will everything fall into place. *(Ren Zhengfei: Speech at the PSST Managers' Meeting, 2008)* Instead of prioritizing R&D and marketing & sales departments, we must ensure balanced development across the company. Outstanding managers are needed in all departments. We can't stop deploying managers to departments simply because they fail to succeed in a given market. We must consider how to achieve balance among all segments of the company. *(Ren Zhengfei: Comments on the Reserve Pool, 2010)*

During process execution and business operations, we need to combine reviews with decision making and delegate decision-making authority over issues to experts. In this way, we can establish a highly-efficient operational mechanism and maximize the value of experts. Financial departments need to develop and appoint more experts. Managers need to focus more on people management, and take responsibility for developing both the organization and managers. *(Ren Zhengfei: Comments at a Meeting with Managers from Finance, 2012)*

4.6.4 Putting the company's principles before personal feelings

A good manager should put the company's principles before personal feelings. *(Ren Zhengfei: Meeting Minutes, 1997)*

Department heads who cannot identify good managers are not qualified to hold managerial positions, because they lack management capabilities. We would rather they step down and take non-managerial jobs. Top experts can also receive high pay, sometimes even higher than some department presidents. As long as managers are in managerial positions, they should show no favoritism. Rather, they must adhere to our company's principles and completely implement the value assessment system while keeping the company's interests at heart. *(Ren Zhengfei: Speech at the CEO's Staff Team Meeting, 1998)*

Managers at all levels need to phase out employees who are inefficient and make no contribution. It is not acceptable to tolerate slackers simply because they are on good terms with their colleagues and managers. Those who don't understand how to build effective teams by replacing inefficient employees are not qualified to be department heads. *(Ren Zhengfei: Continuously Improving Per Capita Efficiency and Building a High-performance Corporate Culture, 2004)*

When addressing problems, managers should avoid representing their employees all the time. Instead, managers should promote self-reflection within teams. When there are problems, managers should not try to take the blame for everything. Instead, they should help those who have made mistakes realize what went wrong and how to improve in the future. We are not conducting an election. Why should we bother to represent our employees so much? If you have done this, then you are not a qualified manager, because you haven't provided your employees with the right guidance. What you should do is self-reflect to identify the problem's root cause and discuss with your employees how to improve in the future. *(Ren Zhengfei: Fully Implementing the Position-based Accountability System, 2005)*

Managers at all levels must adhere to the company's principles and have the courage to manage. Those who dare not dismiss low-performing employees are harming the company's interests. These managers should be removed from their positions. We should begin streamlining our organization by demoting unqualified managers. *(Source: EMT Meeting Minutes No. [2008] 037)*

As everyone can see, the economy is currently experiencing extreme difficulties. Only our company is continuing to carry out reforms, including those related to salary. This is an indicator of our business strength. If we improve contract quality this year, we will have more capital at our disposal to carry out reforms, which may offer us great opportunities for further development. I believe we can improve our teams so long as everyone remains dedicated and is down-to-earth. We must demote managers who are not qualified and transfer them to other positions. To do this, we need to put the company's principles ahead of personal feelings. *(Ren Zhengfei: Speech at the Mid-year Conference of Regional Presidents, 2011)*

Managers at all levels must take responsibility for managing, have the courage to manage, and be adept at managing. As the company develops, there will be an increasing number of younger managers in charge of older or more senior employees. But the problem is that some young managers do not dare, or are unwilling to manage those "older" managers or experts, or even leave them out in the cold. Many of these older managers and experts are experienced, ambitious, and diligent, and think independently, but are unable to create value because they have not been in the right position for a long time. So managers at all levels need to have the courage and be willing to manage all their employees, regardless of their age and experience. In addition, managers need to recognize these employees' value and contributions in order to motivate them and get the most out of them. *(Ren Zhengfei: Uniting as Many People as Possible, 2013)*

4.6.5 Avoiding treating your subordinates rudely

Many senior managers are very strict with their subordinates and often criticize them. As a result, a lot of managers would rather not make any decisions to avoid being criticized. Therefore, when we see middle managers not making any decisions, senior managers should also be held accountable. Managers at all levels need to avoid treating their subordinates rudely. More importantly, managers need to help their subordinates make the right decisions and develop skills. When criticizing subordinates, managers should focus on the issue, not the person. When subordinates make wrong decisions, managers need to address these mistakes objectively and give their subordinates the opportunity to explain what happened. At the same time, subordinates should also take the initiative to communicate with their managers and improve their own communication skills. *(Source: EMT Meeting Minutes No. [2008] 021)*

Our corporate culture does not welcome tough and ferocious managers. It instead provides employees with a soul, a centripetal force for cooperation, and values for interpersonal relationships. According to these values, managers must be able to solicit admiration and conviction among employees. Toughness and ferocity are signs of incompetence and inner weakness. These kinds of managers act against Huawei's corporate culture and are not capable at all. We must replace them immediately. *(Ren Zhengfei: Deepening our Understanding of the Corporate Culture of Staying Customer-centric and Inspiring Dedication, 2008)*

Many managers at Huawei have a bad attitude and rarely communicate with their subordinates. We should learn from Western companies to understand that communication between managers and subordinates is very important. It is not enough for managers to only communicate with employees who will be promoted. Collecting ideas from employees before making decisions is also a good chance to communicate more. During this process, you can learn more about your subordinates and identify managerial candidates. In addition, managers need to place employees in positions where they can unleash their potential and recognize employees who do a great job. In this way, we can develop a positive culture. *(Ren Zhengfei: Speech at the EMT ST Meeting, March 29, 2013)*

It is important to create an atmosphere where employees respect and trust one another. Those who are able to create value, especially managers and experts above certain levels, usually have very strong self-esteem and independent thinking capabilities. So managers need to respect them, trust their capabilities, and exchange ideas with them on equal footing. Being humiliated by managers is a common reason why employees choose to leave the company. The company cannot provide unlimited incentives or opportunities, but respect and trust are an effective way to encourage employees to continuously create value for the company. Managers at all levels need to improve their management and communication skills, listen to employees, and recognize their contributions promptly to make full use of their potential and creativity. *(Ren Zhengfei: Uniting as Many People as Possible, 2013)*

CHAPTER 5

REQUIREMENTS ON MANAGERS

The key responsibility of managers is to lead their teams. A manager's conduct sets the tone for his or her team – it is crucial to the team's morale and effectiveness. That is why Huawei focuses on cultivating managers' conduct, and why it sets high requirements in this respect.

Managers must be the first to bear hardships and the last to enjoy comforts; they must be in the vanguard during the advance and in the rearguard during retreat. Managers must lead by example and hold themselves to strict standards. At Huawei, junior managers are expected to commit themselves to their work; practice what they preach; pay personal attention to every detail; and achieve resolute execution, strict management, effective monitoring, as well as integrity and compliance. Middle and senior managers are expected to remain mentally dedicated; devote themselves to their work; possess a sense of sacrifice, mission, and urgency; and practice self-reflection. The success of Huawei today is not the story of one dedicated individual, but the stories of selfless leadership and teams with an unyielding spirit. Any company not founded on the spirit of dedication will not last long.

Managers must give absolute priority to facts. They must speak the truth, never hide facts, and report successes as well as problems. Huawei pays special attention to managers who voice dissenting opinions. They have good motives when they offer their opinions to corporate executives. They care about the company and have no regard for personal interests, so Huawei must take good care of them. Managers must unite as many people as possible, including those who voice dissenting opinions, and view them as like-minded partners in the pursuit of individual and organizational goals. Managers must build a tightly knit team that works hard to achieve the goals in spite of difficulties.

Fairness and objectivity are vital if managers are to gain the support of their subordinates. Managers must be selfless and treat their subordinates objectively, and adopt a result- and responsibility-oriented approach to assessments. Only when managers are selfless can they be fair and objective, and tightly unite their teams. Only when managers are selfless can they fearlessly uphold principles. Only when managers are selfless can they dare to criticize themselves and others, and address their own shortcomings. Only when managers are selfless can they become open-minded and set their sights high. Only then can they tolerate all that must be tolerated, and be able to shoulder responsibilities.

Openness, compromise, and *huidu* are the essence of Huawei's corporate culture. They are also the right ways for managers to think. A closed culture does not seek to absorb the best qualities of others, and will gradually be marginalized – and there will be no way out. Without tolerance, there is no compromise; without compromise, there is no *huidu*. If managers cannot apply a certain level of *huidu* under different circumstances, they will not be able to make the right decisions. The key to openness and compromise lies in the mastery of *huidu*.

Self-reflection helps managers refresh their thinking and open their minds. Willpower is more important than skill; character is more important than willpower; but an open mind is the most important of all. Self-reflection is essential to developing a good character and an open mind, which in turn make it possible to tolerate all that must be tolerated.

Starting a business and keeping it going are both difficult. But if the difficulties are understood, it is no longer difficult. The past successes of hi-tech companies are often the mother of failure. In this rapidly changing information society, one must remain vigilant in order to survive.

Chapter Five explains Huawei's requirements on managers' conduct from multiple perspectives.

5.1

Managers Must Remain Dedicated Over the Long Term

5.1.1 The HR system must encourage employees to forge ahead and remain dedicated

I believe everyone present is a hard worker, but I don't know whether all of you are mentally dedicated. These are two totally different things. To become a senior manager, you need to be mentally dedicated. Hard work alone does not make a good manager. *(Ren Zhengfei: Building the Development and Pilot Department to Act as a Sieve, 1996)*

In a fiercely competitive market, success favors the bold. We must therefore not relax in our pursuit of managerial excellence. This is the only way we can survive. When studying corporate documents, you must grasp their essence. An anti-gambling document, for example, should not be merely taken at face value. Its essence concerns dedication, though its basic idea is to prohibit gambling. We place strict requirements on senior managers. If we don't, the company would have long since failed. We cannot condone any managers who slack off. There is no way back: We can only forge ahead. *(Ren Zhengfei: Comments to Staff of the United Arab Emirates Representative Office, 2004)*

We train employees so that they can dedicate themselves to realizing the company's goals. If managers are not dedicated, their teams will gradually slack off – just like a frog that is slowly boiled alive – and the company will decline. *(Ren Zhengfei: Guidelines for Human Resources Management Transformation, 2005)*

Regarding employee development, Huawei gives priority to outstanding employees who are dedicated and have made significant contributions.

Dedication does not necessarily mean working in hardship regions; you can also show dedication in other positions. *(Ren Zhengfei: Adapting the Appraisal System for Managers to Challenges Facing the Transforming Industry, 2006)*

Managers at all levels are the key to building a culture of dedication. This is clear from case studies at Huawei and elsewhere, as well as from our successes and failures. Great leaders make great teams. If managers are not dedicated, their teams will inevitably fall apart. *(Source: EMT Meeting Minutes No. [2008] 021)*

The success of Huawei today is not the story of one dedicated individual, but the stories of selfless leadership and teams with an unyielding spirit. We will not compromise on dedication. Those who are not dedicated and those who play it safe will be dismissed. This is necessary to ensure the company's long-term stability. *(Ren Zhengfei: Timely, Accurate, High Quality, and Low Cost Delivery Calls for Professional Process-compliant CFOs, 2009)*

Our HR system must encourage employees to forge ahead and remain dedicated. But how can we inspire long-term dedication? The performance appraisal mechanism is the key: In addition to comparing employees, it also assesses each employee's progress, comparing his or her current and past performance. Our policy of eliminating poor performers aims to inspire employees to make progress in an all-round manner. If you fail to improve, you will be replaced. This makes for a natural cycle of renewal. If we guarantee the positions of middle and senior managers, we will ruin the future of talented employees, who will have no way to rise in the company. We should build an open stage where everybody can dance. Even those who leave the stage will have the chance to return. *(Ren Zhengfei: Human Resources Must Be Oriented Towards Forging Ahead and Refrain from Being Dogmatic and Rigid, 2009)*

To become generals, managers must commit themselves to dedication and adhere to our code of conduct; these are the simplest and most fundamental requirements for those who want to become generals. *(Ren Zhengfei: A Prerequisite for Becoming Generals Is Commitment to Dedication and Adherence to a Code of Conduct, 2009)*

The essence of our HR policy is maintaining our spirit of dedication. This spirit must never change, and neither should our sense of mission, urgency, and hunger. Without them, we will slide into crises and will never recover. In some ways, a crisis is already upon us: Some middle managers have become slack. To address this crisis, our Human Resources Committee must develop guiding principles and systematic methodologies. *(Ren Zheng-fei: Speech at the EMT ST Meeting, 2009)*

As part of our efforts to cultivate a spirit of dedication, we have incorporated customer centricity and customer service into the recruitment, promotion, training, and appraisal of every employee and every manager. For example, we attach great importance to employee contributions to customer service. Customer satisfaction is now a KPI for every manager, from presidents down. We have also included customer centricity in the competency model for managers and employees during their promotion and development. It is even included in the templates we use for recruitment interviews. *(Source: Huawei's Core Values, 2007)*

5.1.2 Managers must focus on their work

Managers must focus on their work – this is a solemn requirement. At present, some managers seem much more interested in leisure, which is breeding a negative climate within their teams. The market is always changing, and we have to keep our attention firmly fixed on it if we wish to spot windows of opportunity and achieve success. *(Ren Zhengfei: Continuously Improving Per Capita Efficiency and Building a High-performance Corporate Culture, 2004)*

Junior and middle managers must learn to be good at their jobs. Managers who are great at playing office politics but lack capabilities end up making a complete mess of things, because they spend much of their time communicating and holding meetings. However, managers with strong capabilities know very well how to get their job done. In the meantime, office politicians can remain busy with meetings and communication. Our purpose is to achieve success – this is a simple principle. The reason internal communication is so complicated is that a lot of people without strong capabilities have been appointed to managerial positions. If you can change this, you will see hope ahead of you. *(Ren Zhengfei: Acting Boldly at Work, Behaving Humbly, and Following the Patterns of Consumer Products in the Pursuit of Maximum Growth and Success, 2011)*

Some managers have misunderstood one principle: First learn to be a good person, then learn to be good at your job. By "learning to be a good person", I mean complying with business ethics, adhering to a code of conduct, and honing skills. But a lot of people took it to mean "learning to play office politics". When these people become department heads, they have no idea of how to do their job. They hold meetings all day long and complicate coordination and appraisal processes, leaving their subordinates exhausted. To avoid this, we must appoint those who know their job inside-out as junior and middle managers. A meeting is necessary only when a conflict arises. We must reduce the number of meetings, reports, and coordination activities; simplify appraisals; and ease the burdens on employees. All field departments must focus their attention on customers and daily work, rather than on preparing PowerPoints for their managers or filling out forms for the HQ. In certain departments, everyone – from managers to junior employees – goes crazy all day long, preparing PowerPoints and leaving their work uncompleted. Why is this? It's because an executive is going to attend their meeting. If they impress the executive with incredibly dazzling PowerPoints, it could mean a promotion. This phenomenon is detrimental to our effectiveness. For this reason, we must demote managers who are good at currying favor with supervisors or embellishing the accomplishments of subordinates. These managers must be removed from managerial positions and transferred to other positions where they can give full play to their abilities. Be on guard when a subordinate gives you a gift, because he or she is going to ask you for a favor. *(Ren Zhengfei: Success Is Not a Reliable Guide to Future Development, 2011)*

We need to separate people management from business management to a certain extent. The latter is a responsibility of staff teams (STs). I believe administrative departments can organize their own ST meetings. The chair position of an administrative team (AT) should not be filled by one of its team members, but by a core member of the upper-level AT. An AT can cover several business departments (two or three) and manage issues from end to end. This will allow us to break down departmental silos, facilitate manager mobility, and avoid blind decisions regarding employee deployment. In addition, we will make managers' performance appraisal results, both current and previous, known to their subordinates so that they can see if their managers have done a good job. *(Ren Zhengfei: Success Is Not a Reliable Guide to Future Development, 2011)*

We must demote managers who are incompetent and spend most of their time holding meetings. Why do they have meetings all day long? It's because they are incapable and indecisive. At Huawei, there are too many lengthy meetings with many attendees. We must reduce meeting hours per capita by 30%. Maybe we should make this a rule: If the number or duration of meetings exceeds a certain limit, the involved managers should be held accountable. They must come to the HQ to give a report explaining why there are so many meetings, and pay for their own plane tickets. They would not receive their salary during this period, either. *(Ren Zhengfei: Speech at the EMT ST Meeting, March 30, 2012)*

Managers at all levels must focus their efforts on value creation and business improvements. They should continuously improve their business capabilities, increase service quality, reduce operating costs, simplify processes, optimize organizations, and reasonably reduce the workforce. These initiatives will allow our company to enhance competitiveness and improve the extensive relationship with customers. We must not misunderstand customer relationships. In my opinion, we can improve customer relationships so long as we do our jobs well, enhance service quality, and reduce service costs. *(Ren Zhengfei: Remarks to the China Region at the Xinsheng Building, 2012)*

5.1.3 Slackness is the major type of corruption

Any company not founded on the spirit of dedication will not last long. Some of our managers and employees have become spoiled and complacent. They indulge themselves with worldly pleasures and become less disciplined. They are scared of hard or laborious work and thus no longer take their jobs seriously. They constantly think about their compensation and benefits. We must combat these bad habits. Regarding managers who fail to get rid of these habits, we will need to let them go. We must all be on lookout for those employees, especially senior managers, who have slacked off and given up on our fine tradition of dedication. We need to bring on board those who identify with our core values and are willing to work hard. In addition, we must remind more managers and employees of the importance of dedication – it is something they should take pride in. *(Source: Hard Work Will Pay Off Eventually, 2006)*

Effective performance appraisal and benefit distribution mechanisms are crucial to our current transformation. Let's say one employee basically lies to get resources and ultimately succeeds by using excessive resources, but another employee does not get enough resources and thus fails. Should the second employee be given a bonus? This dilemma poses a huge challenge to our HR management policy, and will continue to complicate management over the long run. I expect you to think about this carefully. Don't imagine that once you've got your bonus, you feel good, and you can slack off. The major type of corruption is slackness. Those who don't do their job after having earned some money are slacking off. Those who remain in their comfort zone after getting rich, or those who don't want to make progress are slacking off. Those who curry favor with others, deceive their supervisors and subordinates, and form cliques are slacking off. This year we will distribute lots of money to employees, but the HR department reports that they are very worried. The more employees earn, the more danger the company will face. Why do I say this? Because employees may slack off once they become well-off. Internal corruption is the only barrier to our development. By internal corruption I mean slackness. Therefore, we must accelerate the demotion of unqualified managers to allow middle managers to feel a sense of urgency. This is also true for senior managers as they are selected directly by the company. We can see how well senior managers work; if they lag behind, they will have to step down. Throughout this process, Huawei will keep going forward and never stop. To stop is to regress or even die. *(Ren Zhengfei: Simple Interpretations of Three Success Principles, 2010)*

5.2

Managers Must Work Hard and Make Sacrifices

5.2.1 Managers should be assessed based on their drive and commitment to dedication, not just their skills

We have four criteria to determine whether a manager is competent and loyal. First is working hard. We can judge this by asking a few questions. Do you take your job seriously? Have you tried every means of improving? Will you continue to improve? Second is a spirit of sacrifice. Our value assessment system cannot ensure absolute fairness, which requires managers not to be calculating. If we use Cao Chong's[1] buoyancy method of weighing an elephant during C&Q assessments, we can achieve fairness. However, if we use a precision balance scale, we will never achieve fairness. It is impossible for us to be absolutely fair. Therefore, a spirit of sacrifice is a very important factor during manager assessments. If managers haggle over minor details, they are not good managers. A manager may have many subordinates. If he or she is selfish and calculating, how can subordinates cooperate with him or her? Employees without a spirit of sacrifice must not be promoted to managerial positions. Managers must have a spirit of sacrifice. Third, managers must have a sense of responsibility. Fourth, managers must have a sense of mission. Do all of our employees have a sense of responsibility and a sense of mission? If not, why would they even want to become managers? *(Ren Zhengfei: Huawei's Hard Winter, 2001)*

Those who lack a spirit of sacrifice, haggle over personal gains, and cannot bear with it when being wronged should not be promoted to managerial positions. It's not possible for the company to continuously delay key projects simply to negotiate compensation with employees. It is even worse for employees to demand payment when they are halfway through. An enterprise is not a supernatural being that can ensure things are always fair. There is no absolute fairness. As long as our leaders are truly dedicated to our company's goals, you may be treated unfairly once, but the next time they will perhaps correct their mistake. You may experience several unfair situations, but eventually things will balance out. If you are made of gold, you will shine sooner or later. *(Ren Zhengfei: Guidelines for Human Resources Management Transformation, 2005)*

Managers must have strong willpower and a spirit of sacrifice, which means making appropriate compromises when necessary. Managers must also learn how to take control of an expanding business environment as the company continues to grow. *(Ren Zhengfei: Speech at the PSST Managers' Meeting, 2008)*

Managers should be assessed based on their drive and commitment to dedication, not just their skills. Those who fail to meet these two criteria must be removed from managerial positions. Those who are not dedicated must not lead teams. *(Source: EMT Meeting Minutes No. [2008] 009)*

When the going gets tough, managers must step up, pull their teams into line, and navigate through difficult times. There are some managers who spread rumors, lose confidence in the company, fail to calmly meet challenges, or always whine about how hard their projects are. These signs indicate that these managers have difficulties fulfilling their responsibilities. We need to help them step down from leadership or key positions, and quickly replace them with competent successors who can bear up under pressure. We are at a crucial moment, which is a touchstone for all of our managers. I believe most of our employees will become heroes. *(Ren Zhengfei: Critical Moments Are a Touchstone for Managers at All Levels, 2012)*

5.2.2 Managers must have a sense of responsibility

We want to promote employees with a strong sense of responsibility and mission, good organizational skills, excellent capabilities, team spirit, and a spirit of sacrifice. We can then turn them into a large, effective, and organized team of managers. In addition, we need to demote managers who muddle along, play it safe, embellish results, or cover up problems. We will continue our work against corruption, against the wasting of time and energy, and against slackness. We will also strengthen the management and supervision of managers. *(Ren Zhengfei: The Most Courageous Will Survive in a Tight Competition, 1998)*

Selfishness leads to a poor sense of responsibility, a weak spirit of dedication, and slackness. If Huawei is to survive, our managers must never slack off or be corrupt. There are still managers who are irresponsible and unprofessional, so we need to keep clearing them out. Today is a new beginning, not the end. Every department and employee must think about this problem carefully. Manager assessments must emphasize both current and previous performance. If a manager has always been irresponsible, what is the point of keeping him or her in the company? There is no such need. *(Ren Zhengfei: Encouraging Self-reflection and Avoiding Naive Actions Are the Long-term Principles of Huawei, 1999)*

We must demote managers who fail to assume managerial responsibilities according to process requirements. We must also demote managers who are unwilling or unable to assume responsibilities and who play it safe by avoiding responsibilities. A professional management team with a sense of responsibility, a sense of mission, and strong management skills must grow and thrive through continuous improvements. Of course, this team must also be continuously optimized according to the laws of natural selection. *(Ren Zhengfei: Key Points for Management, 2001)*

Candidates for Huawei's strategic reserves must have a strong sense of responsibility and mission, a spirit of dedication and sacrifice, and be loyal to the company. They must also have made outstanding contributions. *(Ren Zhengfei: Speech Regarding Huawei University and Strategic Reserves, 2005)*

Managers should not find excuses to not do what they are supposed to do. Their mission is to help Huawei resolve difficulties and attain goals, not to create internal pressures on the company. What is the point of keeping managers who pose additional threats to the company when it is in trouble? All managers must strive to create value for Huawei and build a favorable business environment. Managers who fail to meet these requirements will be replaced, no matter how senior they are. *(Ren Zhengfei: Speech at a Workshop on Europe's Business Environment, 2012)*

5.2.3 Managers must be down to earth

By requiring our managers to be down to earth, we are actually protecting them. This requirement will force those who talk big to come back down to earth. A mismatch between employees' talents and their positions is a failure in staff deployment. We must never condone improper manager deployment, such as deploying a manager to a certain position because of his or her seniority. As technologies become more complex and our scope of services expands, more conflicts of interest will arise. If you don't love your job and always think about changing it, how will you be able to unleash your potential? How can you demand a higher salary? If you want to eat, you have to work; no one will do your job for you. Ask yourself what you have done. Regarding your accomplishments, we don't care how well you tell stories; we only care about what you have done and how well you have done it. At Huawei, there are many big talkers, but there are only a few hard workers with a strong sense of responsibility. When Huawei was a small company with only several employees, I used to explain my Lotus Theory. Hard workers are like the lotus roots that maintain a strong grip deep in the ground. By taking nourishment from these roots, lotus leaves and flowers have the strength to sway in the air. Like these leaves and flowers, our senior managers lead the way forward; like the roots, our dedicated employees remain down to earth and get things done. At Huawei, there must be more doers than big talkers. *(Ren Zhengfei: Speech at the CEO's Staff Team Meeting, July 24, 1996)*

In the coming year, we will demote managers who love to discuss theory and strategy during management, but do not get involved in field operations, or do not take responsibility for supervision. We will replace them with managers who are down to earth and responsible. *(Ren Zhengfei: The Most Courageous Will Survive in a Tight Competition, 1997)*

Huawei's early employees committed themselves to making the company what it is today. R&D employees have also devoted themselves to developing high-quality products. Managers must also commit themselves to making continuous management improvements. I'm not asking them to sacrifice their lives for this. Rather, I expect them to work meticulously and tirelessly in the pursuit of product success. I often receive grand development plans from some employees; I throw them straight into the trash. I'm more than happy to receive suggestions and criticism from employees who have optimized management or improved their own work. Committing to management improvements does not necessarily mean you have to study how to catch up with IBM. Rather, you have to study how your management domain can become the best in the world. Catching up with IBM is not your job, because you have neither the experience nor the qualifications. All you have to do is to face reality and take measured steps to improve management. That is crucial to our company. At Huawei, we have more big talkers than doers, and more immature than mature managers. A sense of commitment is something we must advocate in managerial activities. Managers who lack commitment must be removed from their positions. *(Ren Zhengfei: Do Not Be a Temporary Hero, 1998)*

We should be clear that manager development is mainly about being down to earth. We will tamp our management team like you tamp the earth: driving out the airy parts and leaving a solid foundation for development. Any manager who is not down to earth will be removed from his or her position. *(Ren Zhengfei: Focusing on a Down-to-earth Approach to Seize Opportunities for Development, 1998)*

---

[1] Cao Chong was a son of Cao Cao, a warlord who rose to power towards the end of the Han dynasty and laid the foundation of the state of Cao Wei in the Three Kingdoms period. A child prodigy, Cao Chong is best known for his ingenious method of weighing an elephant using the principle of buoyancy.

5.3

Maintaining Team Diversity and Discouraging Cliques

5.3.1 Collectively discussing manager deployments

For manager deployments, we should conduct collective discussions rather than have only a few people make decisions. We must focus on managers' strengths. However, we must also identify their weaknesses. Most importantly, we must not form cliques in promoting or demoting managers. We must not support managers just because we were the ones who recommended them. Instead, we need to consider the interests and survival of our company. *(Ren Zhengfei: Seeing the Situation Clearly, Having Confidence, and Being Open-minded and High-spirited Through Hard Times, 2002)*

Fairness and objectivity are vital if managers are to gain the support of their subordinates. In the absence of fairness and objectivity, even a pat on the back and a word of praise will ring hollow. Therefore, managers must be objective and fair when determining job promotions, bonus distribution, and other matters. If they manage to do so, they will earn the respect of their subordinates. Even if they haven't yet earned respect, they will sooner or later. Of course, it is not easy to be objective and fair. Some managers are unable to identify the best performers on their teams and lack management capabilities, so they have to sacrifice their own interests. On the one hand, this unnecessary sacrifice means these managers are not qualified; on the other hand, it indicates they are unable to motivate outstanding employees. Achieving objectivity and fairness is easier said than done, but it is worthwhile to try as hard as we can to earn recognition and raise team morale. *(Ren Zhengfei: Speech at the PSST Managers' Meeting, 2008)*

At Huawei, senior managers must not form cliques or factions within the company – this is our hard and fast rule. *(Ren Zhengfei: Speech at the HRC Meeting, 2009)*

All leaders must lead by example. Senior managers must possess a leadership mentality and keep the big picture in mind. They must be selfless and treat their subordinates objectively, and adopt a result- and responsibility-oriented approach to manager assessments. They should never allow their personal biases to enter into the equation. *(Ren Zhengfei: Uniting as Many People as Possible, 2013)*

5.3.2 Uniting as many people as possible

The most distinctive feature of Huawei's HR strategy is that we recognize natural leaders – those who unite and win the support of many people. A leader of a group of three can become a sales manager. A leader of a group of 20 can become a regional manager. The more people a leader brings together, the bigger managerial role he or she can play. Managers must make every effort to help, unite, and inspire people to forge ahead, thus turning Huawei's sales team into a strong force. Huawei will succeed only when all employees work hard and commit themselves to developing markets. *(Ren Zhengfei: There's No Guarantee for Success, But Boldness Makes a Difference, 1996)*

Managers must unite as many people as possible, including those who voice dissenting opinions, and view them as like-minded partners in the pursuit of individual and organizational goals. We must treat our employees and managers kindly in order to build a tightly knit team that works hard to achieve the company's goals in spite of difficulties. We must also encourage employees and managers to unleash their initiative and creativity to drive Huawei's growth in strategic businesses. *(Ren Zhengfei: Uniting as Many People as Possible, 2013)*

Inspiring dedication – that's what we must always do. The goal of achieving unity is to bring together employees who are willing and competent at doing their job. We are not pursuing unity for unity's sake. As for those who are unwilling and incompetent, we need to demote or transfer them. *(Ren Zhengfei: Uniting as Many People as Possible, 2013)*

A hundred rivers flow into the sea, which is great only because it contains them all. Inclusiveness matters most, and we must make our culture and systems more inclusive. We also need to maintain an open mind, develop a broad perspective, and be considerate of others. There are several ways to unite outstanding employees and inspire long-term dedication. First, we can assign different types of employees to appropriate positions by studying industry best practices while taking employees' personal interests into account. Second, we can design diversified work modes and deployment strategies. Third, we can use various monetary and non-monetary incentives. These approaches are crucial to encouraging outstanding employees to remain dedicated. *(Ren Zhengfei: Uniting as Many People as Possible, 2013)*

5.4 Continuously Improving Our Thinking and Practicing Openness, Compromise, and *Huidu*

5.4.1 The key to openness and compromise is the mastery of *huidu*

Any absolute idea – be it black or white – can be very inspiring. But we don't need this. What we need is *huidu*. Maintaining a proper level of *huidu* – which means a balance of the grayness between black and white – is difficult, but that is what leaders and mentors should aspire to achieve. *(Ren Zhengfei: Key Points for Management, 2003–2005)*

Tolerance is the key to leaders' success. Only by being tolerant can we unite the majority of our employees to focus on a common direction. Only by compromising and reducing resistance can we achieve our goals. *(Ren Zhengfei: Huawei University Must Become the Cradle of Generals, 2007)*

Every manager who is likely to undertake critical tasks in the future must understand openness, compromise, and *huidu*. These principles represent the most important mindset and work approaches for those who seek to become leaders. Managers should take time to digest these principles. *(Ren Zhengfei: Comments to Staff of the Core Engineering Department, 2009)*

Huidu, compromise, and tolerance lead to a clear and resolute direction. We often say the most important quality of managers is their ability to set direction and pace. Their managerial competency lies in their ability to master *huidu*. *(Ren Zhengfei: Openness, Compromise, and Huidu, 2010)*

Junior employees are not required to study the principles of openness, compromise, and *huidu*. It's all right if they learn these principles to improve their interpersonal relationships, though they often seem to misunderstand the ideas.

Senior managers must study these principles in order to achieve internal unity and create synergy to seize the most opportunities in the global market. We have made Huawei what it is today through over two decades of continuous efforts, and it would be really bad if our slackness ruined the company. Along the path we are on now, we aim to become even bigger and stronger. This will be impossible if we fail to create unity or synergy and if there are many internal conflicts. All the arguments we are hearing now are exactly what we want. In the new era, our managers must remain united and take up the great historic task ahead so that we won't let our employees down. *(Ren Zhengfei: Speech at the Meeting of the New Board of Directors and the New Supervisory Board, 2011)*

5.4.2 "In a group of three people, there is always someone I can learn from"

There is an old saying that "anyone who can haul himself up out of the mud is a sage". Our R&D department must remain open, pursue innovation, and tolerate failure. I believe only those who are not afraid of losing face will succeed. Confucius was one such person. He said, "In a group of three people, there is always someone I can learn from." And Confucius didn't say three *brilliant* people. They might just have been three shepherds. How can shepherds possibly be teachers? That's why I describe Confucius as someone who was not afraid of losing face. With his willingness to learn from anyone, he became China's greatest sage. If you overemphasize face, you will end up neglecting self-reflection. Openness forms the basis for Huawei's survival. A lack of openness will spell doom for our company. To be open, we must hone our core capabilities and cooperate openly with others. Openness is our lifeline and we must remain committed to it. *(Ren Zhengfei: Speech at the PSST Managers' Meeting, 2008)*

An integral part of Huawei's core values is openness and initiative, but our EMT members have been divided on this for quite a long time. Huawei is now a strong innovator, so is openness really so important? Due to our past successes, our confidence, pride, and complacency have increased, and we are becoming increasingly self-absorbed. To change this, we need to be open and learn more from others. Only by doing this can we set new goals, truly examine ourselves, and develop a sense of urgency. *(Ren Zhengfei: Openness, Compromise, and Huidu, 2010)*

5.5 Respecting Facts, Speaking the Truth, and Avoiding Covering Up Problems

5.5.1 Managers must not be overly obedient and play it safe

Good managers respect facts, stick to principles, and pay attention to subordinates, not just their supervisors. We must be cautious of those who are overly obedient and ingratiate themselves with supervisors. They are not working for the good of the company, but rather for themselves. This has been proven many times. *(Ren Zhengfei: Being Mentally Dedicated and Trying Your Best to Successfully Complete Your Work, 1996)*

We should pay special attention to managers who voice dissenting opinions. They have good motives when they offer their opinions to corporate executives. They care about the company and have no regard for personal interests. We don't want managers to be like obedient children; we want them to be bold enough to assume responsibilities. *(Ren Zhengfei: Key Speech at the Review Meeting on the Regulations on Managing Huawei's Corporate Committees, 1998)*

All departments should be aware of bad management practices: exaggeration, one-sided reporting, self-justification, hiding the truth, and talking in abstractions. We must be careful not to appoint people like this to managerial positions unless they change their ways. *(Ren Zhengfei: Key Points for Management, 1999)*

We must boldly shoulder responsibilities at work in order to make our processes flow faster. Those who play it safe and shirk their responsibilities must be demoted. Huawei compensates its employees well, so some people play it safe just to keep their job and associated benefits. Selfish people must be replaced, because they are obstacles to transformation. Is it possible for us to demote managers who have not made any improvements or committed even one mistake in the past year? They may argue that they did not even make one mistake. Can this be an excuse for them to continue to be managers? The truth is they have not done anything to improve. I think we need managers who have greatly increased the department's per capita efficiency even if they have made some mistakes in their work. Managers who have never made any mistakes or any improvements must be demoted immediately. *(Ren Zhengfei: Huawei's Hard Winter, 2001)*

I'm not afraid of criticism. It's a good thing to be criticized. I don't expect employees to act according to my moods or see who I like or who I tell off. They must focus their attention on customers rather than on me. As long as customers recognize you, you can take out your frustrations by coming to my office and kicking me. But if you spend your time watching me instead of customers, I will kick you out no matter how good you make me feel. In that case you're not contributing to the company, you're just a drain. So you must correctly understand the relationships between supervisors and subordinates. Managers should listen to different voices. The worst thing for a company is to become an echo chamber where we can't hear critical voices. If we are happy about the fact that nobody raises objections, we will be doomed when crises arise. *(Ren Zhengfei: Speech at the Communication Meeting with Employees of the Intelligent Network, Master Control, Signaling, and Documentation Departments, 2002)*

We have built hierarchical management organizations and appointed managers level by level. No absolute authority or absolute truth should be allowed to exist in the company. Rather, we must leave sufficient space for good ideas to develop, and we must avoid the situations where we miss opportunities and fail to correct our mistakes due to the limitations of certain individuals. *(Ren Zhengfei: Key Points for Management, 2003–2005)*

All departments and managers must improve themselves and remain down to earth. Managers must boldly uncover, reflect on, and resolve the company's problems. Those who cover up problems must be removed. *(Source: EMT Resolution No. [2006] 017)*

Managers must give absolute priority to facts. They must speak the truth, never hide facts, and report successes as well as problems. They must be even-handed with their subordinates and peers; they must have the courage to call out problems with the company and with their supervisors. People who are excessively obedient or play it safe by shirking their responsibilities are unfit for managerial positions, and managers like this will be replaced in 2010. Managers who do not dare to shoulder responsibilities or always look up to their supervisors' stance are not mature. *(Ren Zhengfei: A New Year Message for 2010, 2009)*

There is an unfortunate climate in this company. Managers have so much authority that their subordinates focus more on them than customers. Employees make fabulous PowerPoints for their boss. They spend a lot of time and effort arranging an elaborate itinerary for their boss on a business trip. Is there any time left for them to look after customers? They are not paying enough attention to customers, not to mention developing extensive customer relationships. Also, many employees are afraid of laborious work. When they get rich, they spend a lot of their time and energy investing or playing the markets. They don't focus on their work like they used to. Can you feel Huawei changing? Why are our processes now so lengthy? Why is decision-making so slow? If Huawei goes public one day, will it continue to fly with its golden wings? Huawei might not even exist if the successful companies of the past had managed to stay humble, cautious, and dedicated, because they wouldn't have left the door open for us. We will disappear into darkness, too, unless we can clear out managers who neglect their duties and play it safe, and replace them with ambitious people. *(Ren Zhengfei: From "Philosophy" to Practice, 2011)*

Every department needs to get rid of managers who are well liked but don't actually do anything. The first to go should be those who are great at currying favor with their bosses and embellishing their subordinates' accomplishments, but are scared of seeking the truth. These types of people are a big drain on the company. The audit report on the members of the Executive Management Team has been published on the *Xinsheng Community²*. The reason for conducting an audit was not to find faults, but to discover sycophants. We will also audit regional presidents and general managers of representative offices, in order to uncover sycophants. Why don't we get rid of those who curry favor with supervisors and play office politics? *(Ren Zhengfei: Developing Managers Based on the Selection Mechanism, Reviewing and Streamlining Organizations Based on Processes, and Promoting the Open and Balanced Development of Organizations, 2011)*

5.5.2 Managers must take responsibility for issues

While developing managers, should we advocate a system of being responsible for issues, or a system of being accountable to a supervisor? In my speech at a meeting with senior managers, I emphasized the importance of the former. I explained the difference between the two: A system of being responsible for issues is expansive and goal-oriented, while a system of being accountable to a supervisor is a control-based management system. The latter has many drawbacks: It may encourage the abuse of personal relationships and opportunistic actions. When recommending managerial candidates, we should put aside cronyism and instead be goal-oriented. You may go unrecognized for a year or two or even longer, but you will eventually shine as long as you keep working for the company's goal, and not for your supervisor's favor. *(Ren Zhengfei: On Transforming the Management System and Developing Managers, 1998)*

There is a fundamental difference between being responsible for issues and being accountable to a supervisor. The former is expansive whereas the latter is constricted. Why do we emphasize that we must build process-based, up-to-date systems? Because our managers continue to ask their supervisors for directions on all issues, even when there are processes in place. This is wrong. We have regulations and standard practices, and there is no need to ask for directions. Just follow the processes and act quickly. People who follow processes are responsible for issues. That is what we call a system of being responsible for issues. People who ask for directions on all matters are accountable to their supervisors. This is a constricted system. We must reduce unnecessary confirmations and unnecessary process segments. Otherwise, how will our company be able to operate efficiently? *(Ren Zhengfei: Huawei's Hard Winter, 2001)*

We advocate a system of being responsible for issues. We want to promote employees who are not opportunists, but responsible; who know how to manage and coordinate; who can see the big picture; who tell their supervisors the whole truth without exaggeration or embellishment; and who are innovative and down to earth. Those are the employees we want in management. *(Ren Zhengfei: Key Points for Management, 2003–2005)*

What kind of people do I believe are the best managers? Those who turn their eyes to customers and work, with their backside to me. They are like thoroughbreds, and I will only be able to see their backsides, or perhaps their hooves. As they race past, a stray hoof might kick me. These are good managers, and they are always doing their job. That's the kind of talent I want to find and promote, not those who are office politicians. During this year's organizational transformation, we must clear out managers who don't know how to do a good job, and transfer them from managerial positions to expert positions, rather than to lower-level managerial positions. If they are unqualified for expert positions, they need to compete with others to see which job level they are competent for. If they end up getting a level 13, then they should be given a level-13 job. Who says that we can only knock a level-20 manager down to level 19? In a nutshell, those who work the hardest will climb the highest. At Huawei, there is no room for opportunistic action. *(Ren Zhengfei: Developing Managers Based on the Selection Mechanism, Reviewing and Streamlining Organizations Based on Processes, and Promoting the Open and Balanced Development of Organizations, 2011)*

---

2   The *Xinsheng Community* is Huawei's online forum for all employees to freely discuss company matters.

5.6 Leading by Example and Continuously Improving Professionalism

5.6.1 Managers must be the first to bear hardships and the last to enjoy comforts

The trials of the past eight years have taken their toll on the health of many of our executives. But all of the frustrations have only made them more determined, and they have improved their management skills. Our executive team is committed to the company's success, not personal gain. They are role models in the way they devote themselves to their work, and they avoid fraudulent acts and involvement in political issues. They have the courage to criticize themselves and others, and impose rules to discipline themselves. They are visionary and fearless in the face of challenges. They follow the principle of *from each according to his ability, to each according to his labor*, and always show concern for employees' interests. That's why I believe that our executives are qualified to lead our company, and that they will lead us to success. *(Ren Zhengfei: Current Situation and Next Steps, 1995)*

Our Marketing & Sales managers are collaborative, self-disciplined, and lead by example. They are clear-eyed and open-minded, and have the courage to criticize themselves and others. They know very well that resources can be exhausted, only culture endures. That's why they have strengthened the development of a positive culture in the Marketing & Sales Department, to foster team unity and positive practices in management and organization operations. These are the first steps in building a strong team. *(Ren Zhengfei: Toasting Those Who Succeed and Offering a Helping Hand to Those Who Fail, 1997)*

At Huawei, junior managers are expected to commit themselves to their work; practice what they preach; pay personal attention to every detail; and achieve resolute execution, strict management, effective monitoring, as well as integrity and compliance. *(Ren Zhengfei: Mission and Responsibilities of Professional Managers, 2000)*

When we say *lead by example*, we don't expect you to take it too far. You don't have to be perfect in every detail. If you focus all your attention on the small things, you will lose your perspective on the big things. It doesn't matter if you wipe your nose on your sleeve, or have socks hanging out of your jacket pocket. But when you produce documents or develop software, you must lead by example and strive for excellence. The most important thing is how you manage: You must clearly tell your subordinates what you expect of them, and what standards apply in each case. *(Ren Zhengfei: Making Progress While Remaining Down to Earth, 2000)*

Managers should take the initiative and work in overseas field offices to hone their skills. Organizations at the HQ will be downsized and our focus should be on field offices. Hence, managers at the HQ must take the lead to work in overseas field offices and stay there until the entire projects they are engaged in are completed. *(Ren Zhengfei: Establishing an Open Cooperation System and Accelerating the Strategic Transformation for Internationalization, 2000)*

5.6.2 Managers must focus on building systems and proactively fulfill responsibilities under the systems

Only professional management practices and process-based operation mechanisms can help a large company increase its operating efficiency and decrease management costs. Over the next two to three years, Huawei will initially achieve IT- and process-based management from end to end. By then, professional managers will be responsible for standardized operations within their own section of a process. Think of a train running from Guangzhou to Beijing: Along the track there are hundreds of switchmen, and dozens of drivers will take shifts driving the train. You wouldn't say that the driver who has been assigned the last shift and brings the train into the Beijing station is the hero of the entire process. Even when one individual has to step forward to accept a bouquet, the last driver does so as a representative of the whole team, not because he is the only hero. *(Ren Zhengfei: Speech to Executives on the Exam on Writing an Essay on "Non-action in Management", 2000)*

Over the past ten-plus years, we have promoted many high-profile managers who are good at loudly proclaiming their achievements. But now we need to change this practice: We must promote a professional working climate that inspires managers to remain down to earth, work hard, maintain a low profile, and focus on details. *(Ren Zhengfei: Speech at the CEO's Staff Team Meeting, 2001)*

Trust is not a good basis for financial management. We need systems. Trust is elusive and can't be measured by fixed standards. That is why financial management in the West is entirely system-based. As long as you follow the system, you can be trusted, no matter who you are. But if you don't follow the system, you can't be trusted. Before establishing a system, we must conduct all necessary validation. After the system is established, we should make it authoritative; otherwise, our push for the Four Unifications (processes, systems, controls, and coding) will lead nowhere. Within the finance department, we must deploy an authorization system, a checks and balances mechanism for exercising authority, and an accountability system. First, we must establish an effective authorization system and a rigorous system for overseeing managers in exercise of authority. Authorization pushes responsibility down the organization and allows junior managers with a full understanding of the business to assume responsibility. Second, a checks and balances mechanism must be created based on internal control requirements, and the scope of authority and responsibility relating to processes must be clarified, to ensure that processes are implemented flawlessly to guarantee smooth business operations. Third, we must establish an accountability system to track how authority is exercised, thus urging managers to fulfill their responsibilities. The accountability system needs to be incorporated into processes. Appraisal and disciplinary requirements must be clarified for all positions and roles in processes. Responsibility must be specified for each individual. Particularly, responsibility for managing key monitoring points must be specified for each manager. Once violations are identified, all involved violators must be identified from the top down and their managers must first be held accountable. *(Ren Zhengfei: Integrity and a Sense of Responsibility Are Key Criteria for Selecting Finance Managers, 2006)*

The EMT has decided that directors of business departments are responsible for monitoring. First of all, it must be made clear that process owners shall take responsibility for three tasks: proactive reviews, internal control checks and assessments, and the development of an authorization system. Current operations have yet to be standardized; the monitoring management department should do something in this regard. They should assign monitoring responsibilities to process owners, and implement internal control checks and assessments as a way to urge business owners to fulfill responsibilities within their business scope. With the right of appraisal, the monitoring management department should participate in appraising managers and can impeach managers if necessary. We need to manage employee conduct first, and then the implementation of accountability systems for processes at all levels. Once we formulate the code of conduct, position responsibilities, disciplinary rules, and rewarding regulations, process owners will not dare to slack off. *(Ren Zhengfei: Speech Regarding Regional Monitoring Work, 2007)*

Senior leadership mentors can veto manager appointments. The decision-making process for appointments should be accelerated. If a manager appointment is vetoed, the Executive Committee can discuss the appointment and submit it again, which may be vetoed by us senior leadership mentors again. If you committee members have given it due consideration, then the third time you can simply go ahead with the appointment and inform us of your decision. This will ensure that nothing is held back because of our veto. We reserve the right to continue reviewing the performance of managers after they are appointed to new positions. We also reserve the right to review managers whose appointments have not been vetoed. If they don't do a good job, you can impeach them. The right of impeachment creates considerable deterrence for managers. Of course, the right of veto is also important. However, we should leave some leeway – the Executive Committee should have the right to place a manager in a specific position, even if his or her appointment has been vetoed twice. After the appointment, we reserve the right to impeach the manager at a later date. This prevents everything from reaching an impasse. After managers are impeached or their appointments are vetoed, we should have a talk with them and give them a second chance to reflect and change. I think system development is crucial. Systems will last a long time and will have a profound impact. I will never give up on the development of systems. *(Ren Zhengfei: Speech at the EMT ST Meeting, July 28, 2011)*

The separation of administrative management from business decision making will help us improve operating efficiency. The Global Process Owner (GPO) has the authority to replace the random behavior of individuals with standard processes, methodologies, and regulations to keep internal operations relatively stable and standardized. *(Ren Zhengfei: Comments to Staff in Mauritius, 2013)*

5.7 Practicing Self-reflection

5.7.1 Self-reflection is the precondition for tolerance

Any manager who is incapable of self-reflection should not be promoted. Managers who have not been criticized at all should be carefully scrutinized. Managers who have been sharply criticized should be classified and treated differently. If they have no ethical problems, we should still provide them with development opportunities. People have a natural inclination towards laziness; they are not born with innovative capabilities. Huawei will fade away rapidly if our managers fail to practice self-reflection from time to time. Over the next few years, we will emphasize that anyone incapable of self-reflection will not be considered for a managerial position at Huawei. *(Ren Zhengfei: On Transforming the Management System and Developing Managers, 1998)*

Self-reflection helps managers refresh their thinking and open their minds so they can endure criticism from others. Instead of asking others to criticize managers, we should ask managers to first criticize themselves, and then let others judge if they can pass. Managers must be open-minded, accept criticism from others, and engage in self-reflection. The Chinese philosopher Confucius said, "Every day I examine myself on three counts." I believe this is a great idea. I have had a lot of experiences in my life, and I have been critical of lots of people. But I have been even more critical of myself. Every day I think about which things I have done right, and which I have done wrong. Self-reflection won't drag the company down, nor will it make people feel inferior. Even if self-reflection does evoke a feeling of inferiority, it can be offset by rapid development, and this balancing process will allow our managers to become more capable, composed, and mature. I think for someone who is self-reflective, capable, and experienced, the more criticism he or she receives, the better he or she will perform. *(Ren Zhengfei: Speech at the Communication Meeting with the Steering Committee on Self-reflection, 2006)*

Managers must be realistic and down to earth. All senior managers, from deputy directors upwards, must reflect on their mistakes and make them publicly known. If they publicly admit mistakes that they previously covered up, then they are showing signs of improvement. But this does not necessarily mean they have met our requirements on self-reflection. *(Ren Zhengfei: Adapting the Appraisal System for Managers to Challenges Facing the Transforming Industry, 2006)*

There are two defining factors for manager appointments. The first is self-reflection: If someone always thinks that they are in the right, they will be excluded from promotions. They have to know where their own problems lie – that's the kind of person we want to promote to managerial positions. The second factor is character: People of weak moral character cannot be promoted. *(Ren Zhengfei: Speech at the Annual Meeting of the Domestic Market Finance Department, 2006)*

Willpower is more important than skill; character is more important than willpower; but an open mind is the most important of all. Self-reflection is essential to developing a good character and an open mind, which in turn make it possible to tolerate all that must be tolerated. *(Ren Zhengfei: Famous Battles Do Not Automatically Produce Generals, but All Generals Were Once Heroes, 2006)*

When giving work reports, managers must be realistic and tell the truth, without deliberately keeping a low profile or exaggerating their achievements. They should reflect on and boldly reveal the problems and mistakes they've made over the past year. This is the only way to continuously improve. No manager or employee should be afraid of making mistakes. When a mistake has been made, we must have the courage to grasp the nettle. *(Source: EMT Resolution No. [2006] 017)*

Employees will never become generals if they don't know where they've gone wrong. If they know when, where, and how they made mistakes, they will learn valuable lessons. Generals grow by learning from their mistakes and continuously improving. *(Ren Zhengfei: Employees Will Never Become Generals If They Don't Know Where They've Gone Wrong, 2007)*

Our senior managers need to be more frank and open. When asked about an issue, they are expected to tell the whole truth, clearly and without evading. We will never be completely error-free. We should make this a standard practice: If a senior manager gives a report, it should be the whole truth; otherwise, don't report. We have never said that senior managers cannot make mistakes. The important thing is that we keep on reflecting on ourselves and learning lessons from our mistakes. A company will reach a dead end if every employee considers him or herself to be perfect and refuses to admit mistakes. A company without the spirit of self-reflection is doomed to fail, so Huawei must infuse this spirit into every employee. In addition, managers who cannot see their own flaws or problems should not be promoted any higher. Why not? Because they can't find any room to improve. Their mindset is too narrow and can't be expanded. Organizations at all levels must not promote this type of manager. *(Ren Zhengfei: Speech at the EMT ST Meeting, June 30, 2011)*

We should start by asking senior managers to engage in self-reflection and listen to more objections. Critical voices from our customers and competitors should be published in *Improvement³*. This will prevent us from becoming the proverbial frog in a well who thinks the tiny patch of light above it is the whole sky. *(Source: EMT Meeting Minutes No. [2012] 028)*

5.7.2 Managers should be happy to hear criticism and promote openness

Managers at all levels must foster a more open culture. Everyone needs to be accepting of criticism, both internal and external, even when that criticism is expressed in an inappropriate way. Managers should also be happy to hear criticism and rapidly correct their mistakes. Continuous improvement is an important way for managers to become more open, so they should keep learning to better themselves. In addition, they should be willing to unite with all critics, including those who criticize wrongly. *(Ren Zhengfei: Key Points for Management, 1999)*

Middle and senior managers must have the courage to shoulder responsibilities and adopt an open mindset. They need to accept different opinions, as a great weight of responsibility rests on their shoulders. They need to believe the old adage: "Every person has a quality to contribute, and one can become a sage by combining the qualities of one hundred people; every person has an opinion to express, and one can make a key decision by relying on the opinions of one hundred people." *(Ren Zhengfei: Key Points for Management, 2003–2005)*

Over the next three to five years, Huawei will undergo a thorough shake-up, from top to bottom. We will need managers who dare to speak the truth, practice self-reflection, and accept criticism from others. Huawei can only survive during tough times if we have these kinds of people filling every managerial position. Some people may believe that Huawei is currently doing well and there is no need to worry too much, but I think that a company does well only when its employees dare to speak out honestly and managers are willing to hear the truth. *(Ren Zhengfei: Speech at the Communication Meeting with the Steering Committee on Self-reflection, 2006)*

Managers must speak the truth and be willing to accept criticism. They should be humble and responsible, and improve their conduct to boost their teams' morale and productivity. *(Ren Zhengfei: Speech at the Communication Meeting with the Steering Committee on Self-reflection, 2006)*

Don't feel pressured if I criticize someone or something; otherwise we will end up without a single person left working with us. I believe that every one of you will make mistakes; I make mistakes, too. But what matters most is that we work hard to correct errors, in order to improve Huawei's standardized operations and set it on the right track. Not everyone can move forward at the same pace. When we demote a general manager of a representative office who is making slow progress, we don't mean to ruin him or her. What is the problem if he or she ends up as an account manager? Job adjustments won't necessarily embarrass managers. Judging from the corruption in several regions, we need to increase manager mobility. Managers who are disciplined should not panic or feel as though they have been marked for life. That is not how it is. The company is objective in assessing managers, allowing those who have performed well to rise once again. As long as you admit and thoroughly reflect on your faults, why shouldn't you be able to work your way back up to where you were before? *(Ren Zhengfei: Speech at the EMT ST Meeting, June 30, 2011)*

No manager dares to say that they do everything right. Everyone makes mistakes, but as long as we are able to see and explain our errors, that's OK. We have never said that when someone admits an error, he or she must be disciplined, and that is even truer for the most senior managers.

Every single person may get things wrong, and everyone needs time to realize mistakes. Our executive board members are not supernatural beings and are thus likely to make mistakes. In countries like the UK, the US, France, Germany, and Japan, entire national and cultural ideologies support the existence of well-functioning systems, which can lead to fewer and fewer mistakes. I don't think that all of the decisions we've made have been correct. But we would not make a decision at all if we have known it is wrong. If decisions made and approved by the seven-member Executive Committee are all wrong, this means the members are not competent enough and should take time to improve by engaging in self-reflection, repeatedly reviewing their decisions, and promptly reporting how the decisions are executed. Our Executive Committee must practice self-reflection more often. Self-reflection is the biggest advantage of the Japanese people, and we must learn from them. *(Ren Zhengfei: Speech at the EMT ST Meeting, July 28, 2011)*

---

3 *Improvement* is an internal publication at Huawei aimed at improving all aspects of management.

Maintaining a Sense of Urgency and Remaining Vigilant in Order to Survive

5.8.1 The past successes of hi-tech companies are often the mother of failure

Starting a business and keeping it going are both difficult. But if the difficulties are understood, it is no longer difficult. The past successes of hi-tech companies are often the mother of failure. In this rapidly changing information society, one must remain vigilant in order to survive. *(Ren Zhengfei: Spring of Northern Country, 2001)*

For the past ten years, I've worried about failure every single day and paid no attention to success. I have no sense of pride or superiority, just a sense of urgency. This might be the reason for Huawei's survival. If all of us try to figure out how we can survive, we may survive for a much longer time. No matter what, we will fail one day. Please be prepared for that. This is my unwavering point of view because it is a law of history. *(Ren Zhengfei: Huawei's Hard Winter, 2001)*

Are we going to be left behind by the times? Or can we afford to be left behind? These are important questions. Many great inventors failed to expand on their initial successes. These include Marconi, who was the first to use radio waves to invent wireless telegraphy; Motorola, pioneer of cellular communications; Lucent, inventor of optical transmissions; and Kodak, creator of the world's first digital camera. They failed because they didn't see the future clearly, or because they didn't have the courage to reinvent themselves or give up their vested interests when they did. Large companies have their advantages, but if they fail to keep pace with the times, they will vanish in the blink of an eye. *(Ren Zhengfei: Speech and Comments at the Carrier Network BG's Strategy Retreat in Huizhou, 2012)*

5.8.2 Senior managers must have a sense of mission; middle managers a sense of urgency; and junior managers a sense of hunger

Managers must have a sense of mission to create vitality for the organization, much like cells that produce blood for the body. By attempting every means of achieving a goal, managers produce the vitality that is the lifeblood of a vigorous company. *(Ren Zhengfei: It's Not Always Easy to Enjoy the Shade Under a Big Tree, 1999)*

Today, Huawei is still growing. It is a practical requirement that our senior managers have a sense of mission, our middle managers a sense of urgency, and our junior managers, to a certain extent, a sense of hunger. We must use our HR policies to create a sense of mission, urgency, and hunger, and to develop systems to transform these feelings into the driving forces behind the dedication of our staff. *(Source: EMT Meeting Minutes No. [2007] 009)*

Middle managers must maintain a sense of urgency. We will demote managers who rank in the bottom 10% of performance appraisals, and transfer them to positions that handle routine matters. This way, middle managers will feel a sense of urgency. Senior managers must maintain a sense of mission and avoid slackness as they get rich. *(Ren Zhengfei: Speech at the EMT ST Meeting, 2009)*

In the future, we will gain more revenue and our employees will earn higher income. However, the company will face greater risks, as more and more employees will lose their sense of mission. What is a sense of mission? With a sense of mission, we work out of passion, regardless of the payment. At Huawei, there are only a limited number of managers with a sense of mission. Junior and middle managers should have a sense of urgency. What is a sense of urgency? It means 10% of managers will be demoted each year. As a manager, you have been given trust and opportunities. If you fail to put these to good use, the company will have no choice but to demote you. We must resolutely demote unqualified managers. Only in this way can we rank and screen managers, drive them to remain energetic under pressure, and help our teams maintain their effectiveness. *(Ren Zhengfei: Simple Interpretations of Three Success Principles, 2010)*

5.9 Putting Organizational Interests Before Personal Interests

5.9.1 Managers must prioritize the company's interests over personal interests

We should adopt a correct attitude towards transformation. What is this? Transformation is the process of redistributing benefits. A powerful management organization is necessary to support benefit redistribution and transformation. During transformation, we will gradually move away from the previous balance of benefit distribution to a new one. This cyclic process of balancing is necessary for an enterprise to enhance its core competencies and increase efficiency. However, there will never be a perfect balance when it comes to benefit distribution. As we transform our positions, we will face challenges in benefit redistribution. Regardless of your rank, you need to adopt a correct attitude towards transformation, or it will be unable to take root or succeed. *(Ren Zhengfei: Huawei's Hard Winter, 2001)*

Our company is transforming. Managers at all levels should not worry too much about personal gains or losses. To transform means to change the principles of benefit distribution. Our employees must not worry too much about personal gains, but instead be open-minded about our transformation. Since its inception, Huawei has attached great importance to employee benefits and the interests of its partners. The combination of these two factors has led to Huawei's success. We will continue to adopt such practices, and we hope all of our employees can understand and support this. Why is there resistance to transformation? Because it often involves changes in benefit distribution. *(Ren Zhengfei: Speeches During the Early Years of Huawei, 2001)*

Everyone should truly understand why the company needs to downsize in order to get through these difficult times. Of course, organizational re-structuring may affect some people. We will downsize gradually, because doing everything at once would cause chaos during our transformation. Also, different departments can restructure their organization in different ways. For example, R&D may need to increase its number of managers. In-stead of having a huge department, R&D needs small departments. Where redundancies cannot be avoided, we should first find other internal posi-tions for redundant staff, and these employees should adopt a correct atti-tude. To give their role into full play, managers must correctly understand and embrace transformation. *(Ren Zhengfei: Seeing the Situation Clearly, Having Confidence, and Being Open-minded and High-spirited Through Hard Times, 2002)*

We should adopt a flexible approach to downsizing. We won't do what some Western companies often do. They may say: "This year revenue has dropped 20%, so we need to cut this many people to keep our financials in order." This is a rigid approach, and we are not going to do that. We need to be flexible. At present, we focus on assessing each and every department and position. Certain organizations will disappear when the IPD and ISC pro-cesses are streamlined. Where should we place the managers of these organ-izations? We must prioritize manager deployment over the growth of finan-cial indicators. In addition, our approach to downsizing must be reasonable, which can be guaranteed by our system and process transformations. We will only downsize the part of our workforce that can no longer make con-tributions, not the people we still need. Large organizational consolidation will take place in February of next year, when the IPD and ISC processes are streamlined. By then, we will be able to identify which departments and po-sitions are redundant. Employees who lose their positions during the organ-izational restructuring will be made redundant not because they didn't work hard, but because of the company's actions. The Committee of Ethics and Compliance should help assess which managers in redundant organizations are key talent worth retaining. After assessments, we must make every effort to deploy these managers to new positions as soon as possible. *(Ren Zhengfei: Seeing the Situation Clearly, Having Confidence, and Being Open-minded and High-spirited Through Hard Times, 2002)*

A proper attitude and an enhanced sense of service are essential. Managers must be understanding when it comes to position adjustments caused by transformation, and place organizational interests before personal interests. Once the organization's positioning is defined and processes are running smoothly, we will reselect managers for positions according to process requirements. Any department that cannot meet process requirements must be restructured, and the type of required managers must be defined accordingly. Managers should be accepting of both promotions and demotions based on their performance. Unqualified managers should be transferred to positions that match their competencies; those who disagree with the transfers can resign. *(Ren Zhengfei: Building a Professional Financial Team That Has Solid Integrity, Dares to Shoulder Responsibilities, and Sticks to Principles, 2006)*

Ninety-three managers – including middle and senior managers – have voluntarily accepted demotions and salary cuts. My thanks go out to them! And I'd also like to thank the employees who have voluntarily resigned from their previous positions and applied for new jobs on a competitive basis! Their understanding and support will help drive Huawei's long-term development. This adjustment will become one of Huawei's historical milestones. We sincerely hope that the managers who have been repositioned will continue improving through self-learning. Those who do not improve will be left behind. Dedicated employees will always be given more opportunities. *(Source: Notification on the Status of the Human Resources Management Transformation, 2007)*

5.9.2 Selflessness inspires courage

Only those who are selfless and committed themselves to the company wholeheartedly will dedicate themselves to grooming successors who will surpass them. *(Ren Zhengfei: Speech at the Group Resignation Ceremony for All Marketing & Sales Staff in Primary Leadership Positions, 1996)*

Since Huawei's foundation, we have maintained internal unity. Unity brings power, eliminates internal friction, and gives birth to cohesiveness and team spirit. Because our senior managers are selfless, they do not form cliques or pursue personal gains. They can thus focus more efforts on the company's operations, development, and management. As a result, a positive climate has taken shape across the company, enabling our core values and value assessment and distribution systems to take hold. Based on self-reflection, our unity is not aimed at maintaining unprincipled harmony. We are united because we all identify with the corporate core values and follow a code of ethics. *(Ren Zhengfei: Huawei's Opportunities and Challenges, 2000)*

Since the day I founded Huawei and became CEO, I have been caught between internal and external conflicts – conflicting interests and temptations. I'm well aware that I shoulder great responsibilities. How can I calmly cope with various conflicts and contradictions? How can I make resolute choices and trade-offs when faced with dilemmas? And how can I resist temptations and distractions of personal desires on a long-term basis? The only option is to put aside my personal biases and interests. Otherwise, I would not have been able to strike an appropriate balance between different groups. Being unbiased and selfless is my baseline for being CEO. It is also the baseline for being a senior executive at Huawei. Only when we are selfless can we be fair and objective, and tightly unite our teams. Only when we are selfless can we fearlessly uphold principles. Only when we are selfless can we dare to criticize ourselves and others, and address our shortcomings. Only when we are selfless can we become open-minded and set our sights high. Only then can we tolerate all that must be tolerated, and be able to shoulder our responsibilities. *(Ren Zhengfei: Speech at the Declaration of Self-discipline, 2007)*

5.9.3 Remaining dedicated, bearing with it when being wronged, and adopting a balanced and flexible approach

There is no absolute fairness, and errors in judgment are inevitable. However, unbridgeable divides or calling right wrong will not occur. You must tolerate unfairness, even if you have worked well. If you lack endurance, how will you be able to shoulder responsibilities in the future? Our company strives to offer equal opportunities. However, opportunities favor those who are down to earth. *(Source: Out of Chaos, 1998)*

Managers need to have a strong sense of mission and responsibility, and need controlled passion that allows them to work hard and methodically. Governing a great state, as the saying goes, is like frying a small fish: You can't take your eye off the ball for even a moment. So stay disciplined and don't be cocky. Be a little more levelheaded, a little less impetuous. *(Ren Zhengfei: Key Points for Management, 2001)*

Don't grumble too much – it will sap your willpower. Try to take a long-term view when making decisions. Our middle and senior managers need to be tough enough to endure hardships and unfairness. *(Ren Zhengfei: Living with Peace of Mind, 2003)*

If a manager has been demoted, he must reconcile himself to this, reflect on himself, and tackle his new job with renewed energy. Don't complain or hold grudges. If we fall down, we should pick ourselves back up and carry on. In particular, managers who have been demoted due to an incorrect decision made by the organization should continue working hard without complaint, and prove themselves in their work. They are the company's valuable assets and will assume more important roles in the future. *(Ren Zhengfei: Continuously Improving Per Capita Efficiency and Building a High-performance Corporate Culture, 2004)*

All managers must learn how to conduct themselves, particularly senior managers who shoulder major responsibilities. They should raise the standards of conduct for themselves as well as their teams. We are all educated people, and we should behave like it. In our work, we sometimes have to throw our weight around; but in life, restraint is a virtue. *(Ren Zhengfei: Key Points for Management, 2003–2005)*

Still waters run deep. All managers should learn the art of calm reflection. *(Ren Zhengfei: Speech at the Communication Meeting with the Steering Committee on Self-reflection, 2006)*

In their spare time, junior and middle managers should study a little philosophy; senior managers should learn a little history. All managers should avoid political issues, stay away from inappropriate social interaction, and try not to form unsuitable friendships. Managers need to mature. So I recommend that managers focus on their work and not comment on things beyond their experience, particularly sensitive issues. They should not be a burden on society. *(Ren Zhengfei: Adapting the Appraisal System for Managers to Challenges Facing the Transforming Industry, 2006)*

Hardships are blessings in disguise. Generals are forged through adversity; in fact, smooth, unobstructed progress does not lead to growth. *(Ren Zhengfei: Employees Will Never Become Generals If They Don't Know Where They've Gone Wrong, 2007)*

Always keep the following in mind. First, remain dedicated. Second, bear with it when being wronged. Third, adopt a balanced and flexible approach. Instead of seeking fame or fortune, managers should fulfill their duties in a down-to-earth manner and face the future with peace of mind. Huawei has only one key value proposition, which is serving customers. Don't attach too much importance to your career path, or you will certainly not succeed at Huawei. Only those dedicated employees who constantly serve our customers will get opportunities. *(Ren Zhengfei: Timely, Accurate, High Quality, and Low Cost Delivery Calls for Professional Process-compliant CFOs, 2009)*

Everyone should work hard in the pursuit of personal goals and dreams, no matter whether his or her efforts are recognized or not. I was not recognized when I was young. If I had given up working hard because of that, wouldn't I simply be someone you'd pass on the street without giving a second look? Don't overemphasize recognition from the organization or company. Obsession with external recognition can't produce great scientists, artists like Van Gogh, musicians like Beethoven, or great inventions like the helicopter. The ancient Chinese poet Bai Juyi said, "Imagine if we died with our stories incomplete, who could know the truth or fiction of our lives?" Self-motivation is the most important impetus in life. *(Ren Zhengfei: Comments to Trainees of the Tenth Session of the Senior Management Seminar at Huawei University, 2011)*

We should learn from the wisdom of *the survival of the fittest*. It's imperative that we show a certain degree of understanding and tolerance towards others. Discomfort is perpetual, whereas comfort is merely transient. Only by surviving in extremely uncomfortable environments can we fully develop ourselves. Difficulties and setbacks – if seen from a broader perspective – are actually blessings in disguise. *(Ren Zhengfei: Comments to Staff from Finance, 2011)*

CHAPTER 6

SELECTING AND DEPLOYING MANAGERS

At Huawei, we don't focus on developing managers. Instead, we select outstanding employees for managerial positions and demote incompetent ones. We only select managers from among those who have successful field experience. In China we have this saying: "A valiant general always starts as an ordinary soldier, just as a prime minister always starts as a local official." HQ personnel who have no field experience cannot become managers, just as those who know nothing of battles cannot be commanders. Therefore, successful field experience and project management experience are required to become a manager.

Commitment is the first thing we look for when selecting managers at Huawei. Our core values are the basis for evaluating managers while integrity and work ethics are our minimum requirements. Excellent performance is also a key condition. When promoting a junior manager to a middle managerial position, we look at their performance and ability to sustain high performance; when making a middle manager a senior manager, we look at integrity first.

We follow three principles when selecting managers. First, we give priority to employees from successful and high-performing teams. We can thus develop a group of managers who are bold enough to charge forward, thus energizing our organization and manager management systems. Second, we prioritize employees working in our major markets, field offices, and hardship regions. Exceptional managers are usually born from hardships, just as generals usually emerge from tough battles. Third, we examine and select managers based on their performance during key events that influence the company's long-term development, especially when the organizational interests conflict with personal interests. Key employees are those the company can rely on during its development, especially in times of crisis and major internal and external events. They share in both the company's successes and failures and work hard in whatever positions they assume. When we discuss our focus on results and responsibilities in performance appraisals, our assessment of responsibilities is not based on our subjective judgment, but on performance during key events.

We are realistic about employees' skills, and don't expect them to be perfect. We want to bring out their strengths and tolerate their weaknesses. Those who have obvious strengths often have obvious weaknesses as well. We need to focus on their strengths rather than weaknesses. We should be able to accept courageous but flawed people who adhere to our core values.

We need both employees with a strong sense of social responsibility and employees with a strong sense of personal achievement. We aim to cultivate the former into leaders, and develop the latter into heroes. If there are no heroes among our junior employees, the company will lose its vitality and hope.

At Huawei, selecting managers is like a horse race; only the fastest thoroughbreds will be picked. However, we should also give foals a chance to be selected as senior professionals in regional offices. We need to promote those with strong leadership capabilities right away so that they can make a bigger contribution while they are young. If we don't quickly promote them, they might become too old to contribute more when they finally have a chance. The HRC thus needs to fast-track promotions for outstanding employees. This is necessary to encourage and retain them. Although in general we advocate a step-by-step approach in managerial promotions, we need to be flexible and fast-track those who have made exceptional contributions to the company in accordance with our goals and business development requirements, and also our established procedures.

Manager development is a bottleneck at Huawei. We should leverage global capabilities and resources to become an industry leader and adopt a global vision when selecting managers. We need managers who have deep market insight and a broad knowledge base. We should bring in non-Chinese professional managers and experts to work alongside Huawei's exceptional young employees and form a mixed team.

We should adopt a long-term policy to ensure that managers are demoted or promoted based on their performance. As Huawei continues to move forward rapidly, we must create a mechanism that helps outstanding employees develop; otherwise, the company will fail despite the heights to which it has risen. In other words, if nobody joins or leaves, our company's development will be affected as all human beings are hurtling towards the inevitable. To enable our company to develop sustainably, we must demote unqualified managers, and never give anyone a free pass. Our system of demoting the unqualified is primarily targeted at managers rather than employees. We must develop a systematic, measurable approach for demoting unqualified managers and dismissing underperforming employees based on performance and facts, and integrate this approach into the performance management system. Managers who are demoted temporarily need to stay positive and be prepared for a future comeback. At Huawei, we believe that from the ashes the phoenix is reborn.

The goal of manager deployment is to develop a strong team to enable business success. To this end, we should avoid leaving positions vacant and, instead, fill them with qualified managers, even if they are not perfect. We should have the courage to appoint managers as quickly as possible and then wait and see how they do on the job. We identify talent through practice, and demote or promote managers based on their performance.

This chapter focuses on Huawei's criteria and principles for selecting managers, its views on talent, and its policies and principles relating to manager deployment.

6.1   Successful Field Experience Is Critical

6.1.1 Selecting managers from those with successful field experience

Field experience is the most important criterion for selecting managers. *(Source: EMT Meeting Minutes No. [2005] 022)*

We should select managers from among those who have successful field experience, no matter how small their success is. We should never select managers from among those who are just good at talking. Managers who have succeeded have developed their own methodology and have leadership skills; it's therefore easier for them to absorb the company's management methodologies after they are trained. *(Ren Zhengfei: Guidelines for Human Resources Management Transformation, 2005)*

Why do we select managers from among those who have successful project experience? It is because no matter how small a project is, they can succeed because they have developed their own methodology and they are able to put their knowledge into practice. After they are trained, they can improve further and contribute more to the company as they are skilled at self-reflection. *(Ren Zhengfei: Guidelines for Human Resources Management Transformation, 2005)*

Our managers are cultivated in the field. At a meeting, the EMT asked: Why don't we learn from the practice of promoting outstanding soldiers straight from the trenches as seen during China's War of Liberation? Why must we assign managers from the HQ to field offices? Why don't we select managers directly from successful regions? This is the trend of our times. If we focus too much on qualifications or seniority when it comes to promotion, the company will fail. *(Ren Zhengfei: Speech at the Mid-year Market Conference, 2006)*

We need to improve how we manage our managers. Field experience is required for promotion. We will never promote someone who doesn't have successful field experience. Managers in financial departments need to frequently communicate with field teams overseas and enrich their field experience. People without field experience cannot be promoted to managerial positions. Managers who lack such experience need to improve in that respect before they get pay raises or shares distributed based on their job levels. In the future, if someone doesn't acquire six months' field experience within three years, he or she will be considered to have no field experience. We will not allow those who have never worked in field offices to sit at the HQ and give directions to field offices. All managers should go to work in field offices and solve real-world problems. *(Ren Zhengfei: Building a Professional Financial Team That Has Solid Integrity, Dares to Shoulder Responsibilities, and Sticks to Principles, 2006)*

Managers who lack field experience must be sent to the field as soon as possible. This needs to be integrated with management succession planning. *(Source: EMT Meeting Minutes No. [2008] 021)*

When selecting a manager, we will first look at whether he or she has successful field experience and is able to draw upon past experience to sustain success. Then we will listen to his or her vision for the future to see if he or she is the right person for the position. *(Ren Zhengfei: Speech at the EMT ST Meeting, 2009)*

We need to select managers from among those who have successful field experience. As the old Chinese saying goes, "A valiant general always starts as an ordinary soldier, just as a prime minister always starts as a local official." We encourage our employees to face challenges, put their personal interests aside, and work where they are needed most. *(Ren Zhengfei: A New Year Message for 2010, 2009)*

When selecting managers, we must prioritize results and responsibilities, and then consider competence. Also, we need to emphasize field experience. HQ employees who have no field experience should be called professionals and not be promoted to managerial positions. If they want to become managers, they must work in field offices; otherwise, they can only be experts. Although some Western value assessment systems may not be suitable for us, there are many effective management approaches in the West that we can learn from while adhering to our own values. *(Ren Zhengfei: Speech at the EMT ST Meeting, August 31, 2011)*

Project finance is the best way for financial staff to hone their skills. Being involved in a small project from the beginning to the end can help them better understand finance and business, and prepare them for becoming CFOs. *(Ren Zhengfei: Comments to Staff from Finance, 2011)*

During the early years of our enterprise business, all managers need to work in the field, so that they can develop quickly and learn how to lead their teams. Those who succeed in the field will likely grow into managers and expand their organization. They will become heroes, and an effective command system will be developed. We need to allocate more human resources, including managers, to high-value regions and industries. We also need to set job levels based on performance rather than positions and bring on board talented professionals who identify with our culture. These people do not necessarily have to be high-end, as our enterprise business is still in the start-up and development stages. This will help us avoid high costs. *(Source: EMT Resolution No. [2011] 001)*

A key standard for selecting BG and EMT members is whether or not a candidate has successful field experience and project management experience, as managers are always developed through practice. *(Source: EMT Meeting Minutes No. [2011] 008)*

We need to control the number of managers promoted from among those without field experience. Those who have never acted as junior managers should not be promoted to managerial positions at the HQ. Those who have already become managers should be provided with opportunities to work and gain more experience in field offices. *(Ren Zhengfei: Do Not Expand Blindly and Do Not Assume That We Are Already Strong Enough, 2012)*

You should move your project team to the country where your project will be piloted, instead of staying at the HQ. Personnel at the HQ will be replaced by project members and become ordinary staff members, and their positions and salaries will be reset accordingly. Are there any volunteers who want to work in field offices, participate in a project, and analyze its problems like we did with our Guangzhou Representative Office? If we hadn't dived deep into the office, we would not have identified so many problems in the field. If we simply remain at the HQ and learn nothing about what's going on in the field, how can we establish an effective management system? Our backup managers, especially those for senior managers, need to work in hardship regions, so that they can experience hardships and figure out how to set the quota for work hours, and others will be willing to follow them. *(Ren Zhengfei: Speech at the EMT ST Meeting, August 31, 2012)*

Managers need to have experience in their specific business domain or other related business domains. Anyone who has previously succeeded must have some ideas about success. I can understand things relating to HR because I have experience in this field. Many people in our company have never succeeded so they cannot understand which issue is the most important for their success. They work hard but go nowhere and incur high costs. So managers must be able to identify and focus on the most important issue and know how to address it to ensure success. We require our managers to have successful field experience because such managers understand the most important issue. Such approaches are the most efficient and least costly. Currently, certain managers at the HQ need to return to the field to gain more experience. I think we can put them in charge of small projects, as this will allow them to learn everything they need. After the projects are completed, we can evaluate their performance. They will be considered competent if they pass this evaluation. *(Ren Zhengfei: Speech at the EMT ST Meeting, July 27, 2012)*

The HRC must focus on increasing organizational vitality, as one of our biggest challenges in the future will be slackness among our employees, including managers. Currently, our objective is to inspire passion across our organization and motivate our employees to forge ahead and grow. As the Chinese saying goes: "A valiant general always starts as an ordinary soldier, just as a prime minister always starts as a local official." Similarly, managers must have successful field experience. We will look at whether our managers of level-2 departments or above have such experience. For those who do not, we will not consider them for promotions, pay raises, and share distributions, or transfer them to other departments at the same level. Right now we have too many meetings. This is because managers have no successful field experience and tend to make problems complicated. These managers are incompetent and do not have the courage to take on responsibilities. *(Source: EMT Meeting Minutes No. [2012] 016)*

To become a department head at the HQ, you must have experience working as an account department director at a large representative office, or at least as a general manager of a mid-sized office. Deputy directors normally cannot become directors at the HQ, because there are huge differences between these two roles. Being a director is more challenging because the person in this role has to make decisions in the face of huge uncertainties. Once assigned to the HQ, the director can streamline management. However, those who have no field experience tend to make things complicated and have one meeting after another whenever problems arise. This can be really frustrating for employees, so we must do something to change the current situation. *(Ren Zhengfei: Remarks at a Meeting with Staff of the Guangzhou Representative Office, 2013)*

6.1.2 Managers need work experience overseas

HQ managers must be the first to go to work overseas. They need to be involved in a project from end to end. *(Ren Zhengfei: Establishing an Open Cooperation System and Accelerating the Strategic Transformation While We Go International, 2000)*

We need to streamline our HQ organizations while putting effective supervision in place. If possible, we should minimize the number of managers at the HQ. Of course, I do not mean that we should not have any managers at the HQ. Rather, we need to send some HQ managers to work in positions where they can directly create value. *(Ren Zhengfei: Huawei's Hard Winter, 2001)*

It is always costly to appoint someone who knows nothing about battle as a commander. Similarly, HQ managers must possess successful experience in their specific business domain, be able to provide timely and accurate services, and be willing to serve others. Non-managerial staff at the HQ must also have experience in their own business domain. *(Ren Zhengfei: Speech at the Mid-year Market Conference, 2006)*

The HQ must change its role from a management and control center to a service and support center. We thus need to reduce the number of deputy directors and the total number of HQ staff. Deputy directors and lower-level managers at the HQ will be repositioned as professionals. Directors with decision-making authority must come from field offices and be rotated regularly. In the future, we will not select directors from among existing deputy directors at the HQ. One of the most important criteria for selecting directors is field experience. What do we mean by the phrase, "building command centers near the battlefield"? Our purpose is to delegate project authority to field offices, with the HQ playing a support role. We cannot blame field offices and say their reports have problems if the resources they requested did not arrive on time. Instead, the HQ should be held accountable. *(Ren Zhengfei: Speech at the Mid-year Market Conference, 2006)*

Deputy directors and lower-level managers at the HQ need to be gradually replaced by professional managers with successful field experience. Deputy directors will not be delegated decision-making or command authority. We will widen the compensation gap between deputy directors and directors. In this way, the HQ will become a place for professional managers, not a place for relaxation. Directors at the HQ need to be selected from among managers working in field offices rather than deputy directors at the HQ. Also, we need to adopt a policy stating that managers at the HQ can only serve for a specific term and they have to return to field offices regularly. *(Ren Zhengfei: Adapting the Appraisal System for Managers to Challenges Facing the Transforming Industry, 2006)*

If Chinese employees who return from overseas have good language skills and outstanding performance results, they can replace some of our current managers at the HQ. All managers at the HQ must rotate to field offices. Managers who do not have experience overseas or field experience need to figure out how to compensate for this. Every manager, from the top to the bottom of our organization, must review whether they have obtained such experience. We must ensure that our managers at the HQ have field experience and understand how things work in the field. *(Source: EMT Meeting Minutes No. [2007] 030)*

We plan to send every manager of the functional departments at the HQ to the field within three years to make sure our managers have field experience. Those who are sent to the field cannot come back until their performance is well recognized by departments that they are working with. *(Ren Zhengfei: Speech at a Meeting with Field Representatives on Organizational Optimization, 2008)*

Managers and employees at the HQ should understand that their job is to serve and support field offices, not the other way around. They should never ask field offices to report everything to them; otherwise, the HQ will become more bloated and bureaucratic. *(Ren Zhengfei: Who Calls For Artillery and How Do We Provide Timely Artillery Support, 2009)*

After a selection process within each BG, we will conduct more screening processes to eliminate those who lack successful field experience. An incompetent manager knows nothing about what is going in the field and is only able to issue orders to his subordinates, which decreases efficiency for the whole team and other teams they are working with. I have emphasized that HQ managers with no successful field experience will be demoted to non-managerial positions. We should make it clear that non-managerial staff who have never worked in the field will not be deployed. We must differentiate between employees at the HQ who have field experience and project management experience and those who don't. Those who lack such experience cannot be promoted to managerial positions. Otherwise, they will create additional bureaucracy and make more trouble, because they know nothing apart from holding meetings. This is really frustrating for their subordinates. While selecting managers, we should stress their ability to forge ahead. *(Ren Zhengfei: Speech at the EMT ST Meeting, May 31, 2011)*

6.1.3 Manager selection is like a horse race; only the fastest are chosen.

Those who are not competent in their current jobs will of course be unsuitable for more important work. *(Ren Zhengfei: Do Not Be a Temporary Hero, 1998)*

We can hold a race for all our thoroughbreds. Those who are among the top 25% will be considered for further evaluation. I do not care who you select, as long as they are from among the fastest. *(Ren Zhengfei: Eight Points Made After Receiving the "2008 Business Plan and Budget" Report at the EMT ST Meeting on January 31, 2008)*

At Huawei, selecting managers is like a horse race; however, we should give foals a chance to be selected as senior professionals at regional offices. Experts in network maintenance at representative offices can also be selected through this competitive process. *(Ren Zhengfei: Staying Customer-centric, Inspiring Dedication, and Persevering Are Key to Our Success, 2010)*

6.2 Selecting Managers from Successful Teams

6.2.1 Talented employees grow in high-performing teams

We should select backup managers from among those who are courageous and willing to work under harsh conditions. Hardships will not necessarily produce generals, but we believe that generals are usually born out of hardships. If a leader cannot even lead a small team, how can he or she lead a large team? When we say not to judge a hero based on a single success or failure, we are referring to the entire management team. For junior managers, however, we need to ensure that they have the ability to succeed together with their team. *(Ren Zhengfei: Guidelines for Human Resources Management Transformation, 2005)*

Once a project succeeds, we can promote some of the project members to managerial positions. It is simply impossible that no one on the team would be competent for a managerial position. We cannot always assign an outsider as a team leader. However, senior managers, such as general managers of representative offices, may not be promoted locally, but instead come from other regions. *(Ren Zhengfei: Speech at the Mid-year Meeting Regarding the Work Report by Regions to the EMT, 2008)*

We should allow the Core Engineering Department to fully play its role. The department can first send some of its members to work on projects in selected countries. We will choose those who perform well to become managers, and they will then be assigned to other countries. We can repeat this process to include all countries. *(Ren Zhengfei: Speech at the EMT ST Meeting on August 31, 2012)*

Our policy is to offer more rewards to high-performers. We should select more managers from among successful and high-performing teams. *(Ren Zhengfei: Remarks at a Meeting with Staff of the Guangzhou Representative Office, 2013)*

6.2.2 Developing employees who are courageous enough to charge forward

We need to develop employees who are courageous enough to charge forward. They will then energize our organization and manager management systems. Although they are not expected to take responsibility for further development in the areas they are working in, they may well grow to be experts in this respect. *(Ren Zhengfei: Embracing the Enthusiasm of Youth and Living a Life Without Regrets, 2008)*

Those who have charged forward will not necessarily be promoted to managers. We need to train 25% of the employees selected according to certain criteria and then select 8% of those who have been trained to become backup managers. We then need to provide them with opportunities to obtain hands-on experience. After gaining this experience, those who still do not possess the necessary qualifications can be recognized as heroes. Heroes may not necessarily be generals. *(Source: EMT Meeting Minutes No. [2008] 028)*

Prioritizing Major Markets, Field Offices, and Hardship Regions in Manager Selection

6.3.1 Generals usually emerge from tough battles

If managers in hardship regions and countries are also competent and willing to take on marketing and sales jobs, we can promote them to managerial positions rather than keeping the positions vacant. Different standards should be applied to identify and select managers in different regions. Managers in regions can grow into general managers or deputy general managers of representative offices. After that, their salaries should be increased accordingly. If we need managers, we must have incentives. *(Ren Zhengfei: Speech at the Third Quarter Meeting Regarding Marketing in China, 2004)*

We need to develop and select managers from hardship regions. Does this mean that we will not promote managers in developed regions? Of course not. Managers in developed regions need to be more professional because their competitors and customers are much more professional than they are. If they want to work in hardship regions and apply new methodologies there, like the Canadian doctor Bethune did in the Spanish Civil War, they are more than welcome to go there. *(Ren Zhengfei: Remarks at a Meeting with Employees of Huawei Nigeria, 2004)*

You may not necessarily become a general even if you are very knowledgeable. Otherwise, teachers at world-famous military colleges would have all become commanders. This is also true for professors. Knowledge needs to be developed into experience and capabilities through practice. Therefore, we believe that employees who have a good education should be sent to field offices and hardship regions to achieve success. The more people that you unite around you, the more successful you will be. *(Ren Zhengfei: Guidelines for Human Resources Management Transformation, 2005)*

We could deploy more deputy directors with clear job responsibilities to hardship regions and field operating units to develop backup managers so that they can step up as managers in the future. *(Source: EMT Resolution No. [2006] 027)*

Our previous strategy was to first establish a presence in rural areas be-fore making inroads into urban areas. Now we need to change this strategy. We should first win key accounts before extending our reach into small and medium-sized operators, and establish our presence in big cities before expanding into the countryside. I believe that we are now capable of focus-ing on the central areas first. We need to be clear about who our primary strategic partners are in each area and what their relationships with us are. We will then serve them with our best resources, such as service managers and sales managers. Managers must be developed in our major markets and also selected from these markets. In this way, the salaries, bonuses, and positions of employees in different regions will be differentiated. We must change the way we operate. *(Ren Zhengfei: Eight Points Made After Receiv-ing the "2008 Business Plan and Budget" Report at the EMT ST Meeting on January 31, 2008)*

6.3.2 Commitment is the most important criterion for selecting managers

When selecting managers, we emphasize two things. First is commitment; the Reserve Pool should train managers to be committed. Second is meth-odology; we should not overemphasize knowledge. *(Ren Zhengfei: Speech at the Regular Meeting of the Reserve Pool on June 24, 2009)*

We should select junior and middle managers who are totally commit-ted, have achieved high performance, and have successful field experience, to become BG EMT members. These junior and middle managers can be developed into backup managers. When an executive visits field offices, his or her primary job is to identify potential managers rather than focus on business performance or specific projects. *(Source: EMT Meeting Minutes No. [2011] 008)*

We need to replace current managers with those with commitment, ability, and integrity. Currently, departments at all levels tend to bargain with the HQ and set low objectives for themselves. Nobody volunteers to take on tough projects. Do you dare to replace some of your managers? I hope that you can promote outstanding, committed, and capable employees to replace existing managers. Those who are replaced will not be fired, so do not worry about that. I am confident we will win the market. If no one is willing to work in field offices, then I will. *(Ren Zhengfei: Speech at the EMT ST Meeting on January 20 – Increasing Investment to Seize Strategic Opportunities, 2011)*

Our company is becoming increasingly open and, as a result, employees understand each other better. When selecting managers, apart from integrity, I think capability and commitment are also important. If someone is capable and committed, we should let him or her take a managerial position regardless of seniority. This will enable a group of young managers to develop quickly and assume important roles. We can never become the best in the world if we only rely on our current managers. *(Ren Zhengfei: Speech at the Mid-year Regional Presidents' Meeting, 2011)*

6.3.3 Selecting managers with a global outlook

What qualities are we looking for in future managers? I think they are expected to have a deep understanding of the markets and a broad knowledge base. It is helpful if managers know something about everything. All senior managers must have a broad knowledge base. To that end, managers need to rotate between different positions to learn more about different business fields. Personally, I think this is very important and meaningful, and also a great opportunity for managers to develop. *(Ren Zhengfei: Speech at the Farewell Meeting for R&D Staff and Managers Sent to Field Offices, 2001)*

To meet the challenges of going global, we need to recruit international and professional staff members in different areas, including technical services, supply chain, procurement, strategic cooperation, branding, overseas public relations, human resources, and commercial affairs. We only need to hire a limited number of high-end employees, who can act as seeds to increase our overall capabilities. The Human Resource Management

Department needs to provide support in terms of compensation policies and recruitment. *(Source: EMT Resolution No. [2005] 005)*

We mainly recruit two types of high-end talent: professional managers and seeds. The former will assume managerial positions and work together and share success with their teams. The latter will increase the overall capabilities of the entire team. We can offer higher compensation to the latter if necessary. *(Source: EMT Meeting Minutes No. [2005] 029)*

Manager development will be a bottleneck for our company. We can promote those who have at least two years of overseas work experience to managerial positions in technical services and sales departments at the HQ. All middle and senior managers will be required to possess international work experience. This will enable all our managers in technical services, sales, and finance to acquire a global outlook within two years. *(Source: EMT Meeting Minutes No. [2005] 029)*

We need to hire more high-end talent, which we now lack in our global operations, especially experts who can improve our end-to-end processes and make up for our weaknesses in business operations and management (e.g. quality, processes, finance, deliverables, architecture design, marketing, turnkey projects, and human resources). These experts can help us adjust the structure of our business staff and professionals and further expand in the global market. *(Source: EMT Resolution No. [2006] 023)*

When deploying our human resources, we need to have a global vision and follow our business strategies. Currently, the HQ is not globalized enough, and this is a major obstacle to deploying more local managers in overseas markets. Once English becomes a common language within our company, this problem will be resolved. *(Source: EMT Meeting Minutes No. [2006] 018)*

Our basic policy is to recruit a few proven leaders at a high cost, and develop a large number of talented professionals at a low cost. These leaders can develop their teams based on their prior experience and methodologies. Our employees are mostly young, passionate, and quick learners, but they lack experience and methodologies. They will do a great job if they receive appropriate guidance from an expert. *(Source: EMT Meeting Minutes No. [2007] 030)*

For positions open to external hires, we can appoint qualified high-end talent as presidents of level-1 departments. Otherwise, we can appoint them as vice presidents or advisors to the presidents. *(Source: EMT Meeting Minutes No. [2007] 030)*

We need to hire groups of high-end talent. Otherwise, it will be difficult to create the kind of work atmosphere we expect. *(Source: EMT Meeting Minutes No. [2007] 030)*

We need to accelerate the process of localization, especially the promotion of local employees. Currently, we have many Chinese employees working overseas. But they cannot stay there forever. We need to develop local employees so that they can work independently. We should first localize service delivery. Ericsson has no European employees in its Venezuela office. All of the employees there are locals. But our problem is that if we only hire local employees, they will be unable to communicate with the HQ. So we need to improve how we work at the HQ. In the future, we can bring those who have worked overseas for years back to the HQ and appoint them to managerial positions; we can send HQ managers who have no overseas experience to field offices. In the past, we failed to assign employees who returned from deployment overseas to suitable positions. As a result, some left. We should consider inviting them back to help the HQ go global. Finance has already gone global, and we need to do the same for Supply Chain and GTS – and quickly. This will help us become a true multinational company. *(Ren Zhengfei: Generals Will Never Become Generals If They Do not Know Where It Goes Wrong, 2007)*

We can set a growth target for local managers. Every year, we can bring more local managers on board based on the target, but we should not rush it. For low-level local employees, we need to be extremely strict in the recruitment process. *(Source: EMT Meeting Minutes No. [2007] 030)*

Supply Chain and GTS should go global more rapidly. To that end, they should hire more high-end professionals with a global vision and appoint them as department directors. Supply Chain should hire an executive from Japan or Germany as their vice president. Audit should recruit high-end talent from the US. We aim to have non-Chinese members in the Staff Team (ST) of every level-1 department and regional office in 2008. *(Source: EMT Meeting Minutes No. [2008] 013)*

We cannot simply rely on resources in China to become a global industry leader. We cannot develop by destroying others. Instead, we must leverage capabilities and resources from all over the world to become a leader. We need to continue investing in technologies overseas, which may decrease our profits in the short term. But if we can develop our expertise in multiple fields via investment, profits will grow in the long run. We have a huge R&D center in China, but it lacks experience and efficiency. If we do not hire top talent from around the world, we will still be working on low-level technology and there will be lots of duplicate work. We currently lack architects with a big picture, so we should further increase cooperation with countries that possess the expertise we require. *(Ren Zhengfei: Speech at the Workshop on the Business Environment in Europe, 2012)*

We need to bring in more non-Chinese CFOs and experts to work with our outstanding young employees and form a mixed financial team. We need to provide opportunities for capable employees to work as managers or experts. In the past, we were not open enough and, as a result, some excellent employees could not live up to their potential and left the company. Now we'd like to welcome them back to work with us. *(Ren Zhengfei: Comments to Managers from Finance, 2012)*

Examining and Selecting Managers Who Excelled During Key Events

6.4.1 Key employees must have a clear stance in key events

When selecting backup managers, we need to review their stances and conduct during key events and emergencies, and when their personal interests are in conflict with the company's interests. *(Ren Zhengfei: Speech Regarding Huawei University and the Strategic Reserve Pool, 2005)*

Employee loyalty is most evident during key events, when employees out-compete our rivals and protect our interests. We focus on employees' attitudes and conduct during key events. A key event could include circumstances when the company faces an operational crisis, adopts a strategic approach, significantly changes business or employee management policies, or when the company's business development requires employees to sacrifice their short-term, personal interests. Key employees must have a clear stance and stick to principles to protect the company's interests during key events. When selecting key employees, we first look at their loyalty demonstrated during key events, and their loyalty is expected to stand the test of time. *(Source: EMT Meeting Minutes No. [2008] 006)*

Key employees are those the company can rely on during its development, especially during times of crises or major internal and external events. They share in both the company's successes and failures and remain dedicated in whatever positions they assume. *(Source: EMT Meeting Minutes No. [2008] 006)*

When selecting key employees, we look at loyalty and capabilities. We have to make sure our key employees are capable so that they can play a key role in their positions when the company faces major opportunities or risks. The company welcomes all capable employees; however, not all of them can be selected as key employees. We must ensure that the loyalty demonstrated by key employees can stand the test of time and the test of key events. *(Source: EMT Meeting Minutes No. [2008] 006)*

6.4.2 Selecting those with a strong sense of professional responsibility as our key employees

When evaluating department directors, we should look at their leadership during key events rather than simply focusing on what they have achieved. *(Ren Zhengfei, Speech at the UK Representative Office, 2007)*

We need to select those who have a strong sense of mission and professional responsibility as our key employees. These employees are expected to make more sacrifices than others. Our job is to maintain network stability. The nature and character of a nation are evident during times of crisis. The Japanese people demonstrated great character during the recent earthquake, which is an excellent example for us to learn from. The mayor of Suzhou cried when he told me about the deaths of 50 heroes who went to the Fukushima nuclear plant right after the disaster. Nothing is impossible if we have such great people. We witnessed similar character in our employees during the evacuation from Libya. They stayed calm and showed great care for others. They even requested that other people evacuate first. This kind of behavior is really inspiring. When Ken Hu reported this to me, he said he almost burst into tears. Our employees who have been working in the most dangerous areas, and their families who have accompanied them, should all receive our respect. Without their sacrifice, we could not have such a comfortable life. During the earthquake, tsunami, and nuclear crisis in Japan, our local team, under the leadership of our chairwoman, did not retreat, but stayed calm and played an active role in the relief efforts. During that time, we learned from the Japanese people and also demonstrated the character of a Chinese company to Japanese carriers. We showed them that our employees, both Chinese and Japanese, worked through difficult times together and also demonstrated our corporate culture. We should have an upright character and do our jobs well. *(Ren Zhengfei: Speech Regarding Cherishing Life and Fulfilling Job Responsibilities, 2011)*

6.5 Focusing on Employees' Strengths and Not Demanding Perfection

6.5.1 Focusing on employees' strengths rather than their weaknesses

If we select managers rigidly based on our C&Q criteria, they would be perfect people, or sages. This is not we want. Instead, we need a group of effective managers. During C&Q assessments, we should adopt a scientific evaluation system to significantly improve our previous management style, which relied too much on emotion. But one typical characteristic of this type of management is that we do not expect anyone to be perfect. *(Ren Zhengfei: Establishing an Organization and Mechanism That Facilitates Enterprise Survival and Development, 2000)*

Decision-makers should not seek perfection or appoint managers who make no mistakes at all, but cannot do anything. We need to have a transparent system for selecting managers. Managers should not be passive; instead, we expect them to be willing to take on responsibilities, face challenges head-on, and make sacrifices for the company when necessary. *(Ren Zhengfei: Staying Close to Customers by Going Where You Are Most Needed in the Field Office, 2011)*

We need to be tolerant of managers as long as they have no moral or ethical issues. I have always been a controversial individual during my life. If people around me were not tolerant, I would not have gotten to where I am today. *(Ren Zhengfei: Seeing the Situation Clearly and Accelerating Organizational and Reserve Pool Development to Embrace Huawei's New Development, 2005)*

We should choose department heads that have obvious strengths and are capable of leading teams. People with obvious strengths also tend to have obvious weaknesses, which may prevent them from becoming competent managers. We should not expect people to be perfect. We should focus on our employees' strengths rather than weaknesses. *(Source: EMT Meeting Minutes No. [2007] 025)*

When assessing new managers, we need to focus on their strengths rather than their weaknesses. No one in the world is perfect. But if a person has moral or ethical problems, we will not promote them no matter how capable they are. We should stick to our principles when selecting managers. The Committee of Ethics and Compliance has the right to veto the appointment of managers with ethical problems. Despite this, we still have many competent managers with integrity, so we must have the courage to develop more managers. Every generation has bright sparks and we should fan them into a roaring fire. *(Ren Zhengfei: Speech at the Mid-year Meeting Regarding the Work Report by Regions to the EMT, 2008)*

When promoting managers in our Consumer BG, we should avoid overemphasizing strategic thinking and years of experience. We should not require our managers to be perfect. Instead, the Consumer BG should remain realistic and focus on results and responsibilities when selecting managers, and promote more young employees to managerial positions. *(Source: EMT Meeting Minutes No. [2009] 041)*

We need to give opportunities to employees who are young, motivated, and hard working, and have the potential to take on greater responsibilities to see if they are competent for managerial roles. When it comes to manager selection policies, I still believe that we should not expect people to be perfect and should be more open to promote young people. The HRC needs to be involved in this. Otherwise, we may be unable to select the managers we need as departments may be shortsighted. When selecting managers, we should break our old rules and give preference to those who are hard-working, have successful experience, and make a great contribution. We can fast-track those who are really capable. *(Source: EMT Meeting Minutes No. [2009] 022)*

6.5.2 Fast-track outstanding employees

Why can't we fast-track outstanding employees? Why can't we learn from the American military? During the Normandy landings, Ridgway was just a major general, in command of the US 82nd Airborne Division. In the Korean War, he was appointed as the Commander-in-Chief of the United Nations Command. Later, he succeeded General Dwight D. Eisenhower as Supreme Commander, NATO. These promotions all took place within just eight years. I think Huawei can follow suit in this respect. We should select some strategists to help us grab markets of strategic importance. Can the Human Resource Management Department make Richard Yu a vice president? He can then recruit and develop his own thoroughbreds. At Huawei, we now have no secrets, so we will not say who is reliable and who is not. Now, we will promote those with ability and integrity. We will never promote those with moral or ethical problems, no matter how capable they are. *(Ren Zhengfei: Speech at the EMT ST Meeting on January 20 – Increasing Investment to Seize Strategic Opportunities, 2011)*

We should fast-track outstanding managers. We used to place too much emphasis on fairness. We have already built a baseline of fairness, and now need to fast-track exceptional employees. For junior employees, we can give a pay raise to those with excellent performance. We do not need to fear that other employees will quit because of this, as there is no absolute fairness in the world. We need to promote those with strong leadership capabilities right away so that they can make a bigger contribution while they are young. If we don't quickly promote them, they might become too old to contribute more when they finally have a chance. The HRC thus needs to offer fast-track promotions to outstanding employees. Otherwise, our managers may leave us and join other companies and help them expand into the international market. *(Ren Zhengfei: Speech at the Self-reflection Session of the Executive Committee of the Board of Directors from May 24 to 25, 2012)*

While practicing our core values, we also need to be tolerant of our heroes' weaknesses so as to motivate them rather than restrain them. We cannot expect them to be perfect. For outstanding professionals, results are more important than work attitude. But for other employees, since it is sometimes difficult and costly to clearly assess results, we should assess their work attitude. But we must make sure that no department uses poor work attitude as an excuse for not promoting outstanding employees. In the future, those who are fast-tracked will be mostly experts. For managers, however, after the appointment system is well on track, the evaluations of most managers will be fair. Some experts unknown to most people may be promoted all of a sudden. *(Ren Zhengfei: Speech at the EMT ST Meeting on July 27, 2012)*

We should fast-track outstanding employees. To enable our company to grow sustainably, we should develop more managers and experts, inspire passion across our organization, and enable exceptional managers and experts to take on greater responsibilities and develop faster. We plan to establish a fast-track promotion mechanism for outstanding employees in accordance with existing manager deployment and job level management rules and procedures. After a discussion at the EMT meeting on July 27, 2012, we reached the following resolutions on management principles and implementation requirements.

1. Definition of fast-track promotion: Employees who meet certain criteria can be directly appointed to positions that match their responsibilities, regardless of their existing job levels, and their job levels can be raised to match their new positions, irrespective of the existing rules and requirements. In principle, job levels can be raised by no more than three levels at a time.

2. Fast-track promotion is applicable to the following groups:
   - Employees who have achieved outstanding performance over a long period and are role models for employees at the same job level;
   - Employees who take the initiative to work long-term in hardship regions or take challenging positions, and make outstanding contributions;
   - Key employees who assume great responsibilities and produce outstanding performance in key projects, competition projects, or corporate transformation projects;
   - Managers who are bold enough to undertake risks and meet challenges head-on in new business areas and achieve outstanding results;
   - Managers and key employees who assume responsibilities at critical moments, overcome difficulties, and achieve complete or nearly complete turnarounds in operations or management.

3. In principle, employees must meet the following conditions before being promoted via the fast track: Employees who have worked in their positions for at least one year or have completed tasks for at least one cycle of key projects and achieved positive performance results (assessment results on work attitude are not a mandatory condition for fast-track promotion). In addition, they must identify with and practice our corporate core values and remain responsible and committed, without passing the buck or making unfounded complaints.

4. The authority to approve fast-track promotions for the above employees and managers can be delegated according to specific procedures. In principle, existing processes can be implemented to approve such fast-track promotions. If no processes are available, a special approval process can be developed to complete approvals in a standardized yet flexible manner.

5. The Human Resource Management Department shall formulate operational standards, approval procedures, and authorization mechanisms according to the above requirements, and implement them upon approval by the HRC. (Source: EMT Resolution No. [2012] 034)

6.5.3 Our goal in manager selection is not to look good, but to succeed

Our HR management transformation aims to encourage employees to forge ahead. We need to develop a strong team that is courageous, tenacious, and able to achieve success. We won't select a well-coordinated gymnastics team that is full of attractive, strong, graceful, and agile people. Our goal is not to look good, but to succeed. *(Ren Zhengfei: Guidelines for Human Resources Management Transformation, 2005)*

We should be adept at finding new, capable managers and putting their advantages into full play in different environments and under different conditions. We cannot use a fixed, rigid model to evaluate and select managers. We do not need a well-coordinated gymnastics team; instead, we need a group of managers who are able to seize major projects. *(Ren Zhengfei: Seeing the Situation Clearly and Accelerating Organizational and Reserve Pool Development to Embrace Huawei's New Development, 2005)*

6.5.4 We need employees with social responsibility and also employees with a strong sense of personal achievement

Our company recognizes these kinds of employees. Here, I am talking about social responsibility in a narrow sense – employees who have a strong sense of mission and responsibility towards our company's goals. These employees provide more and better services to others, without seeking personal achievements. We also support employees who have a strong sense of personal achievement. We want to develop employees with a strong sense of social responsibility into leaders, and cultivate those with a strong sense of personal achievement into heroes. If we have no heroes, our company will lose its vitality and hope. Therefore, we need both leaders and heroes. However, we cannot promote heroes to top management roles unless they develop a sense of social responsibility; otherwise, these heroes might easily cause disunity or even breakup in our company. A manager's responsibility is to mould his or her subordinates into heroes, and to become a leader themselves. *(Ren Zhengfei: Bringing Life into Products, 1998)*

We emphasize the promotion of outstanding employees. We look at two things when differentiating managers: social responsibility (in a narrow sense) and a sense of personal achievement. Social responsibility refers to employees' strong sense of mission and responsibility towards our company's goals, which is more than a sense of personal achievement. The social responsibility that Fan Zhongyan[1] talked about is of a broader sense, and involves a politician's talents. The social responsibility we are talking about relates to a manager's talents. We will recognize, support, and trust those who have a strong sense of personal achievement and cultivate them into role models for heroes. We need heroes among our junior employees as they give vitality and hope to the company. So we use both social responsibility and personal achievement as criteria for selecting managers. We do not promote passive people. It is fine if you make mistakes, but it is unacceptable to be passive. A sense of responsibility and mission is different from a sense of self-achievement. Managers need to understand that their role is to help their subordinates become heroes and provide necessary services to help them achieve their goals. Being a leader means providing services to subordinates. *(Ren Zhengfei: How Long Can Huawei Survive, 1998)*

Great leaders have a strong sense of social responsibility, and do not seek personal achievements. They do not need to be motivated with big rewards. At Huawei, we have many unsung heroes. We need to rely on them to create a better future, so we should enable them to fully play their roles. We should develop a manager management system and use our value assessment system to institutionalize the values that we cherish, which will help the company thrive well into the next century. *(Ren Zhengfei: Bringing Life into Products, 1998)*

---

[1] Fan Zhongyan was a prominent politician and literary figure in China's Song dynasty. One of his famous quotes was: "Bear hardship and bitterness before others, enjoy comfort and happiness after them."

6.6

Key Behavioral Criteria for Managers

6.6.1 Integrity and ethics are the minimum requirements for managers

We need to avoid a one-sided understanding of what appointing people according to their character means. Professionals with strong expertise are not necessarily people of good character, but those with high integrity are. We hire people who identify with our corporate culture, rather than just appointing the people we like. Our managers must identify with our corporate culture, and we focus most on integrity when selecting middle and senior managers. We are determined to remove corrupt managers, and will never condone their corruption. We will have made a serious mistake if we do not develop outstanding managers. We must be strict with our managers today to ensure they have a better tomorrow. *(Ren Zhengfei: Minutes of the CEO's Staff Team Meeting, 1997)*

Integrity is the most important trait when it comes to promoting managers. It is never easy to measure this. However, it is relatively easy to see if someone is obsessed with gossip and likes to talk about others behind their backs. Gossiping about others is something we need to avoid, even if it is based on facts. Those who gossip without any respect for facts will be considered unprincipled. We should not promote them to managerial positions. *(Ren Zhengfei: Focusing on a Down-to-earth Approach to Seize Opportunities for Development, 1998)*

When selecting employees, we should attach great importance to integrity. To enable thoroughbreds to run fast, we need to give them complete trust, and provide guidance to help them improve. When making a middle manager a senior manager, we prioritize integrity. When making a junior manager a middle manager, we put ability first. As standards for selecting employees are constantly changing, we need to develop a long-term strategy for employee selection. *(Ren Zhengfei: How Long Can Huawei Survive, 1998)*

When selecting middle and senior managers, we must put integrity first. Discipline, integrity, loyalty to the company, and advocacy for collective interests are important standards to consider when we select managers. We must not merely focus on ability in manager selection. *(Ren Zhengfei: Living with Peace of Mind, 2003)*

For managers, the most important requirement is integrity. Integrity is an umbrella term that covers not only honesty, but also the willingness to work in hardship regions, the courage to bear hardships, and the boldness to take on responsibilities. We prioritize employees with high integrity during manager selection. History has shown that most reforms fail during prosperous periods. Such periods create opportunities for opportunists, who will turn against the reformers as soon as it suits them. We should learn lessons from this, and select managers with high integrity in our good times to ensure the company develops sustainably. *(Ren Zhengfei: Speech at the Third Quarter Meeting Regarding Marketing in China, 2004)*

Currently, Huawei is developing steadily. We need to increasingly focus on integrity during manager selection. Integrity is an umbrella term that covers not only morality and ethics, but also a sense of responsibility and mission, dedication, the willingness to work in hardship regions and grow through practice, and the ability to manage teams effectively. Currently, we are developing quickly, and it is critical for Huawei to select good managers. At Huawei, dedication is the only way for managers to succeed. *(Ren Zhengfei: Remarks at a Meeting with Staff of the United Arab Emirates Representative Office, 2004)*

When selecting backup managers, we put integrity and commitment first. During training at Huawei University and daily cultivation activities, we stress skills and competence, with an emphasis on integrity throughout the process. *(Source: EMT Meeting Minutes No. [2005] 022)*

ATs are mainly responsible for people management. We should never appoint people to become ATs who are not strong-minded or who are unethical. Such people can remain ordinary managers or experts. *(Ren Zhengfei: Speech at the EMT ST Meeting, August 31, 2011)*

6.6.2 Prioritizing high performance in manager selection

We need to focus more on competence when selecting senior managers, and attach more importance to performance when selecting junior managers. While performance is generally objective, assessing competence tends to be subjective and involves ambiguity and misunderstandings. *(Ren Zhengfei: Speech at the Meeting Regarding the Hay Pilot Project, 2000)*

During manager management, the competence requirements for senior managers versus junior managers are dramatically different. While the former are expected to demonstrate high competence, the latter are expected to achieve high performance. When assessing professionals, we should focus on competence closely related to their job responsibilities. When it comes to managers, we should have high expectations for their overall competence. *(Ren Zhengfei: Remarks at a Meeting with Employees, 2000)*

We cannot simply measure competence when assessing and promoting employees. We also need to look at performance and results. The assessment of integrity is largely influenced by managers' personal preferences and the limitations of their perspectives. Performance and results are concrete and objective. We have requirements relating to responsibilities and results for all our senior managers. We always look at results before reviewing the actual process for producing them and examining whether key events reflect competence. *(Ren Zhengfei: Speech at the Meeting to Convey the Main Ideas of the Human Resources Conference, 2002)*

High performance is a prerequisite for managers. The manager selection process is only applicable to those who have achieved high performance in actual work and rank among the top 25%. We do not recognize "dumplings in the teapot". *(Source: EMT Meeting Minutes No. [2005] 053)*

We must select managers with successful field experience. However, "successful" does not necessarily mean sales amount. We cannot simply focus on sales revenue and blame our result-oriented assessment system because we couldn't achieve the expected results. *(Source: EMT Meeting Minutes No. [2008] 009)*

We should focus on the ability to forge ahead when selecting BG EMT members and future managers. All business units should focus on increasing revenue rather than discussing how to distribute revenue. *(Source: EMT Meeting Minutes No. [2011] 008)*

6.6.3 Leadership is key to continuous high performance

When promoting and deploying promising managers who are responsible and have achieved outstanding performance, we need to review their competence levels and key events. *(Ren Zhengfei: Continuously Improving Per Capita Efficiency and Building a High-performance Corporate Culture, 2004)*

We select and cultivate those who are loyal, dedicated, high-performing, and outstanding in key-event-based appraisals. Competence is often mistaken as a combination of academic degrees, knowledge, and skills. Actually, it refers to capabilities that are consistently demonstrated through key behavior and key events in achieving performance and results. Therefore, we should avoid using the term "competence" in corporate documents to minimize misunderstandings. In written documents, we can use "has consistently demonstrated key behavior" to clarify our intended meaning. *(Source: EMT Meeting Minutes No. [2005] 040)*

How can we assess whether an employee possesses the necessary leadership skills? We need to conduct appraisals based on practices and key events. It is not a good idea to rely on incomplete, subjective, and uncertain methods when selecting managers. As performance and successful field experience are objective, they should be the basis for manager selection. But they are not enough. Therefore, we still need to assess if the candidates have leadership skills. In other words, when selecting managers, we need to base our decisions on actual facts while complementing our decisions with subjective assessments. *(Source: EMT Meeting Minutes No. [2005] 053)*

In my opinion, there are three manager qualities: decisiveness, execution, and comprehension. If one possesses comprehension, he or she is competent for a managerial role at HQ. If one is competent at execution, he or she could serve as a deputy director. If one is good at making decisions, he or she could serve as a department head. *(Ren Zhengfei: Speech at the Meeting Regarding the Work Report of the Asia Pacific Region, 2006)*

We use four manager qualities as core standards. We select managers with successful field experience, and demote underperforming managers. Decisiveness, execution, and comprehension are the three main standards for manager selection. First, if managers cannot comprehend what they hear, how can they execute tasks and get things done effectively? Second, we need to improve the execution capabilities of middle managers, and the decisiveness of senior managers. Later on, we add interpersonal connection and we thus have four quality requirements for managers. Together, these four qualities will ensure teamwork and willpower. The qualities will be assessed through key events, not through exams. *(Ren Zhengfei: Human Resources Must Be Oriented Towards Forging Ahead and Refrain from Being Dogmatic and Rigid, 2009)*

To be a good leader or manager, you need to read extensively, broaden your horizons, and be sharp enough to understand industry trends. Only in this way can we standardize operations within the company. If you merely focus on internal issues without paying attention to external changes, you will be demoted after you have achieved standardized internal operations. You may ask why. It's because you failed to adapt to future changes. I always emphasize the importance of vision, which is complemented by experience and learning. *(Ren Zhengfei: Speech at the EMT ST Meeting, March 29, 2013)*

Our strategic leaders still focus too much on specific issues and do not have a big picture. This is different from the United States, where strategic leaders emerge rapidly and become leading global experts in a short period of time. Currently, we have many young, outstanding business leaders. To help Huawei succeed in the global market, our business leaders need to open up their minds and field of vision to think more about how Huawei can succeed globally, rather than simply focusing on the success of individual projects. Otherwise, our business leaders will never become strategic experts or strategic leaders. We need to learn from the United States and great Western companies that focus more on issues related to the global landscape rather than specific tasks. *(Ren Zhengfei: Speech at the EMT ST Meeting, March 29, 2013)*

Apart from vision, integrity, and willpower, our successors must possess long-term thinking regarding our value assessment system and be able to navigate the business ecosystem. They are also expected to have a global view; conduct transactions and support goal achievement; have an in-depth understanding of new technologies and customer needs; open up to constantly improve themselves; and manage the business operations, logistics, and cash flow of the company from end to end. *(Ren Zhengfei: Summary of the Speech at the Representatives' Commission Meeting, March 30, 2013)*

6.7
Basic Principles for Deploying Managers

6.7.1 Deploying managers in accordance with business development plans

Our operating model focuses on seizing opportunities; gaining competitive advantages in product technologies and price/performance ratios through heavy R&D investment; creating a positive feedback loop in the shortest time possible through large-scale marketing campaigns; and earning huge profits from windows of opportunity. We never stop optimizing our mature products. By avoiding price competitions, we will secure a dominant position in strategic markets. To support this operating model, we need to align organizational structures and develop talented professionals to constantly improve the company's overall operating efficiency. *(Source: The Huawei Charter, 1998)*

Currently, we are facing a serious shortage of marketing staff outside China. Many representative offices only have one or two marketing employees. So we have decided to assign outstanding, experienced marketing staff abroad. That is a strategic decision, because marketing staff have a sharp market sense, and can clearly understand local market trends. *(Ren Zhengfei: Speech at the Farewell Meeting for R&D Staff and Managers Sent to Field Offices, 2001)*

Department heads at all levels who are able to develop and implement strategies in regions need to be allocated globally. *(Ren Zhengfei: Speech at the Mid-year Market Conference, 2006)*

We should first assign outstanding managers to new business domains and subsidiaries engaging in such domains, laying a solid foundation for our future capital operations. *(Source: EMT Resolution No. [2006] 024)*

Backup managers and managers in the succession pipeline should be developed in accordance with Huawei's business development strategies and plans, and managerial position requirements. ATs at all levels must develop succession plans for all managerial positions, including candidates who are ready now and who need to further gain experience in one or more positions. *(Source: EMT Resolution No. [2007] 025)*

We need to continue downsizing support functions and reducing the number of support staff. However, we should make sure that we have enough employees in our operating teams. Also, when downsizing support functions, we have to make reasonable decisions based on facts. *(Ren Zhengfei: Speech at the Regular Meeting of the Reserve Pool, March 25, 2009)*

The HRC should be bold enough to rotate managers via training programs, without too much emphasis on seniority. Our goal is to become a key player in the global market. We will offer opportunities to those who can help us succeed, so long as they do not have any ethical problems. Competence and performance are key, not seniority. When a project begins, it is almost impossible for us to wait for someone to get ready. *(Ren Zhengfei: Quickly Building Our CFO Team to Support IFS Deployment, 2009)*

6.7.2 Allocating high-quality resources to valued customers

A crucial factor in our sustainable growth is establishing a presence in three areas: valued customers, valued countries, and mainstream products. Therefore, product lines and regions must reasonably allocate human resources; priority will be given to these three areas, rather than to product domains and regions with low growth momentum. We must expand our competitive presence in these three areas in order to support our sustainable growth. *(Source: EMT Resolution No. [2009] 002)*

Our overarching guideline is to provide quality services to customers. The aim of our transformation is to channel high-quality resources to valued customers. For employees working in outstanding teams and service platforms, we can rate them at higher job levels. We don't need to overemphasize balance between different representative offices. If your representative office earns profits, we can assign higher-level service staff to you to help you better serve customers. In that case, customers will see the value of

Huawei, as we will help them succeed. *(Ren Zhengfei: Remarks at a Meeting with Staff of the Guangzhou Representative Office, 2013)*

High-quality resources should be channeled to valued customers. When I say high-quality resources, I mean junior managers with higher job levels. The job levels of these managers can be constantly increased. In this way, we can allocate high-quality resources to serve our valued customers. *(Ren Zhengfei: Remarks at a Meeting with Staff of the Guangzhou Representative Office, 2013)*

We are assigning people with a major-general's capabilities as company commanders. Only offices that are profitable can be assigned major-general company commanders. I'm not sure if any of you would like to act like Lei Feng, doing many good things and wanting nothing in return. Well, I'm not a supporter of this idea. Lei Feng here is simply an idea; it cannot be used as a mechanism. We must start the transformation at profitable representative offices that can afford senior experts and managers. In this way, high-quality resources will be channeled to valued customers. To have more high-quality resources, you first have to make more money from such customers; otherwise, where will you get the money to support such high-level people? *(Ren Zhengfei: Speech at the Huawei Annual Management Conference, 2013)*

6.7.3 Selecting managers based on the company's positioning and managers' advantages

Once the organization's positioning is defined and processes are running smoothly, we will reselect managers for positions according to process requirements. Any department that cannot meet process requirements must be restructured, and the type of required managers must be defined accordingly. *(Ren Zhengfei: Building a Professional Financial Team That Has Solid Integrity, Dares to Shoulder Responsibilities, and Sticks to Principles, 2006)*

At Huawei, we select outstanding employees for managerial positions, rather than developing managers. We assess and deploy employees based on what they can do, regardless of their seniority. This is supported by our increasingly clear processes and systems. In the future, we will promote more high-end talent. Our selection mechanism will act as a great enabler, offering enormous opportunities to those with integrity, ability, and accomplishments. Currently, many departments are dismissing long-time employees, because they think these employees are not capable enough even though they have stayed at Huawei for quite a long time. However, our Group CFO is strongly against doing the same thing in the finance system. She pointed out that some long-time employees are satisfied with their current positions, and are willing to stay even with less pay. Why should we drive them away? We can keep them in accounting positions. Financial data from previous years will remain relevant in the future. If all finance staff are new hires, who will be able to explain historical financial data? We can keep long-time employees and help them focus on their jobs by providing stable salaries and benefits. Meanwhile, we can provide opportunities to young employees so that they can forge ahead and grow. The company is very vocal in calling for heroes to come forth in great numbers. Finance needs to pick up the pace because progress has been slow. Last year, I fast-tracked the promotions of 183 finance employees. However, those employees have not made sufficient progress. They have let me down. *(Ren Zhengfei: Minutes of the Meeting with Staff of the Romania Accounting SSC, 2011)*

Huawei's early success is attributable to its emphasis on marketing's guiding role in R&D efforts. As a result, many of our managers have a marketing background. But now, marketing staff can no longer lead the company, because they don't understand our future direction. To solve this problem, we will assign R&D managers to the marketing & sales departments to see if they are able to drive the company forward in the future. Thus, the source of our managers will change. *(Source: Speech at the EMT ST Meeting, March 30, 2012)*

6.7.4 Never leaving a position vacant until there are more qualified candidates

We should promote managers at a fast but measured pace. As an old Chinese saying goes: "When one does not hold any office, he or she does not need to consider policies." If we want our managers to grow quickly, we need to put them in real-world positions. *(Source: EMT Meeting Minutes No. [2005] 029)*

We should step up efforts to select and promote managers from among employees working in hardship regions. We cannot leave managerial positions in hardship regions unoccupied until more qualified candidates are found. High-performing employees should be appointed to vacant positions as soon as possible, so that we can observe and develop them while they are gaining hands-on experience. *(Source: EMT Resolution No. [2006] 015)*

When promoting managers, we should assess their performance, competence, and integrity. Once we identify qualified candidates, we can give them a chance to try a new position. If they can't do a good job, we will coach them and help them adapt to the new position more quickly. Once they are competent in the position, we can promote them and then give them a pay raise. We will continue to check whether they are competent in their position. If we stick to such an inclusive manager selection mechanism, we will be able to select qualified managers more quickly. *(Ren Zhengfei: Speech at the Annual Meeting of the Domestic Market Finance Department, 2006)*

Critical and key positions must not be left vacant. Timely incentives must be provided to employees who have proven to be competent through appraisals. *(Source: EMT Resolution No. [2006] 029)*

We should not allow positions to remain unoccupied following the demotion of underperforming managers. We need to identify and promote those with outstanding performance and leadership potential, and give them opportunities to take on new responsibilities. *(Source: EMT Resolution No. [2007] 022)*

We should establish new rules for replacing managers before discarding the old rules. After we have established principles and standards, we can implement them step by step. Currently, the company has a large business volume. We need to be practical so as to keep things going. A large number of managers at HQ are really good managers. The only problem is that they don't know much about operations in field offices. I believe they will be even better managers after gaining hands-on experience in the field. Managers assigned from HQ will not necessarily work in managerial positions in field offices. *(Source: EMT Meeting Minutes No. [2007] 030)*

Regarding manager deployment, we should establish new rules before discarding the old. We should not leave positions vacant until more qualified candidates are found. We will not allow our business or management to come to a standstill because of a lack of managers. *(Source: EMT Meeting Minutes No. [2007] 015)*

We should expand our workforce and promote managers at a fast but measured pace, so as to help managers gradually improve their management skills and meet the needs brought about by the company's increasing size. *(Source: EMT Meeting Minutes No. [2008] 011)*

We need to carry out management improvements and adjustments, such as adjusting processes and organizations and improving operating quality, while ensuring everyday business continues as usual. This is also true for managerial succession planning. We can't afford to stop everything in order to make adjustments. *(Source: EMT Meeting Minutes No. [2009] 038)*

We must not implement rigid systems or mechanisms. To seize strategic opportunities, we can flexibly deploy managers irrespective of their seniority, because success is more important than seniority. We should strive for success, without being overly concerned about disrupting the balance. *(Ren Zhengfei: Do Not Expand Blindly and Do Not Assume That We Are Already Strong Enough, 2012)*

6.7.5 Setting different criteria for selecting directors and deputy directors

How can we effectively select directors and deputy directors? Can we set different criteria for developing and selecting these two types of directors? Deputy directors must focus on fine-grained management to help achieve the organization's intent. Directors must dare to forge ahead; clearly understand corporate strategies; be adept at strategic planning; show traits such as determination, willpower, perseverance, and the willingness to make sacrifices; and lead their teams to breakthroughs. Therefore, those who are careless are not suitable as deputy directors, and those who focus too much on details or are too modest, are not suitable as directors. When appraising directors, we should look at their leadership during key events rather than simply focusing on what they have achieved. *(Ren Zhengfei: Speech at the UK Representative Office, 2007)*

We will gradually replace deputy directors at the HQ with professional managers who have successful field experience. Meanwhile, we will select those who have management experience in field offices to serve as directors at the HQ, and rotate them with managers in field offices regularly. In principle, we do not directly promote HQ managers, especially HQ deputy directors, to HQ directors' positions. *(Source: EMT Resolution No. [2006] 027)*

To avoid potential problems in organizations, we normally do not appoint deputy directors to directors' positions, when the previous managers in these leadership positions were demoted due to poor performance. *(Source: EMT Resolution No. [2007] 022)*

Directors must have distinctive qualities, including a clear direction; a sense of responsibility; decisiveness; and the ability to develop appropriate strategies, formulate well-thought-out plans, and develop organizations and capabilities. When making inroads into markets, these directors must sacrifice their individual interests and display such traits as determination, willpower, and perseverance. *(Source: EMT Meeting Minutes No. [2007] 025)*

Directors should be clear about the company's strategic direction, focus on the most important issue and the factors that influence the issue, and then figure out where to go. Deputy directors at a higher level may not be suitable as directors at a lower level. *(Source: EMT Meeting Minutes No. [2007] 025)*

Managers in deputy-level positions must focus on fine-grained management and pay attention to details once inroads into markets have been made, so that the markets can be secured. Directors must develop a wolf pack. Wolves have three key characteristics: a keen sense of smell; a pack mentality; and tenacity. In addition, directors must have a clear strategic direction and willpower, and be strategic and willing to make sacrifices. *(Ren Zhengfei: Comments on Employee Training, 2007)*

6.7.6 Limiting the number of part-time and deputy-level positions

We should set a cap on the number of part-time jobs (including administrative positions and committee memberships) we assign to managers. This will enable managers to focus their time and efforts on their principal responsibilities. In addition, it will also give new managers more opportunities and room to grow. *(Source: EMT Meeting Minutes No. [2009] 019)*

The number of HQ deputy-level positions should be determined based on the complexity and scope of businesses and services. The headcount for deputy-level positions must be fixed. We expect to cut the number of HQ deputy-level positions by at least 30%, after this round of people-job matching. *(Source: EMT Resolution No. [2006] 027)*

All divisions must plan and define the responsibilities, number, and C&Q criteria of deputy-level positions according to their actual business needs. Deputy-level positions must not be set arbitrarily or treated as honorary titles. We should appraise current managers in deputy-level positions against the selection criteria to see if they are still competent. We will reposition those who are no longer qualified and adjust their salaries. *(Source: EMT Meeting Minutes No. [2008] 002)*

6.7.7 Deploying managers in a balanced manner to overcome weaknesses

There are four elements in sales: solutions, customer relationships, financing, and delivery. In the past, we only focused on customer relationships, and neglected delivery and financing. We ignored the development of the financial system. As a result, we were skilled at solutions and customer relationships, but weak in delivery and financing. We need to change this. In the future, we will deploy managers evenly to ensure the balanced development of the four elements. Otherwise, we may be unable to collect payments, which could lead to the company's collapse. *(Ren Zhengfei: Speech at the Mid-year Meeting Regarding the Work Report by Regions to the EMT, 2008)*

We should place outstanding finance employees in the reserve pool to gain hands-on experience, so that they can become managers with both business and finance knowledge. In the future, managers with a finance background will work in business departments, and vice versa. We will also assign some managers to the procurement department, and implement job rotation. All this is based on the assumption that we have enough employees. But what if we do not? Many of our employees are outstanding college graduates. Have we provided opportunities for them to move up? Is our current method of selecting managers problematic? Is it possible to promote graduates to managerial positions directly? The way we implement HR policies and regulations in the above-mentioned scenario is rigid. Instead of prioritizing R&D and marketing & sales departments, we must ensure balanced development across the company. Outstanding managers are needed in all departments. We can't stop deploying managers to departments simply because they fail to succeed in a given market. We must consider how to achieve balance among all segments of the company. *(Source: Comments on the Reserve Pool, 2010)*

Our company, the HQ in particular, needs to greatly cut the number of middle managers. Those who are fully committed can serve as account managers. Currently, we lack account managers, so we will increase their numbers. We need to assign more account managers to optical networks and private networks. However, most managers are now in legacy businesses which have little potential for further growth, while new businesses with huge growth potential need resources badly. Therefore, we need to deploy human resources from a global perspective. We should shape our R&D

team into a pyramid. Some R&D departments need to rotate their managers at levels 16–17, so that lower-level managers have the opportunity to grow. *(Ren Zhengfei: Speech at the EMT ST Meeting on January 20 – Increasing Investment to Seize Strategic Opportunities, 2011)*

Our HQ has many capable employees, but our key projects in field offices lack key staff and our Customer Centric 3 (CC3)[2] roles that directly engage with customers are weak. Even though our internal control capabilities are strong at the HQ, our operating capabilities have not been improved accordingly. To change the current situation, we need to select and promote daring employees, particularly young ones, and deploy them to managerial positions in field offices despite their lack of seniority, and allocate high-quality resources to valued customers. We should give more opportunities to young employees. By so doing, I think the company will have a brighter future. *(Ren Zhengfei: Speech at the EMT ST Meeting, October 30, 2012)*

6.7.8 Giving preference to female candidates who are as competent as their male peers

There must be a certain proportion of female managers in the reserve pool to ensure the balanced development of our company. *(Ren Zhengfei: Speech at a Meeting with Huawei University and the Strategic Reserve Pool, 2005)*

Management teams must include female members. When selecting managers, we can give preference to female employees. Management teams that have no female members should develop female managers. *(Source: EMT Resolution No. [2005] 009)*

Preference should be given to female employees who are as competent as their male peers. We can make fast-track promotion available to outstanding female managers. *(Source: EMT Resolution No. [2006] 015)*

We need to increase the proportion of female managers on our management team. By the end of 2008, we would like to see at least one female manager in each AT. *(Source: EMT Meeting Minutes No. [2008] 013)*

---

[2]   Customer Centric 3 (CC3): a project-based cross-functional team, consisting of
        three roles: Account Responsible (AR), Solution Responsible (SR), and Fulfillment
        Responsible (FR).

6.8 Promoting and Demoting Managers Based on Their Performance

6.8.1 No lifelong tenure for managers

Huawei is determined to demote those who take up higher-level positions but do not have field experience or understand our corporate culture. This is a lesson I learned from Apple. If we allow these kinds of managers to exist, our corporate culture will be damaged; this will ultimately cause our company to fail. These managers should be assigned to field offices to gain hands-on experience. Once they develop into outstanding leaders, they can establish their position at Huawei. *(Ren Zhengfei: Speech at the Management Training Class, 1996)*

Huawei cannot develop rapidly all the time. Each employee is different in terms of competence, diligence, and their ability to improve. How can they keep the same pace in driving the company forward? I am not sure about the future of the company in the long run. But I do know that we must not slack off; and we should make it a long-term policy that managers are promoted or demoted based on their performance. *(Ren Zhengfei: Speech at the CEO's Staff Team Meeting, 1998)*

We must demote those who slack off, are unqualified, and have little sense of responsibility. They will not even be allowed to work as deputy directors after new directors are selected. As to those who have been acting irresponsibly in their positions for a long time, we can dismiss them immediately. Otherwise, there will be no hope for their teams. You will be in trouble if you don't think it is a problem. Without capable managers, an enterprise is doomed to fail. *(Ren Zhengfei: Encouraging Self-reflection and Avoiding Naive Actions Are the Long-term Principles of Huawei, 1999)*

We cannot sit in the office and discuss how to develop managers. We need to go to field offices and identify how to make adjustments. We will keep competent managers, including senior managers, and demote incompetent ones. We will allow no one to remain idle in his or her position. It's not always easy to enjoy the shade under a big tree. *(Ren Zhengfei: Speech at the Meeting with the Marketing & Sales Department of Huawei Electric, 1999)*

We will focus on survival of the fittest in each department. We will transfer unqualified managers to more suitable positions and ask unqualified employees to leave the company. Otherwise, it will be impossible for us to improve per capita efficiency to a satisfactory level. Some may say this is too cruel. The problem is that the market itself is cruel. In order to survive, we have to be tough and decrease salaries when necessary. It is unrealistic to expect salaries to go up all the time. Sometimes, salaries have to go down in order to achieve our goals. *(Ren Zhengfei: Speech at Marketing Goals Briefing, 2002)*

We do not offer our managers lifelong tenure. Senior managers can be promoted or demoted based on their performance. When their tenure expires, they should be appraised by both the company and their colleagues through their work reports and C&Q applications for the next phase. Their compensation may be adjusted based on results. After all, the waves of a river are pushed by the waves behind them. Without change, there would be no life. It is necessary to dismiss underperformers. The fixed-term system is a gentle way to do this. *(Ren Zhengfei: Continuously Improving Per Capita Efficiency and Building a High-performance Corporate Culture, 2004)*

As Huawei continues to move forward rapidly, we must create a mechanism that helps outstanding employees develop; otherwise, the company will fail despite the heights to which it has risen. In other words, if nobody joins or leaves, our company's development will be affected, as all human beings are hurtling towards the inevitable. *(Ren Zhengfei: From "Philosophy" to Practice, 2011)*

As Huawei has made it a policy for managers to be promoted or demoted based on their performance, it is possible for a 20-something to become a senior manager. If a manager is not competent in their new position after a promotion, we can demote him or her and reduce his or her salary or shares. There is not much to lose. We have been very cautious regarding promotions, and I think it is time for us to take bold action in this regard. *(Ren Zhengfei: Minutes of the Meeting with Staff from Huawei University Institute of Education, 2012)*

6.8.2 No free pass for incompetent managers

We should assign roles based on performance. Through hands-on practice, we can identify people who have done their jobs well and promote them to managerial positions, regardless of their seniority. We need to train promising managers, thus enabling them to shoulder greater responsibilities. At the same time, we must be resolute in demoting unqualified managers to ensure high efficiency. Employees who want to move ahead must be dedicated. *(Ren Zhengfei: Speech at the Mobilization Meeting on Asset Cleanup and Verification, 1997)*

We must demote unqualified managers. Those at the HQ who are not competent for managerial positions can try their hand at other positions. We must do whatever we can to maintain the vitality and effectiveness of the HQ. At Huawei, there is no place for those in managerial positions who just rely on their seniority but do nothing. We cannot simply sit back and wait for a brighter future. *(Ren Zhengfei: Resolutely Implementing ISO9000, 1997)*

All departments must adjust, consolidate, strengthen, and improve themselves during times of rapid development. All adjustments must be practical. All departments must replace some managers, starting from the junior level. We must promote managers who have a strong sense of responsibility and mission, and the courage to take on responsibilities, are practical and good at uniting team members, and safeguard the interests of the company. Meanwhile, we must be resolute in demoting managers who are not practical, muddle along, only have theoretical knowledge of management, and exploit loopholes for their own benefit. Only by doing so will the company achieve greater success. *(Ren Zhengfei: Focusing on a Down-to-earth Approach to Seize Opportunities for Development, 1998)*

Why can't senior managers work as ordinary employees? Senior managers at the HQ can transfer to lower-level positions if they are completely exhausted. This will enable them to settle down without having to worry about frequent business trips. *(Ren Zhengfei: Adapting the Appraisal System for Managers to Challenges Facing the Transforming Industry, 2006)*

We must establish a process ownership system that fully motivates junior and middle managers to take on responsibilities and promptly make the right decisions within their scope of authority. Managers who cannot or do not have the courage to take on responsibilities will be allocated to non-managerial positions. Incompetent managers or managers who play it safe by skirting their responsibilities will also be replaced. Instead of relying on seniority when selecting managers, we shall consider sense of responsibility, competence, integrity, interpersonal skills, and team organization and coordination skills. *(Ren Zhengfei: Deepening our Understanding of the Corporate Culture of Staying Customer-centric and Inspiring Dedication, 2008)*

To enable the company to develop sustainably, we must demote unqualified managers. Any manager can be demoted, including senior managers and the founder; otherwise, the company will be unable to survive. Huawei never gives any incompetent employees a free pass. *(Ren Zhengfei: Staying Customer-centric, Inspiring Dedication, and Persevering are the Key to Our Success, 2010)*

6.8.3 Incorporating dismissal of underperformers into the daily performance appraisal system

It is forbidden to promote anyone within one year of a demotion, especially across departments. We have to prevent any sign of nepotism. If they perform very well, we need to assess them strictly one year later before we promote them again. *(Ren Zhengfei: Continuously Improving Per Capita Efficiency and Building a High-performance Corporate Culture, 2004)*

If a department or team fails to meet the performance requirements for two consecutive years, the head of the department or team will be demoted and everyone else in the department or team should assume joint liability. *(Source: EMT Meeting Minutes No. [2006] 012)*

Our policy of demoting unqualified managers will not only apply to junior managers, but also to middle and senior managers. We need to demote the bottom 10% of managers at each level, and the figure must be higher for departments or teams that have failed to achieve their annual targets. *(Source: EMT Meeting Minutes No. [2007] 022)*

Our policy of demoting underperformers is primarily targeted at managers rather than employees. We must firmly implement our policy of demoting underperforming managers level by level. Currently, our focus is on demoting junior and middle managers whose annual performance is among the bottom 10%. Unqualified managers can be transferred to non-managerial positions that are more suitable for them. *(Source: EMT Meeting Minutes No. [2009] 016)*

We must develop a systematic, measurable approach for demoting unqualified managers and dismissing underperforming employees based on performance and facts, and integrate this approach into the performance management system. *(Source: EMT Meeting Minutes No. [2009] 003)*

We must continue to base our performance appraisals on factors such as sustainable and profitable growth, profits, cash flow, and per capita efficiency improvements. In cases where departments fail to exceed the average score for corporate-level per capita efficiency improvements, heads of divisions, areas, product lines, departments, regions, representative offices, and others will be held accountable. Departments that exceed the average score must be ranked by positive profits, positive cash flows, and strategic goal attainment; senior managers of departments that rank among the bottom will be considered unqualified and will be demoted. *(Ren Zhengfei: Speech Outline at the Honor Awards Ceremony of Sales & Services, 2009)*

We will continue to adhere to our core values of staying customer-centric and inspiring dedication. At Huawei, dedication is the only way. Huawei needs to keep moving forward. To make this happen, we must reposition incompetent managers to more suitable positions. We have changed the performance appraisals for employees at job level 12 and below into absolute appraisal, and applied relative appraisal to employees at job level 13 and above. We will firmly implement our policy of demoting underperformers, especially those in managerial positions. With great power comes great responsibility. To obtain more benefits, one must make greater contributions. We will not allow anyone to obtain benefits without making contributions. *(Ren Zhengfei: Developing Managers Based on the Selection Mechanism, Reviewing and Streamlining Organizations Based on Processes, and Promoting the Open and Balanced Development of Organizations, 2011)*

Currently, our level-2 departments are overstaffed. In this year's organization restructuring, we may find that many employees are redundant. For the good of the company, we should dismiss managers who accomplish nothing, as they cause greater harm to the company. They design programs for their own sake, which slow down overall efficiency and increase costs. We should have no mercy on these managers; otherwise, we may be unable to secure our position in the global market. For those who have demonstrated good traits, we can send them to field offices and let them start over from scratch if they wish. Employees' self-appraisals should be posted on the *Xinsheng Community* for others to review. We should also make employees' performance appraisals public to prevent certain managers from overstating their subordinates' performance for the purpose of winning support at the expense of the company. Those managers are unqualified and should be replaced. We must dare to replace them to improve overall performance. For those who are not qualified, we could send some of them to new positions after a screening by the Reserve Pool. For example, some long-time employees can open Huawei franchised stores in different areas, selling not just devices, but also products relating to home gateways and other service systems. *(Ren Zhengfei: Speech at the EMT ST Meeting on January 20 – Increasing Investment to Seize Strategic Opportunities, 2011)*

Each year, we demote the bottom 10% of managers. This demotion rate is based on their administrative authority. The 10% demoted should not be all junior managers. Those who are demoted can then work as experts, which is not easy. If they are still not competent in their new positions, they will very likely be marginalized. Therefore, demoting underperformers will encourage managers to do a good job. Eric Xu often accused me of looking down on experts. Being an expert is very challenging. Managers will cherish their jobs once they understand how hard it is to be an expert. *(Ren Zhengfei: Speech at a Workshop on Europe's Business Environment, 2012)*

We borrowed the system of demoting underperformers from West Point. The aim of this system is to motivate the organization, encourage high-performing employees, spur on low-performing employees, and ultimately form a new way to select leaders. Those who can endure hardships can shoulder greater responsibilities. We need to drive managers to constantly improve in order to be qualified for high-level positions. We can't expect entry-level employees to become leaders all of a sudden. Instead, they need to work in a relaxed environment, achieve high performance, and earn more money. When appraising entry-level employees, we need to use a clear and simple appraisal system, and set a baseline, rather than assigning a relative proportion of performance ratings. The purpose of implementing an ABC appraisal system is to select managers. However, we cannot squeeze all employees in order to select managers. The purpose of our 360 degree feedback is to identify heroes, rather than find fault with employees. We must manage entry-level and senior employees differently. For entry-level employees, we will distribute value based on labor and allow those who give more to get more. *(Ren Zhengfei: Speech at the Meeting Regarding the Report on the Pilot Program for Absolute Appraisals of Junior Employees in Operational Positions, 2012)*

6.8.4 From the ashes the phoenix is reborn

To meet the company's needs for a larger market share and a larger organizational structure, all directors in the marketing & sales department handed in their resignations along with their work reports. Back then, China's telecom market was complicated and full of challenges. Their act was heroic and will always be remembered. Without their sacrifice, Huawei wouldn't have grown into what it is today. I really appreciate those unsung heroes who have sacrificed so much and contributed significantly to the company's development. *(Ren Zhengfei: Current Situation and Next Steps, 1995)*

As a vanguard of the company, the marketing & sales department has made indelible contributions over the past six years and has earned the trust and respect of customers as well as that of all our employees. I work side by side with them and I am very attached to them. I love them, especially those who sacrifice their interests for a better future for the company. To ensure a better future, we must correct our mistakes today. The resignation of the entire marketing department demonstrates their daring and selflessness. They are setting a great example for all Huawei employees. Therefore, everyone needs to be open-minded and be integrated into Huawei's culture. Those who stay positive and are willing to make sacrifices for the company's survival and development will have a brighter future. They have a clear positioning of their roles, constantly adapt their roles to changes, and are ready to forge ahead. *(Ren Zhengfei: Speech at the Group Resignation Ceremony for All Marketing & Sales Staff in Primary Leadership Positions, 1996)*

An organization may also make mistakes. It is important for everyone to understand that absolute fairness doesn't exist and it may happen that you will sometimes not be fairly treated. But the important thing is to keep a positive attitude, which will give us a lot of strength to move forward. Also, your understanding and support provides the foundation for the company to put more trust and belief in you. *(Ren Zhengfei: Continuously Improving Per Capita Efficiency and Building a High-performance Corporate Culture, 2004)*

There is no absolute fairness, so don't expect too much in this regard. However, we offer equal opportunities to those who apply themselves. Your manager will know if you consistently achieve results. You must tolerate unfairness, even if you have done your work well. "From the ashes the phoenix is reborn" – this is how Huaweiers think and act when they are wronged or feel frustrated. It is also the principle Huawei uses to select managers. If you lack endurance, how will you be able to shoulder greater responsibilities in the future? You are the master of your own destiny. Inevitably, there will be errors in judgment. However, unbridgeable divides or calling right wrong will not occur. You can place your confidence in Huawei. The sun is sure to rise, even if it currently remains below the horizon. *(Source: Welcome Letter to New Employees, 2005)*

We will keep managers who have successfully passed their performance appraisals; for those who fail, we will remove them from managerial positions and place them in other positions if they are willing. If they work really hard and improve themselves, they will still have the chance to be promoted. During the process of becoming more professional, we must make sure that nobody takes advantage of any potential loophole in our policies. *(Ren Zhengfei: Strengthening Professionalization and Localization, 2005)*

Managers who have been replaced need to stay positive and consider the future. If they perform very well in entry-level positions, other positions they are qualified for will be open to them. When we place them in new positions, we should not replace those who are already working in those positions and achieving outstanding performance. Otherwise, there will be chaos. *(Ren Zhengfei: Speech at the Communication Meeting with the Steering Committee on Self-reflection, 2006)*

Do not be afraid of negative reactions from those who receive a pay cut. Decreasing pay or adjusting positions is also an opportunity to test our managers. If a manager stays positive and works hard after being demoted or receiving a pay cut, he or she may still have the opportunity to be promoted again in the future. *(Source: EMT Meeting Minutes No. [2008] 002)*

CHAPTER 7

MOTIVATING AND MANAGING MANAGERS

When assessing senior managers, Huawei focuses more on competence and integrity. Assessments of junior and middle managers are results-oriented and do not simply focus on competence. However, competence and results are correlated. Competence should lead to good results, and if it doesn't, it should not be considered to be competence. The relationship between competence and results is similar to that between motivation and results. It is meaningless to have good motivation if you don't get positive results. Prioritizing results and responsibilities is a long-term policy at Huawei.

While implementing a performance-based appraisal system, Huawei also tracks key events. It investigates every error to figure out what has gone wrong and what can be done to improve. Huawei also tracks key successful factors and identifies outstanding managers based on successful decisions, particularly those made in the process of achieving goals. Both performance-based appraisals and the tracking of key events are very important.

Huawei makes performance appraisal results public in order to let employees supervise the operations of managers and administrative teams (ATs). In addition, Huawei publicizes the names of managers to be appointed, so as to hear what employees have to say about their sense of responsibility, sense of mission, competence, and integrity. Managers are thus supervised by employees. Greater transparency will help Huawei establish a stable structure.

Huawei implements a manager management system that features separation of rights. ATs that manage managers and employees have the right of recommendation. Huawei University and the Profession Committees which help develop and improve capabilities, and HR branches and the Human Resource Management Department which ensure process standardization have the right of appraisal. Management committees that represent the company's overall interest and the HR Auditing Office of the Committee of Ethics and Compliance (CEC) that is in charge of integrity-related issues have the rights of veto and impeachment. By shifting its management model from a one-man leadership system to AT operations and then to separation of rights, Huawei aims to ensure that a fair, objective, and comprehensive approach is adopted and well-informed decisions are made when promoting managers and motivating employees.

When impeaching or disciplining managers, Huawei focuses on helping them correct and learn from their mistakes. It believes that most of its managers identify with its corporate core values. A vibrant drum does not need to be beaten with a heavy mallet.

In this new era, Huawei is improving its management through its corporate culture, systems, and processes. While delegating more authority to managers at lower levels, it is also strengthening supervision. Authority delegation and supervision are like two wheels that should turn simultaneously.

Huawei never allows corruption to infect its senior managers. It does whatever it can to fight against corruption, fraud, and any other kinds of unethical behavior among its senior managers. The company firmly guards against moral decline after employees get rich, and it continuously combats slackness. Huawei believes that systems, not high salaries, ensure that people remain incorruptible.

Huawei has established a closed-loop management system composed of oath-taking, manager self-checks, and independent supervision. Different auditing milestones are set within processes and the supervisory responsibilities are specified for managers at different levels. Huawei implements controls and supervision throughout processes and incorporates services and supervision into end-to-end processes. The company expects its audit team to work closely with managers and supervise them with care. The purpose of supervision is to ensure smooth business operations. Supervision is a means and business success is the end.

A manager who has made mistakes is not necessarily an incompetent or bad manager, while one who never makes mistakes is most likely mediocre. Huawei believes it must not turn its managers and employees into people who hesitate to do anything, because this will make the company ineffective and unable to create additional value.

This chapter begins by analyzing the conflict between results and competence in manager appraisals and mainly discusses how to motivate and manage managers at the system level.

7.1

Appraising and
Motivating Managers

7.1.1 Prioritizing results and responsibilities

Managers at all levels need to be clear about their responsibilities and goals. We think that those who don't have a clear understanding cannot do their job well. *(Ren Zhengfei: Step Forward or Step Down, 1995)*

To improve customer satisfaction, we must establish a value assessment system that is oriented towards results and responsibilities rather than competence. Our enterprise is results-driven, so we must provide customers with products they like. Huawei's value assessment system, including performance appraisals for middle and senior managers, must be redesigned to focus on results and responsibilities. *(Ren Zhengfei: Speech at the Meeting on the Project Report for the Value Assessment System for Junior Employees, 1998)*

When assessing senior managers, we must focus more on competence and integrity. When assessing junior and middle managers, we need to be results-oriented and we should not simply focus on competence. I think competence and results are correlated. Competence should lead to good results, and if it doesn't, it should not be considered to be competence. The relationship between competence and results is similar to that between motivation and results. It is meaningless to have good motivation if you don't get positive results. Prioritizing results and responsibilities is a long-term policy at Huawei. *(Ren Zhengfei: Being Performance-focused and Result-oriented, and Striving to Increase Per Capita Efficiency, 2002)*

We must stick to an appraisal system that is based on results and responsibilities. Managers who fail to meet C&Q requirements must be demoted, removed from their positions, or dismissed. Our company will not always succeed amid increasingly fierce market competition. We therefore cannot tolerate a bloated organization or unqualified managers. We must select and demote managers based on the fulfillment of their responsibilities. Departments with outstanding performance must also cultivate managers. The company has decided that the heads of departments that fail to achieve their goals will be demoted or removed from their positions. Also, it is prohibited to promote the holders of deputy-level positions in these departments as departmental heads; otherwise, these two roles will not work together closely. Starting in 2005, all employees in departments that fail to achieve their goals will receive no pay raise in the following year even if they transfer to other departments. In the future, if an employee from a low-performing department is transferred to a high-performing department, he or she will work in a position lower than his or her previous one. This policy doesn't apply to situations where low performance is due to incorrect decisions made by the company. *(Ren Zhengfei: Continuously Improving Per Capita Efficiency and Building a High-performance Corporate Culture, 2004)*

We should not promote to managerial positions those who are very competent but do not prioritize results and responsibilities. Instead, we need to demote them to entry-level positions lest they become hands-off bosses and create scenarios that merely look good. *(Ren Zhengfei: Building a Professional Financial Team That Has Solid Integrity, Dares to Shoulder Responsibilities, and Sticks to Principles, 2006)*

How should we appraise managers' performance? If a manager's subordinates are highly motivated at work and the department is high-performing and has a positive organizational climate, why would we deny his or her competence? Why would a manager whose team has made outstanding achievements be criticized for a lack of leadership? We hope we can have more outstanding and hardworking managers develop in our company. The criteria for appraising managers' performance do not need to be fixed, as long as the goal is to unite as many employees as possible to create more value. At Huawei, we use monetary and non-monetary incentives to encourage employees to work hard. The harder you work, the more you will get. If every employee works hard, Huawei will have a large, effective team. So we need to focus more on the benefits brought about by appraisals rather than simply complain about the costs they cause. We need to emphasize benefits and risk sharing and keep the system flexible. *(Ren Zhengfei: Speech*

at the Meeting Regarding the Report on the Pilot Program for Absolute Apprais-
als of Junior Employees in Operational Positions, 2012)

Huawei expects its CFOs to be results-oriented and work with business departments to sustainably produce a maximum output with a minimum input. The role of our HQ is to provide timely and effective services to support business development. *(Ren Zhengfei: Comments at a Meeting with Managers from Finance, 2012)*

We need to first be clear about our goals and responsibilities. After that, we should think about how to achieve these goals and fulfill these responsibilities through planning and budgeting. It is important to know where we are going, do the right thing, and understand the opportunities available and the things that need to be managed. Only then can we figure out how to get there. Budgeting is very important, but it is not an easy job. It requires much more than working on one's own. Budgeting needs to be flexibly linked to goals in the process, and its contributions to results need to be reviewed via final accounting. Two similar projects with different contributions will lead to different C&Q assessments for their managers. It's reasonable that some managers will be promoted and others will be demoted after projects are completed. We have a responsibility to select good project managers, who will be able to develop a group of outstanding successors, utilize resources optimally, thoroughly study templates in advance, flexibly apply them in projects, and summarize project experience. These managers create greater profits, recruit employees with higher output but lower costs, distribute bonuses fairly, and effectively manage interpersonal relationships. People like this should be promoted to leadership positions. They distribute bonuses without catering to the likes of their bosses, so they are able to focus on projects and are more likely to succeed. This illustrates our focus on results and responsibilities. *(Ren Zhengfei: Outline of the Speeches at the Enlarged Meeting of the Finance Committee, Business Process & IT Retreat, and Quarterly Meeting of Regional Presidents–Focusing on Strategy and Streamlining Management, 2012)*

The biggest mistake we have made over these years is expecting every employee to become a great leader. We have dozens of KPIs for every employee, so they end up not knowing what they should focus on. This is a distinct feature of our appraisal system. In addition, we have prioritized competence, not results and responsibilities. This has caused huge harm to the company's development over the years. When selecting managers, we need to check if the candidate has achieved positive results and select the one who is the most qualified for a particular position. *(Ren Zhengfei: Speech at a Workshop on Europe's Business Environment, 2012)*

We should select and appraise managers based on sustainable and profitable growth, strategic development, and contributions they make to associated departments. We cannot set growth and competition against profits. During the current economic downturn, what defines good managers? Good managers remain uncorrupted and have the courage to assume responsibilities. We need to work together closely to promote the company's sustainable and profitable development and help it overcome the current economic recession. We should also promote more enterprising managers and create a positive culture that stresses both cooperation and competition. *(Ren Zhengfei: Remarks to the China Region at the Xinsheng Building, 2012)*

Performance appraisals should not contain too many KPIs. Key event-based appraisals are used to select managers. There is no need to consider key events during bonus assessments as long as the final goal has been achieved. If an outstanding employee is assessed using too many KPIs, he or she might feel discouraged and will only focus on hitting KPI targets. Therefore, the number of KPIs must be reduced. *(Ren Zhengfei: Remarks at a Meeting with Staff of the Guangzhou Representative Office, 2013)*

7.1.2 Comparing current performance with previous performance to facilitate continuous improvement

How should we appraise the performance of departments and their managers? The criteria are decreases in headcount and increases in output, quality, efficiency and core competencies. All these criteria are tangible except for the increase of core competencies. However, there is a way to assess it. The fact that you can do something well today doesn't guarantee that you can do it well tomorrow. Therefore, we must strengthen our future competitiveness while doing our jobs today. What if a manager fails to achieve KPI goals? The answer is that he or she must step down. Currently, the term for vice presidents is two years. In the future, departmental heads will also have a specific term set for their position and every employee will need to sign a fixed-term contract with the company. Managers who have finished their current term but have not received an extension will have to find a new position. We will also have KPIs for presidents, who will have to be demoted if they fail to achieve their KPI goals. *(Ren Zhengfei: It's Not Always Easy to Enjoy the Shade Under a Big Tree, 1999)*

We need to adhere to a work report system and a comparison system to appraise and identify managers. How will this comparison system work? For example, I will look at your work report and compare it with the report of the previous year to see if you have improved and what problems you have faced. Those who fail to improve themselves or increase per capita efficiency will first be warned, and then dismissed if the warning doesn't work. The purpose is not to demote someone, but instead to create a sense of urgency for managers at all levels to improve themselves. *(Ren Zhengfei: Staying Close to the Customer by Going Where You Are Most Needed in the Field Office, 2001)*

The assessment method proposed by Gallup is based on how fast improvements are made rather than how much improvement has been achieved. This is actually consistent with how Huawei appraises its employees. At Huawei, we appraise our managers based on their improvements in performance. This may lead to situations where the best managers are frustrated by the fact that they don't know what else to improve. While it may be frustrating for individuals, it is the best Huawei can hope for. *(Ren Zhengfei: Huawei Only Exists to Serve Its Customers, 2001)*

Managers must focus on the results of key indicators during work reports and compare this year's results with last year's. If they have not improved, they will be demoted. Sometimes, we can't recognize problems if we simply compare ourselves with others. But if we require someone to compare his or her current performance with that of last year, he or she may become anxious. It would be great if one could improve by 10% compared with last year; 5% or 3% is also acceptable. If someone doesn't improve at all, he or she will be demoted and receive a pay cut. *(Ren Zhengfei: Speech at the EMT ST Meeting, 2006)*

For departments that cannot be directly assessed by business results, we will compare current with previous performance. The per capita efficiency of these departments must increase by at least 5%. Managers must make progress; otherwise, they will be demoted. They need to make progress every day and bring out the potential of every employee. After that, they will begin to dismiss underperformers in their team instead of giving them unprincipled protection. *(Ren Zhengfei: Speech at the Mid-year Market Conference, 2006)*

Starting in 2008, we have compared the current per capita efficiency of departments with their past efficiency. Managers in charge of departments whose efficiency improvements are lower than the company average will be held accountable. Disciplinary measures include demotions, job level reductions, and salary reductions. We need to put mechanisms in place to encourage managers at all levels to focus on per capita efficiency rather than using resources without considering costs. *(Source: EMT Meeting Minutes No. [2009] 003)*

7.1.3 Combining performance-based appraisals and tracking of key events

While implementing a performance-based appraisal system, we also need to track key events. We must identify and cultivate managers at all levels based on successful decisions, particularly those made in the process of achieving goals. We should also summarize project failures, and identify good managers via these projects. We should avoid using results as the sole basis for appraisals. *(Ren Zhengfei: Key Points for Management, 2002)*

If a manager hasn't taken advantage of the flaws in our system, we need to give credit for integrity. We also need to maintain records of those who are dishonest during the process of expense reimbursement. These are all key events that we need to consider during appraisals. We need to pay more attention to these key events when assessing managers. Manager management needs to align with financial management. We need to maintain records of those who refuse to take advantage of financial flaws, no matter whether they have done so because they are "not smart" or because they are of good character. *(Ren Zhengfei: Speech at the Meeting Regarding the Audit Report, 2004)*

How should we appraise the performance of managers? I don't think there will ever be a perfect method that can achieve absolute accuracy. We can only assess our employees in a relatively accurate way. *(Ren Zhengfei: Comments to Trainees of the Tenth Session of the Senior Management Seminar at Huawei University, 2011)*

We need to try to be objective from an organizational perspective. Currently, our ATs have a lot of authority. Under such circumstances, what can we do to ensure objectivity? The answer is transparency. We need to inform all employees of specific appraisal criteria and ranking methodologies in advance and allow them to express their opinions for preliminary appraisal results which have been made public. Different perspectives may lead to different conclusions. To ensure our appraisals are as objective as possible, we have implemented various policies to adjust the appraisal results given by ATs, including making performance ratings and key events public and collecting feedback. *(Ren Zhengfei: Comments to Trainees of the Tenth Session of the Senior Management Seminar at Huawei University, 2011)*

7.1.4 Making performance appraisal results public

We will make performance appraisal results public in order to let employees supervise the operations of managers and ATs. By doing so, we aim to strengthen transparency. There is no need to be scared about making things public. Starting this year, we will make appraisal results public, which will constrain the authority of managers and ATs at all levels. This will also make it difficult for managers to cheat, as they will be challenged by employees. I have approved a document on performance appraisals submitted by the Human Resource Management Department. I think we need to make both the preliminary and final appraisal results public so that we can solve problems before they become too serious. If only final appraisal results are made public, a lot of people will be involved, and it will be difficult to identify the root causes of problems and resolve them. Admittedly, such transparency will probably create chaos at first, because employees will challenge the results. Being a manager is no easy task. After the appraisal results are made public, incentive distribution will become much easier. Those who have made more contributions will get pay raises and those who don't deserve pay raises will not get any. In this way, we will be able to establish the correct focus and everyone will try their best to make contributions. *(Ren Zhengfei: Developing Managers Based on the Selection Mechanism, Reviewing and Streamlining Organizations Based on Processes, and Promoting the Open and Balanced Development of Organizations, 2011)*

We will strengthen transparency starting with the Reserve Pool. All summaries and articles by trainees will be put online to let everyone know how they have been studying. For future promotions, achievements included in trainees' self-assessments will also be posted online so that others can clearly see whether they have taken credit for successful projects that they didn't deserve. Those who do not want to make their information public can withdraw from the Reserve Pool, and we will not give them a hard time over it. In the future, everything employees have done at Huawei will be made public, including managers' assessments. This will help Huawei establish a stable structure. A company has a dissipative structure. This means the company dissipates its energy between balance and imbalance, and between stability and instability. Huawei is currently doing well, so we must boldly dissipate what we have accumulated, and expose our faults so that we will be relaxed when others are in trouble. We included the Telekom Malaysia event in our New Year Message. Through this message, everyone could see how Huawei, including senior executives, had made mistakes. Success is possible if we are confident enough to reveal our mistakes to the outside world. *(Ren Zhengfei: Developing Managers Based on the Selection Mechanism, Reviewing and Streamlining Organizations Based on Processes, and Promoting the Open and Balanced Development of Organizations, 2011)*

7.1.5 Giving more opportunities to field employees when it comes to pay raises and promotions

Compensation is more than just money. It also involves the positions you are assigned and the responsibilities associated with them. *(Ren Zhengfei: How Long Can Huawei Survive, 1998)*

We need to give more opportunities to field employees when it comes to pay raises and promotions, because unexpected situations occur frequently in field offices and require very experienced employees. We can't simply appraise managers in terms of skills, because managers working in the desert are definitely at a disadvantage compared with those working at the HQ who receive frequent training. We should properly appraise, select, and cultivate managers. If we don't focus more on employees who fight on the frontlines or give them more opportunities, we will bring ruin upon ourselves. *(Ren Zhengfei: Speech at the Mobilization Meeting for a Final Sprint in the Marketplace, 2000)*

We need to establish a flexible job level framework. Specifically, we must have the courage to implement fast-track promotions, disrupt the balance, and strike a new one. On the one hand, we need to maintain the stability of the overall system for determining job levels; on the other hand, we need to disrupt the balance at key points based on business needs. We could start by increasing the job levels of employees in field operating teams, such as employees who are responsible for developing new businesses or markets, or those that have to turn the situation around. We can maintain flexibility in job level ranges during manager deployment and people-job matching for these positions. In addition, we need to be willing to increase the job level and compensation of those who display outstanding performance, so as to reach a new state of balance that is better than the previous one. In addition, we need to be flexible about the gap between different job levels and flexibly control the job level gap between field managerial positions based on actual situations, such as the gap between a primary leadership position and the corresponding deputy-level position, as well as between superiors and subordinates. As for business experts working in the field, we should increase their job level, which doesn't have to be lower than that of their managers. *(Ren Zhengfei: Uniting as Many People as Possible, 2013)*

7.2 Separation of Rights for Manager Management

7.2.1 Establishing a system of checks and balances as well as deterrence so that managers can unleash their potential without breaking rules

Our current manager recommendation system relies too much on the opinions of ATs, and the AT director is the most influential person regarding manager recommendations. This may lead to promotions of managers preferred by the AT and others with huge leadership potential being marginalized. In addition, the current level-by-level recommendation system may result in some outstanding junior and middle managers not being identified or recognized by their managers and the company for various reasons. Therefore, we need to work out some supplementary solutions and add them to our existing manager recommendation system to address these problems. *(Source: EMT Meeting Minutes No. [2007] 025)*

During organizational restructuring, field managers may not strictly follow rules or regulations when executing the authority delegated to them, so enhanced supervision is necessary. Finance and audit departments need to constantly perform spot checks at key control points during the supervision process and establish deterrence to ensure the proper execution of authority. *(Ren Zhengfei: Timely, Accurate, High Quality, and Low Cost Delivery Calls for Professional Process-compliant CFOs, 2009)*

Our managers need to place strict requirements on themselves and focus on their responsibilities. Our manager supervision is based on separation of rights. The purpose is to deter them rather than to veto or impeach them. In this way, managers can unleash their potential without breaking rules. *(Ren Zhengfei: A New Year Message for 2010, 2009)*

The Supervisory Board supervises members of the Board of Directors and other senior executives, while the Audit Committee supervises the company's operations and managers. *(Source: EMT Resolution No. [2011] 035)*

7.2.2 Using separation of rights to achieve checks and balances

We need to implement the separation of rights mechanism in our manager management. Managers will have the right of recommendation, HR branches and the Human Resource Management Department will have the right of appraisal, and the CEC will have the right of impeachment. *(Source: EMT Meeting Minutes No. [2005] 011)*

We need to implement the separation of rights mechanism in our manager management. However, there is still room for discussion as to whether it should be mandatory. Not everything business departments say is good. The CEC and its lower-level organizations have the right of veto based on integrity and self-reflection. ATs appraise manager performance. HR departments and Huawei University are responsible for assessing manager competence. Managers are appraised in these three areas. The purpose of the separation of rights is to make sure that managers focus on their jobs instead of networking or asking for favors. *(Ren Zhengfei: Speech at the Annual Meeting of the Domestic Market Finance Department, 2006)*

Checks and balances are the precondition for delegating authority. When implementing checks and balances, we need to prioritize the company's overall interests over those of departments and balance short- and long-term interests. While ensuring quality, we also need to guarantee operating efficiency. As to how to apply checks and balances among different organizations within the company regarding manager deployment and employee appraisals and incentives, we need to make decisions based on the specific functions and responsibilities of each organization. Guidelines include:

1. Organizations that represent the company's overall business interests and long-term development have the rights of veto and impeachment.
2. Organizations that help develop and improve capabilities during the company's development have the right of appraisal.

3. Organizations that are in charge of daily business operations and directly manage employees and managers have the right of recommendation.

4. Departments that have dotted line relationships with employees via matrix management (including members of management committees) have the right to veto a recommendation during the recommendation phase. When recommending managerial candidates under matrix management, departments that manage these employees and departments for which the employees work have the right to recommend candidates or to veto a recommendation. However, the same department only has either the right to recommend or the right to veto a recommendation, but not both.

5. Higher-level organizations that manage daily administrative affairs have the right of examination. *(Source: Huawei Corp. Doc. No. [2006] 230 Regulations on Establishing and Operating Administrative Teams for Physical Organizations (Provisional))*

We identify outstanding managers by exercising the right of veto against unqualified ones. Such managers who were not identified during the process can be vetoed later during the exercise. The purpose is to ensure that outstanding managers grow quickly. *(Ren Zhengfei: Huawei University Must Become the Cradle of Generals, 2007)*

During our global development, the issue of selecting and developing managers is becoming increasingly important. To ensure that a fair, objective, and comprehensive approach is adopted and well-informed decisions are made when promoting managers and motivating employees, we should specify the criteria for selecting and appraising managers, and at the same time implement a manager management system that features separation of rights. ATs that manage managers and employees have the right of recommendation. Huawei University and Profession Committees which help develop and improve capabilities, and HR branches and the Human Resource Management Department which ensure process standardization have the right of appraisal. Management committees that represent the company's overall interest and the HR Auditing Office of the CEC (in charge of integrity-related issues) have the rights of veto and impeachment. *(Source: Notification on the Status of the Human Resources Management Transformation, 2007)*

By shifting our management model from a one-man leadership system to AT operations and then to a separation of rights, we have made continuous progress in establishing a governance mechanism of checks and balances. Currently, functional department ATs are developing rapidly, the coverage of separation of rights in these organizations is comprehensive, and rights are exercised effectively. However, process-based organizations that link functional departments are still developing, so the coverage of separation of rights in these departments is limited, and rights are exercised less effectively. As more and more management committees begin to operate regularly and more process owners are appointed, we need to delegate more authority to process-based organizations and strengthen their authority execution. *(Source: EMT Meeting Minutes No. [2009] 009)*

The separation of rights aims to make the manager management system more reasonable, but it cannot ensure the system is completely reasonable. ATs must emphasize a single criterion for value assessment: focusing on results and responsibilities rather than competence. This does not mean focusing on sales contracts. How results and responsibilities are assessed reflects the management capabilities of organizations at all levels. By optimizing the separation of rights mechanism, we aim to encourage employees to think creatively, freely express their opinions, and communicate more effectively. *(Ren Zhengfei: Comments to Trainees of the Tenth Session of the Senior Management Seminar at Huawei University, 2011)*

7.2.3 Implementing delegation of authority and supervision concurrently

An important issue for us is how to train, appraise, and manage the promotion and demotion of managers, and also how to make decisions regarding salary, bonus, job levels, and shares. At some point, we may delegate the authority related to salary and bonuses to a sub-committee, which can make decisions with each member's signature. Such level-by-level decentralized management can avoid bureaucracy. In the future, HR sub-committees at all levels may overlap with other management committees, such as those in charge of manufacturing and scheduling. *(Ren Zhengfei: Speech at the Meeting Regarding the Report by Marketing & Sales on Its Organizational Restructuring Solution, 1996)*

In this new era, we will improve our management through our corporate culture, systems, and processes. While delegating more authority to managers at lower levels, we also need to strengthen supervision. Authority delegation and supervision are like two wheels that should turn simultaneously. To help develop future leaders, our Chairwoman and I will serve as ceremonial heads of the Board of Directors. What are the responsibilities of such a role? The answer is the right of veto. After a solution is vetoed, the Board of Directors will have to work out a new one. If both of us still believe the new solution will not work, we will reject the solution and get more people involved in the solution discussion. Such a decision-making process may take longer than when Huawei was a small company, but it can prevent big mistakes and motivate managers. Our right of veto aims to help everyone. As we discussed in our meeting in Sanya, the major responsibility of the Chairwoman will be to impeach unqualified managers rather than selecting managers. We need to follow the processes and policies we have put in place when selecting managers. My role is to coach and play a supporting role in developing policies and the corporate culture. *(Ren Zhengfei: Speech at the Meeting of the New Board of Directors and the New Supervisory Board, 2011)*

As the representative of Huawei's central authority, the Joint Committee of Regions (JCR) and JCR President will supervise and manage regional managers and help improve key regional businesses through individual influence and processes. The JCR and JCR President have no authority to override processes or directly make business decisions. *(Source: EMT Resolution No. [2011] 044)*

At the BG level, there will only be one Executive Management Team (EMT) that makes decisions on business operations and HR-related issues, and no AT or Staff Team (ST) will be established. The EMT director will take responsibility for making business decisions. Regarding important HR issues, voting will be carried out in accordance with AT operating principles. *(Source: EMT Resolution No. [2011] 047)*

7.3 Supervising Managers

7.3.1 Focusing on helping managers correct and learn from their mistakes during manager supervision

When impeaching or disciplining managers, we need to focus on helping them correct and learn from their mistakes. We need to understand that the purpose of impeachment and discipline is to help managers and get them back on track rather than give them a hard time. In addition, we need to treat cooperative violators with leniency, be flexible, and give them a second chance. But it is not a good idea to be overly lenient. We need to strike a balance between leniency and discipline. Departments at all levels should learn to be flexible in this regard. In addition, we won't allow employees to pose a risk to the company. While being lenient towards employees who voluntarily confess their wrongdoings, we will take disciplinary action as necessary. No disciplinary action at all would only loosen corporate management. We should let things go rather than focus on past problems that have been clarified forever. *(Ren Zhengfei: Speech at the EMT ST Meeting, 2009)*

7.3.2 Fighting against corruption among middle and senior managers

We will never allow corruption to infect our senior managers. We will do whatever we can to fight against corruption, theft, fraud, and any other kinds of unethical behavior among them. We will also continuously combat slackness among managers high and low, from presidents to general managers of every department. We will also extend our anti-corruption campaign to junior managers. Every aspiring manager needs to be strict with themselves at all times. *(Ren Zhengfei: Step Forward or Step Down, 1995)*

We will firmly fight against corruption among our middle and senior managers. We will do whatever we can to fight against corruption, embezzlement, theft, fraud, and any other kinds of unethical behavior, as this is the key to ensuring manager integrity. *(Ren Zhengfei: Speech at the Inauguration Ceremony of Finance and Procurement Managers, 1996)*

We firmly guard against moral decline, greed, and corruption after employees get rich, regardless of their positions. *(Ren Zhengfei: Do Not Forget Heroes, 1997)*

We need to fight against corruption to maintain team integrity and competitiveness. The company emphasizes the importance of mental dedication. *(Ren Zhengfei: Key Speech at the Review Meeting on the Regulations on Managing Huawei's Corporate Committees, 1998)*

Currently, we have seen signs of corruption in some employees' lifestyles. We will by no means tolerate this; otherwise, we will not be able to achieve our vision. We expect those who are going in that direction to be strict with themselves in their lives and thus form a strong and upright team. *(Ren Zhengfei: Speech at the Third Quarter Marketing Meeting of the Marketing & Sales Dept, 1998)*

We will continue to fight against corruption, fraud, and other wrong or inappropriate conduct. We expect everyone to set high ethical standards for themselves and live up to them. We also need to ensure that those with moral or ethical issues are not promoted until they have corrected their mistakes. *(Ren Zhengfei: Key Points for Management, 2000)*

The compensation provided by the company will give managers and employees a decent life after retirement. However, as long as they continue to work at Huawei, they need to work hard and create value. If they slack off or get involved in corruption, they will be dismissed. *(Source: EMT Meeting Minutes No. [2007] 029)*

We can't afford widespread corruption. We may be able to deal with it when it is limited in scale, but large-scale corruption will ruin the company. Those who become involved in corruption may get some money, but all their shares, which are actually a large part of their assets, will become worthless after the company collapses. Corruption and low-quality contracts will have a huge impact on the company, and will cause the company to collapse. *(Ren Zhengfei: Comments to Trainees of the Tenth Session of the Senior Management Seminar at Huawei University, 2011)*

History has taught us that widespread corruption will lead to power disruption. Without the constraints of a pyramid governance structure, many of the newly promoted people might be too ambitious and may become even more corrupt than their predecessors. You are already senior managers, and I have delegated authority to you. You must not become corrupt, because your corruption would result in great losses for our company. We need to do what we can to prevent widespread corruption. Currently, we have seen signs of corruption, but they are not very serious so far. The problem is that nobody can guarantee corruption won't get worse in the future. If things get worse and we have to replace all our senior managers, that would not do us any good, either. Therefore, we need to develop policies and regulations to prevent corruption from spreading. Departmental heads at all levels must not assume that they are only in charge of business operations. We have delegated various types of authority to them, including the authority of supervision. *(Ren Zhengfei: Speech at the EMT ST Meeting, July 28, 2011)*

7.3.3 Using systems to keep people incorruptible

High salaries cannot ensure that people remain incorruptible, but systems can. As long as employees create value, we will recognize them, no matter what motivates them. Employees take certain actions because systems require them to do so. We may lack experience in formulating processes, but if we don't delegate authority or supervise its execution afterwards, we will never establish an effective management system. *(Ren Zhengfei: Resolutely Implementing ISO9000, 1997)*

We need to design our system in a way that prevents future leaders from becoming corrupt, selfish, or lacking ambition. If some senior managers in our company use their authority to seek personal gains, this means there are serious problems with our manager selection system and manager management. If we don't identify the root causes of corruption and optimize our system accordingly, we will be doomed to fail, sooner or later. *(Source: The Huawei Charter, 1998)*

7.3.4 Demoting managers who don't identify with the corporate culture and always complain

We need to step up efforts to manage our middle and senior managers and demote those who are irresponsible, slacking, incompetent, always complain, or don't identify with our corporate culture. Senior managers should not be afraid of offending or displeasing anyone or reducing anyone's salary. Those who hesitate to do these things should be replaced by those who don't. *(Ren Zhengfei: Speech at the CEO's Staff Team Meeting, July 24, 1996)*

Those who refuse to correct and improve themselves after making mistakes, don't have the courage to take on responsibilities, and complain a lot should be transferred to non-managerial positions and have their performance appraised in their new positions. Anyone who is working in a certain position needs to take on associated responsibilities. Otherwise, he or she will be considered unqualified for the job. *(Ren Zhengfei: Fully Implementing the Position-based Accountability System, 2005)*

7.4 Policies and Procedures for Supervising Managers

7.4.1 Establishing a closed-loop management system composed of oath-taking, manager self-checks, and independent supervision

The CEC supervises managers' self-discipline with the support from the internal audit and HR departments. We will establish a closed-loop management system composed of oath-taking, manager self-checks, and independent supervision. *(Source: EMT Meeting Minutes No. [2008] 040)*

I think the Offices of Ethics and Compliance (OECs) at all levels need to take responsibility for managing and preventing corruption in their specific organizations. OEC members are managerial candidates and will be promoted if they have done a good job in their area of supervision. During our recent audit of the Hangzhou Representative Office, we discovered that it is an outstanding office. One outstanding manager has cultivated a group of outstanding managers. All offices where supervision is effectively implemented will cultivate a large number of outstanding managers, while offices that have done a poor job in supervision also perform badly in business and other areas. I think OECs need to be held accountable if they have been negligent and haven't noticed anything wrong when there are actually serious problems in the areas in their charge. Members of these OECs are unqualified as managerial candidates. I think the CEC should assume joint responsibility. Two years ago, I had a meeting with 30 OEC members who had done a good job in supervision, but I found that they all focused on business operations and none of them were interested in supervision. I had planned to promote them on a fast-track basis, but had to give up as they were not interested in supervision. Why not promote those who are good at supervision to managerial positions and punish those who perform poorly in this aspect? We should focus on moving forward, and have no time to make compromises. Why should we tolerate those who are unwilling to assume any responsibilities? Our HR policy has changed from developing managers to selecting managers. Are there still confidential departments that do not allow transparency? The answer is no. Then why are we still making promotion decisions based on seniority? Why not promote those who have integrity and are capable and passionate? *(Ren Zhengfei: Implementing Supervision with Care, 2011)*

7.4.2 Audit and internal controls

We need to set different auditing milestones within processes and specify the supervisory responsibilities for managers at different levels. We will not allow junior or middle managers to become hands-off bosses. Junior and middle managers who only focus on principles and the big picture but know nothing about specific operations have to step down. *(Ren Zhengfei: Key Points for Management, 1998)*

We need to build a strong and professional audit team, and should also require all managers to be involved in auditing and implement controls and supervision throughout processes. While ensuring effective controls, we will further delegate management authority to lower levels to enhance operating efficiency and downsize our workforce. *(Ren Zhengfei: Key Points for Management, 1999)*

Standardization is just like a sieve that allows supervision during the service process. We need to incorporate services and supervision into end-to-end processes. Also, we need to adopt a reverse audit method to track accountability, identify outstanding managers, and demote slacking managers. *(Ren Zhengfei: Key Points for Management, 2001)*

The audit team needs to work closely with managers. First of all, the audit team should use factual evidence to help managers prove that they should not be held accountable. But if evidence cannot be produced, managers will be held accountable and must improve. It may take the audit team longer to find the truth by following managers' instructions, but this is better than forcing them to say something. If the audit team is fact-based, managers will not adopt a hostile attitude. The auditors must have plans and must not randomly come up with just anything. Otherwise, managers will be afraid and will not dare to say anything. They will be afraid that the audit team would use their comments to identify loopholes, which would create panic. *(Ren Zhengfei: Implementing Supervision with Care, 2011)*

Internal control teams (including accounting supervision teams) need to work closely with field business departments to ensure efficient operations and appropriate supervision. Engineering inspection teams are currently tasked with combating widespread corruption. Internal control teams need to work with engineering inspection teams to develop policies and methods that ensure reasonable supervision. The purpose of supervision is to ensure smooth business operations. Supervision is a means and business success is the end. *(Ren Zhengfei: Comments at a Meeting with Managers from Finance, 2012)*

7.4.3 Publicity of names of managers to be appointed for feedback, 360-degree feedback, and employee complaints

We will publicize the names of managers to be appointed, so as to hear what employees have to say about their sense of responsibility, sense of mission, competence, and integrity. Managers are thus supervised by employees. *(Ren Zhengfei: Continuously Improving Per Capita Efficiency and Building a High-performance Corporate Culture, 2004)*

We need to publicize the names of managers to be appointed to get feedback from employees. Our aims are to select managers with integrity, good performance, and leadership; standardize the process for appointing managers; make manager appointments more transparent; and strengthen comprehensive assessments for managerial candidates. *(Source: Huawei Corp. Doc. No. [2004] 99 Regulations on the Publicity of the Names of Managers to Be Appointed for Feedback)*

Any employees, including managers, can lodge complaints regarding the work of incumbent managers to the HR Auditing Office of the CEC, which will organize investigations and evidence collection. *(Source: EMT Meeting Minutes No. [2006] 034)*

The purpose of 360-degree feedback is to focus on aspects like integrity, cooperativeness, employee management, and areas for improvement. *(Source: HRC Meeting Minutes No. [2009] 040)*

Why have I mentioned problems with 360-degree feedback? I think there is nothing wrong with the method itself, but the way you analyze the data is problematic. The aim of 360-degree feedback is to identify individual achievements and contributions, and also outstanding employees and managers, rather than weaknesses or problems. However, our current practice doesn't tolerate any weaknesses. Once a weakness is identified in 360-degree feedback, the individual in question is labeled as problematic, which is totally inappropriate. The feedback should focus on achievements and strong points. If a weakness is also identified, we need to analyze how serious the weakness is, how many people have mentioned it, and whether or not it can be overcome. The feedback cannot aim to find weaknesses, which will ultimately destroy our company. *(Ren Zhengfei: Minutes of the Meeting Regarding How to Share Benefits with Dedicated Employees, 2011)*

7.4.4 Accountability system and joint responsibility

We will adhere to an accountability system to hold violators, supervisors, and managers accountable for violations, and discipline them according to the severity of violations. *(Ren Zhengfei: Fully Implementing the Position-based Accountability System, 2005)*

We need to implement an accountability system to discover who is responsible for what has happened and take disciplinary action when necessary. *(Ren Zhengfei: Building a Morally Strong and Professional Finance Team That Is Courageous to Take Responsibilities and Adhere to Principles)*

We must implement the accountability system strictly among our managers at all levels and demote unqualified managers. *(Ren Zhengfei: Adapting the Appraisal System for Managers to Challenges Facing the Transforming Industry, 2006)*

If a manager whose appointment was countersigned by an AT is found guilty of unethical behavior or financial violations, or proves to be unqualified for the position within three years of being appointed, we will hold the manager in question accountable and also the referee as well as everyone in the AT jointly accountable for what has happened based on the nature and severity of the violations. *(Source: Huawei Corp. Doc. No. [2006] 230 Regulations on Establishing and Operating Administrative Teams for Physical Organizations (Provisional))*

7.4.5 Veto and impeachment

The CEC must exercise the rights of veto and impeachment during manager selection. We identify outstanding managers by exercising the right of veto against unqualified ones. Unqualified managers who were not identified during the process can be vetoed later during the exercise of the right of impeachment. The purpose is to ensure that outstanding managers grow quickly. *(Ren Zhengfei: Huawei University Must Become the Cradle of Generals, 2007)*

We will pilot and implement the separation of rights optimization mechanism for manager management. We should also strengthen the roles of committee directors and process owners in selecting, deploying, and motivating managers, and strengthen the roles of supervisory bodies (e.g., the CEC) in impeaching and supervising managers. *(Source: EMT Resolution No. [2009] 002)*

As the owner of authority execution, committee directors have the right of veto against committee members and their managerial positions during new manager appointments and performance appraisal and motivation for incumbent managers. They also have the right to impeach incumbent managers based on negative key events. *(Source: EMT Meeting Minutes No. [2009] 009)*

Process owners will submit a list of key positions that significantly influence the business performance of end-to-end processes to the Human Resources Committee (HRC) for approval. After the list is approved, process owners will have the right to veto recommendations on manager deployment, appraisals, and reward for these positions. *(Source: EMT Meeting Minutes No. [2009] 009)*

Process owners have the right to impeach employees of relevant key positions based on the negative key events that have considerably affected the business performance of end-to-end processes. *(Source: EMT Meeting Minutes No. [2009] 009)*

7.4.6 Application of manager supervision results

A manager who has made mistakes is not necessarily an incompetent or bad manager, while one who never makes mistakes is most likely mediocre. It is fine for managers to make mistakes, so long as they know how to correct their mistakes and improve in the future. However, managers who have made mistakes and their supervisors may need to tolerate unfairness. *(Ren Zhengfei: Speech Regarding Recent Publicity Requirements, 1997)*

After managers make mistakes, we need to analyze the reasons. If they make mistakes because they tried out new things, they can also receive high ratings during performance appraisals. We have to change our concepts in performance appraisals to avoid turning our managers and employees into people who hesitate to do anything. If that happens, the company will become ineffective and unable to create additional value. *(Ren Zhengfei: Speech at the Meeting with Level-1 Committees Under the Human Resources Committee, 1997)*

We need to deal with the results of investigations fairly and objectively. We need to be tolerant of the minor weaknesses of those who are competent, have huge potential, and have the courage to explore and innovate. We must not let these weaknesses affect their deployment and promotions. *(Source: Huawei Corp. Doc. No. [2004] 99 Regulations on the Publicity of the Names of Managers to Be Appointed for Feedback)*

We have implemented an accountability system and have a clear system of rewards and penalties. There is no need for those who have been penalized to be overly concerned because penalties do not close the door for promotions. In addition, those who have not been penalized will not necessarily be promoted. The point is why mistakes were made; for example, did a manager intentionally cover up the facts, or did they simply lack experience? *(Ren Zhengfei: Adapting the Appraisal System for Managers to Challenges Facing the Transforming Industry, 2006)*

In principle, we will take legal action against managers and employees who have committed economic fraud. *(Source: EMT Resolution No. [2006] 026)*

Corrupt managers have to step down, no matter how talented they are or what their contribution has been. Managers who fail to prevent mass corruption within their scope of authority also have to step down. We must be well aware that it will be very difficult to turn the situation around if mass corruption occurs inside an organization. Corruption has long-term negative effects. Even if years of efforts are devoted to turning the situation around, it will still be difficult to re-energize morale. Therefore, we must put out small fires before they spread and ensure manager quality by implementing strict rules and regulations. We need to let our employees know that the company will not tolerate any corruption and show them anyone who is corrupt will be disciplined regardless of their job level. This is the only way we can prevent corruption among managers. *(Source: EMT Meeting Minutes No. [2007] 029)*

When delegating authority to lower levels, we need to strengthen supervision. The primary role of supervision is to make lower levels that have been delegated authority accountable for profits and legal liability. In addition, they will be able to share benefits when they have done a great job, and need to share the losses incurred by their mistakes. The proportion of losses they should bear can be determined via analysis; for example, they can bear 20%, 30%, or 50% of the losses, the rest will be borne by the company, and the relevant losses can be deducted from their bonuses. These losses should be borne by regions. The bottom line is to share losses and avoid abusing strategic subsidies. I think the JCR must have the courage to track accountability. *(Ren Zhengfei: Speech at the EMT ST Meeting, June 30, 2011)*

CHAPTER 8

DEVELOPING MANAGERS

Generals are born of battle. It is difficult for anyone to become a general without experiencing the hardships of the battlefield. Likewise, meditation is necessary to understand the essence of Buddhism. No one should ever stop learning under any circumstances. When it comes to organizational development, Huawei develops its teams through hands-on operations. It focuses the best employees on its strategic markets and key projects. Once success is achieved, it will summarize experience and transfer these employees to other markets and projects. In this way, organizations can be effectively established.

Knowledge acquisition is a process of preparing for work, and this process is something employees should take care of and invest in on their own. Each employee needs to design their own career path. Talent cannot be developed through training. Almost all great people are self-made rather than trained. Huawei selects talent, rather than developing them. Individuals should have the desire to do better. Without the motivation to improve, they will not succeed no matter how much support they get.

Huawei believes training must be practical and focus on teaching managers how to complete specific tasks. The company provides big rewards for small improvements, but only encouragement for "big" suggestions, to encourage employees to be down-to-earth. It trains managers to master systematic and standardized operating methods. Such training is not based on Western training materials. Huawei customizes these materials based on its own business scenarios, and requires managers to learn what is urgently needed and flexibly apply what they have learned. In essence, the company combines systematic and comprehensive training with real-world problem solving.

Huawei focuses on methodologies rather than knowledge during training. The slogan for the managerial candidate team of Huawei University is "broad vision, strong will, and good character". The slogan for the new employee team is "endure mental and physical hardships and assume heavy responsibilities". The company has different expectations for these two teams. At Huawei, many corporate documents are the result of extensive research and embody the wisdom of the senior management team. Managers are expected to study these documents in-depth in order to understand the company's strategic intent and policies.

Job rotation is a must if Huawei's middle and senior managers are to obtain the relevant work experience and broaden their horizons. However, a zigzag development path is applicable only to senior managers and experts with comprehensive skill sets, not to junior managers and employees. The company expects its junior managers and employees to love what they do and excel in their given fields, and doesn't encourage them to transfer to other positions. The company has established an internal talent market to maintain a proper degree of talent mobility.

The priority of management is to focus on bottlenecks. Currently, Huawei has two bottlenecks: managerial candidates and management transformation. The company is badly in need of a large number of young people who are highly motivated, passionate, capable, and willing to sacrifice and work in places where they are needed. It emphasizes developing managerial candidates. Huawei is willing to place junior employees with huge potential on its senior management team. Otherwise, where will its generals come from?

Huawei has two pyramids: managers and experts. The two pyramids share the same bottom layers. At the middle layers, job holders can be rotated back and forth. But when it comes to higher levels, the pyramids are separate. Those who are at the top of each pyramid focus on directions for future development.

This chapter describes Huawei's policies for developing managers from four perspectives: developing managers based on a selection mechanism, training managers, manager mobility, and developing managerial candidates.

8.1

Developing Managers Based on a Selection Mechanism

8.1.1 Generals are born of battle

I hope those who display outstanding performance will work in field offices to find opportunities to advance their careers. This is very important. *(Ren Zhengfei: Remarks to Candidates of the Executives' Office, 1996)*

Huawei University's focus is on developing different levels of managerial candidates, and sending them to work in field offices. Huawei University does not need to quickly become a real university. It mainly aims to develop project managers at different levels, including junior, middle, and senior project managers. Good project managers will then become general managers of representative offices. At Huawei University, certificates are not important. The point is to develop trainees' capabilities so they can accomplish tasks in real-world scenarios. Those with MBA degrees can demonstrate that they possess relevant skills, but the primary role of a manager is to take responsibility. *(Source: EMT Meeting Minutes No. [2005] 049)*

Generals are born of battle. It is difficult for anyone to become a general without experiencing the hardships of the battlefield. Likewise, meditation is necessary to understand the essence of Buddhism. You should never stop learning. Now that you have chosen to work in hardship regions, you will need to study hard; otherwise, you will lose a lot of good opportunities. It would be a great pity if you lost opportunities as a preferred candidate for promotion. *(Ren Zhengfei: Famous Battles Do Not Automatically Produce Generals, but All Generals Were Once Heroes, 2006)*

We need to establish engineering teams, and develop managers in hardship regions and small- and middle-sized projects; for example, projects worth tens of millions of US dollars. Members of these engineering teams will be expected to work hard in hardship regions and endure mental and physical hardships. They need to deliver high-quality service that meets European standards. The top 25% will have the opportunity to be involved in bigger projects and work with consultants and experts. The remaining 75% will be sent to other positions and develop through job rotations. *(Source: EMT Meeting Minutes No. [2006] 040)*

No matter what they plan to do in the future, managerial candidates in the Reserve Pool must first do their jobs well. Only outstanding candidates will be promoted to managerial positions. We cannot simply say who will become managers based on our own opinions. You need to become managers through your own hard work, rather than waiting for others to appoint you. You need to fight for it, and how far you can go will be determined by your results. *(Ren Zhengfei: Speech at the Regular Meeting of the Reserve Pool, June 24, 2009)*

We only select talent, but do not develop them. You can choose whether or not to work in field offices. If you think you are capable, then you need to grow through hands-on practice and find growth opportunities on your own. In most cases, managers are self-made rather than trained by the company. *(Ren Zhengfei: Speech at the Regular Meeting of the Reserve Pool, June 24, 2009)*

Huawei University needs to develop managers with a wide range of expertise through hands-on practice. These managers are expected to lead Huawei in 10 or 20 years. The overall goal of the Core Engineering Camp is to cultivate employees and help them improve. First, the Core Engineering Camp needs to develop managers with a wide range of expertise through hardware installation and other engineering practices. The slogan for the Core Engineering Camp's new employee team is "endure mental and physical hardships and assume heavy responsibilities". The slogan for its managerial candidate team is "broad vision, strong will, and good character". Second, we will restructure the engineering delivery organization and ensure rotation between managerial candidates of the Core Engineering Camp and the current delivery management teams of representative offices. By summarizing industry best practices and the company's successful experience, we will establish a new delivery management system that integrates budgeting, supply, procurement, and planning. We will also integrate the management of delivery projects for software and the enterprise business to develop the capabilities to manage delivery projects from end to end. We will achieve higher project profitability by enhancing the quality of subcontracting, eliminating corruption, and reducing costs. Third, we will develop managers for every area of the company. Future managers with comprehensive capabilities in operations will come from the Core Engineering Camp, but they will not end up there. Instead, they will assume leadership positions in various departments of the company. *(Source: EMT Meeting Minutes No. [2012] 033)*

In my opinion, we need to send employees to field offices before establishing relevant organizations. I have criticized our organizational development in the enterprise business, where we have been busy with organizational development and appointments. If you have not been appointed to a managerial position, you can first work in field offices. If you succeed, promotion will follow naturally. We need to select our managers in this way and assess them based on their actual performance. Generals are born of battle. If an employee makes huge contributions in field offices, he or she will be promoted to a high-level position, and those who follow will be promoted as well. Such a pyramid structure will be very stable. However, if we develop organizations through appointments, and designate a large number of managers worldwide, they will be unable to unite and succeed. *(Ren Zhengfei: Speech and Comments at the Enterprise BG's Strategy Retreat in Suzhou, 2012)*

We need to focus our resources on winning in our target markets. After succeeding, the most capable people will be promoted and be assigned to other markets. Only one manager will remain behind to defend the market we have won. Others who have been promoted will be reassigned to other markets. In this way, they will be promoted to higher-level positions while still in their twenties. To succeed, they need to work courageously in field offices. As long as they work hard, they will be recognized sooner or later. If employees don't make any effort, they will be dismissed. Huawei was also established through hands-on operations. Our managers have been promoted based on their contributions, not through selection. I agree with Eric Xu on how to develop our organization. I think we need to focus the best employees on our strategic markets and key projects. Once we succeed, we will summarize experience and transfer these employees to other markets and projects. In this way, our organizations can be effectively established. If we develop our team through appointments instead of hands-on operations, we will be easily defeated. *(Ren Zhengfei: Speech and Comments at the Enterprise BG's Strategy Retreat in Suzhou, 2012)*

We only select those with certain characteristics as managerial candidates. In addition, we believe those who don't want to be managers can still be good employees. Why is this? They know they are not cut out to be managers, so they don't bother enduring the hardships required to become a manager, such as working in Afghanistan, the Himalayas, or the old-growth forests of Africa. They are satisfied working in Shenzhen, earning an average salary, and enjoying a stable life. If they cannot become managers, there is no point asking them to ensure huge hardships and wasting a lot of company money. However, future managers must ensure hardships. Managers are selected, not trained. Our selection mechanism aims to help high-potential, enterprising, passionate, and responsible talent grow rapidly. Employees who want to become managers are generally eager to learn and succeed. One needs to have the desire to succeed in the first place, and then invest a little money to receive training and take exams. *(Ren Zhengfei: Minutes of the Meeting with Staff from Huawei University Institute of Education, 2012)*

We emphasize selecting talent from project management. Each manager needs to start from projects and work their way up to a senior managerial position. The biggest weakness of senior managers without field experience is that they know very little about how things work in field offices. Therefore, they can easily ignore actual situations. *(Ren Zhengfei: Minutes of the Meeting with Staff from Huawei University Institute of Education, 2012)*

When selecting and assessing managers, we focus on results and responsibilities and the value managerial candidates have created. Generals are born of battle. Good seeds will sprout on their own. We don't need to help them along. I believe talent is selected rather than trained. If we try to find high-potential talent and develop them step by step, the costs will be very high. So at Huawei, we recognize those with high potential and give them opportunities for further development. Whether or not they can rise to higher positions totally depends on themselves. *(Ren Zhengfei: Speech at the EMT ST Meeting, March 29, 2013)*

You need to proactively create opportunities for future development on your own rather than relying on other people to offer you opportunities.

Technological advances are becoming increasingly difficult and complex, and it is very challenging for someone who knows little about technology to work in this field. As a result, you need to make tremendous efforts to work all the way from an ordinary employee to a leader. There are many paths we can take in life. There is a Chinese saying: "A good scholar will become an official." However, there is a limited number of such positions. Because of this, those who excel in study can also choose to be specialists, and many more choose to take jobs that can help them make a living. By acknowledging that those who don't want to be managers can still be good employees, we want to establish career paths for those who aren't interested in pursuing a managerial path. It is perfectly fine if one wants to be a regular employee all his or her life. *(Ren Zhengfei: Comments to Staff in Mauritius, 2013)*

8.1.2 Knowledge acquisition is a process of preparing for work, and employees should invest in their own knowledge acquisition

What is our goal for Huawei University? First of all, it is a university without a fixed premise or organizational structure. Second, it stresses self-learning and aims to help managers and employees achieve their goals by guiding them to make continuous progress and place strict requirements on themselves. Each employee needs to design their own career path. Different people have different career goals, and thus have different training needs and require different training content. However, the company can only satisfy employees' common training needs which also serve the company's overall goals. It would be impossible for the company to provide each employee with personalized training. It is also not necessary for us to do so. However, we have established a guidance system that encourages self-learning. We need to adopt incentives to motivate managers and employees to unleash their potential. During this process, managers and employees can identify their own weaknesses. Our systems help them integrate their common traits and unique personalities, develop them, and become talent. I think talent cannot be developed through training. *(Ren Zhengfei: Training – An Important Path Leading to Huawei's Future, 1996)*

Our current training system aims to turn every employee into a president. It invests heavily in each employee without considering their potential and expects them to develop comprehensively. Despite the high costs, only a few outstanding people have emerged. In my opinion, employees need to rely on themselves to gain the knowledge they need for work. Knowledge acquisition is a process of preparing for work, and this process is something employees should take care of and invest in on their own. We need to change our views about training and development, and be cautious when using the word "development". Employees need to take responsibility for their own learning and broaden their horizons. It's impossible for us to do so. We can't assume unlimited responsibility for employees. We only select talent, but do not develop them. *(Ren Zhengfei: Speech at the Regular Meeting of the Reserve Pool, June 24, 2009)*

If a soldier wants to become a general, he or she must be willing to learn everything about aircraft, cannons, tanks, and guns. If a soldier only wants to be a soldier for their entire life, why bother studying so many things? Knowing about the guns will be enough. Likewise, employees must aspire to grow. To succeed, employees need to communicate with and help each other. In addition, they should have the desire to do better. Without the motivation to improve, they will not succeed no matter how much support they get. *(Ren Zhengfei: Minutes of the Meeting with Staff of the Romania Accounting SSC, 2011)*

Huawei University needs to shift its focus from developing and training talent to selecting talent. Managers and employees need to learn and improve at their own expense. Congratulations to you all for being the first group of trainees to pay for your own training. We will stick to this policy. Apart from paying training fees, those who stop working temporarily while receiving training will not receive salaries until they resume their job. Also, we will charge a high price for training materials. If you want to learn and improve, you are welcome to receive paid-for training here. It is worthwhile to do so. If the training is helpful to you, you will improve your capabilities, achieve better performance, and have more opportunities to be promoted in the future. Even if you fail in the training, you may learn from your failure and make greater progress in the future. So investing in training is worthwhile. We will charge more for the training in the future. The purpose of asking employees to receive paid training without salaries is to motivate them to study harder. In so doing, we aim to help employees improve their skills, help Huawei University operate better with some revenue from training, and help the company develop a large number of managerial candidates. If we can achieve these three purposes, Huawei will definitely thrive and endure. *(Ren Zhengfei: Developing Managers Based on the Selection Mechanism, Reviewing and Streamlining Organizations Based on Processes, and Promoting the Open and Balanced Development of Organizations, 2011)*

A weakness in China's educational system is that it aims to develop high-level employees rather than leaders. In contrast, some schools in Europe and the US aim to develop future leaders. To achieve this goal, they teach history, philosophy, politics, and sociology in high schools. Senior managers and some senior experts at Huawei need to broaden their horizons, think more creatively, focus on leading in strategy rather than tactics, and innovate in business and technical models. Some of them may even become great thinkers in certain fields. Anyway, it is always beneficial to learn something about history and philosophy. *(Ren Zhengfei: Comments to Trainees of the Tenth Session of the Senior Management Seminar at Huawei University, 2011)*

8.1.3 Self-learning and on-the-job training

Self-learning is much more important than training. Who trained Deng Xiaoping and Mao Zedong? Almost all great people are self-made rather than trained. If you can't learn anything without your instructor, you will never surpass them. We should let our employees know that everyone is a teacher and a student at the same time. If someone is not motivated to improve, and even makes the same mistakes repeatedly, it won't make any difference how many training sessions he or she receives. *(Ren Zhengfei: Training Must Be Practical, 1998)*

At work, training is actually happening all around us every day. You cannot expect others to help you grow; otherwise, you will never succeed. Successful people are self-made, and are adept at self-learning. Everyone must continue learning to constantly improve themselves. *(Ren Zhengfei: Answers to Questions from New Employees, 1999)*

We are now cooperating with more than 30 consulting firms. Each of them has its own unique system design and statistical forms, which are actually great learning resources for employees. If these resources are put online, our employees can apply them to their work. These resources are from more than one source, and can inspire employees to create something better. We can then decide which forms we should use. Those companies have spent dozens or even hundreds of years creating and refining these resources, and some people have even worked on them their entire lives. But no one at Huawei thoroughly understands even a small part of them. More often than not, we simply study these resources at face value. To gain a deeper understanding, we'd better make all of them available to employees as they are, and let them study and digest the knowledge on their own. However, asking employees to study everything concurrently will be problematic. We can select one or two resources for employees to focus on. At the same time we need to make other resources available as well. Everyone can understand the ideas behind all of them on their own. Since we are cooperating with these consulting firms, it will be better to use what they offer and then produce a series of training materials based on their resources, so as to ensure reliability and accuracy. The learning and development platform in the Reserve Pool needs to be open to everyone in the company so that everyone can learn and improve. In addition, we need to ensure the learning resources can be downloaded, at least by those in the Reserve Pool. Whether or not other employees can download those resources needs to be decided by department heads. *(Ren Zhengfei: Speech at the Regular Meeting of the Reserve Pool, June 24, 2009)*

Selection and development are not contradictory. We still need to develop our managers and employees after they are selected. We must make all the courses open to all employees so that those who are willing to learn can access them. We encourage our employees to make progress and develop themselves. They should not passively wait to be developed by the company. We will focus on training managers who are selected to work in certain positions and help them overcome their weaknesses. To make other employees feel better, we need to charge those who receive training. In addition, we must change our existing development system from one that provides one-size-fits-all courses to one that caters to the specific needs of trainees identified during manager selection. *(Ren Zhengfei: Comments to Staff from Finance, 2011)*

We should change how we develop managers and employees. We will no longer try to persuade employees to learn. They can learn and receive training if they choose, and we will not give them a hard time if they don't. Whether or not someone can remain in their position should depend on his or her performance, not on their eagerness to learn. Many great people in history didn't spend much time learning, so we should not force employees to learn. At Huawei, we only select talent worldwide, rather than train them. Those who are left behind will be dismissed. We will not send experienced experts to communicate with underperformers and we will not condone poor performance. We need to change some of our past practices. If we follow such a new approach, Huawei University will be a for-profit organization. To survive and thrive, it must make a profit. No money will be allocated to it in the future. The finance department needs to develop settlement methods, and transfer fees to Huawei University for training rendered. To become bigger and stronger, Huawei University will have to invest this money in developing itself. *(Ren Zhengfei: Developing Managers Based on the Selection Mechanism, Reviewing and Streamlining Organizations Based on Processes, and Promoting the Open and Balanced Development of Organizations, 2011)*

With regard to developing managerial candidates, instructors at Huawei University are facilitators rather than teachers. If they are teachers, what students learn will be limited to what they know. We should make learning inspiring. At Huawei University, we don't have lectures. Trainees mainly discuss problems and debate with one another. After the one-month training period, they say goodbye to each other and go their separate ways. No one knows who will become a manager in the future. But time eventually reveals everything. Some of them will certainly become outstanding managers. *(Ren Zhengfei: Developing Managers Based on the Selection Mechanism, Reviewing and Streamlining Organizations Based on Processes, and Promoting the Open and Balanced Development of Organizations, 2011)*

Different courses may require different teaching methods. For example, some instructors may not always use case discussions during training. However, those who extensively apply this method will gradually develop their capabilities and become qualified to provide training under multiple case scenarios. As a result, they will be able to develop many different courses, such as those on leadership and project management. We can encourage employees to study these courses on their own, stop working temporarily to receive training, and engage in hands-on practice. *(Ren Zhengfei: Developing Managers Based on the Selection Mechanism, Reviewing and Streamlining Organizations Based on Processes, and Promoting the Open and Balanced Development of Organizations, 2011)*

I think case-based instruction for the Reserve Pool can be divided into the following four stages:

The first stage begins with inspiring trainees to learn. They need to first read learning materials. Exams can be arranged on a daily basis to make sure students read what they are supposed to. The learning materials compiled under the leadership of Ken Hu and Eric Xu are very good. The quality actually exceeded my expectations. This was made possible through the hard work of the entire editorial board. Maybe such a huge contribution will be remembered forever. After each exam, instructors can post students' answers online (e.g., on the *Xinsheng Community*) before grading the exam papers so that trainees' subordinates and peers can see how they are doing. This will motivate them to study harder.

The second stage is presentation, during which trainees are expected to talk about how their behavior is consistent or inconsistent with the values they are learning. As long as the trainees talk about their own work, it will be acceptable. We will not tolerate those who indulge in empty talk or simply try to flatter others. Whatever they say, they should have three references who can prove what they are saying is actually true. If they don't have any references, we will assume that they are making up stories. They need to provide information about their references, including job title, staff ID, and name. Once they finish their presentation, we will post everything they wrote and said on the *Xinsheng Community*, including their references. When preparing presentations, trainees should try to be concise and focus on the main points. They cannot merely focus on theories; otherwise, they will not be allowed to make a presentation, or the score they receive for the presentation will be reduced.

The third stage is extensive discussions. Trainees are expected to present their opinions and stories. After the presentation, extensive discussion will be held, during which trainees do not have to say only good things about our culture. Our culture is universally applicable, and we have learned it from others. All our employees will understand our core values of staying customer-centric and inspiring dedication. Those who say they identify with our culture may actually not. We need to be tolerant of those who have different opinions. I think they have also thought hard and what they say may make sense, too. We will delegate authority to instructors to let those with different opinions pass the presentation. At Huawei, we welcome dissenters. As for those who say they identify with our culture, we need to make sure they truly understand and support what we advocate instead of simply pretending to do so.

The fourth stage is writing papers and giving an oral defense. After fully sharing opinions and learning from one another during the extensive discussion stage, trainees will need to write papers and make an oral defense. Trainees should not merely talk about theories in their papers. Otherwise, they will not pass. They need to talk about their practice instead and give real-world examples. They can also write about what they have learned from other people's experience and list them as their references. If they cannot find any references for the stories they tell, they will not pass this stage, and will need to complete it later. *(Ren Zhengfei: Developing Managers Based on the Selection Mechanism, Reviewing and Streamlining Organizations Based on Processes, and Promoting the Open and Balanced Development of Organizations, 2011)*

I think short-term training is better than long-term training. Generals are not trained. It is enough for employees to spend one or two months learning methodologies before working in field offices. We have a learning platform where employees can learn online, get to know instructors, and promptly communicate with them via the internet. *(Ren Zhengfei: Minutes of the Meeting with Staff from Huawei University Institute of Education, 2012)*

In the past, I was very optimistic about the future of our company. At the time, new employees working on engineering installations in Chengdu didn't have laptops. They would carry a backpack full of books on engineering standards into the mountains and read them there. They enabled Huawei's promising future. But now, many employees don't have the capability to do many things and simply outsource projects to external parties, such as data generation. Yet, they are receiving a high salary and have lots of shares that they don't deserve. I'm not saying that our managers who have worked at Huawei for years are not competent. Still, we need to identify those who are not competent for their positions and ask them to make up for what they lack and attain the relevant C&Q levels regardless of their current positions. We need to set specific C&Q criteria for the engineering category and make them publicly available so that employees know what is expected of them. The assessment exam may take the form of the Test of English as a Foreign Language (TOEFL), which has a written and oral test. Only those who have passed the written test will be allowed to attend the oral test, and those who can answer various questions during the oral test will prove that they have not cheated during the written test, and will be offered the corresponding C&Q levels. We need to develop a full set of engineering delivery capabilities, but employees do not have to be good at everything. They can have different career development options, such as project manager, project supervisor, or technical expert, who are all needed in a project. We also need to further improve the management of our succession planning. *(Ren Zhengfei: Speech at the EMT ST Meeting, August 31, 2012)*

8.2

Training Must
Be Practical

8.2.1 Teaching managers how to complete specific tasks through training

Training must be practical. Training content used at Huawei University must align with practices in field offices. For example, processes, forms, and code used during training must come from real-world cases in field offices. We must observe the principles of "learning what is urgently needed and applying what is learned to practice". We need to train ordinary employees to run processes or compile code, not about how to be a manager. *(Source: EMT Meeting Minutes No. [2008] 013)*

Training programs should be practical and focus on teaching managers how to complete specific tasks. Currently, many of our senior managers don't know how to do that. They are tasked with developing employee potential. How can they do that if they don't even know how to complete specific tasks? At Huawei, we provide big rewards for small improvements, but only encouragement for "big" suggestions. Why is this? We want to encourage employees to be down-to-earth. For those who claim that they have some really good "big" suggestions, they should have done a good job in their positions, and been identified long ago. We need to ensure all of our training sessions focus on specific tasks, and are linked to C&Q assessments. I think the direction of many of our training centers is incorrect. They are trying to develop their trainees into presidents. Our training must be practical. At Huawei, we have too many smart people. The problem is that smart people tend not to be pragmatic, and that will eventually ruin the company. HR departments need to help training centers adjust our training approach so they can help employees apply what they have learned in training to their work. We should not simply train employees for training's sake. *(Ren Zhengfei: Training Must Be Practical, 1998)*

Managers are responsible for developing employees who can achieve high performance. If managers are busy all day long, developing employees who are not down-to-earth or able to apply what they have learned to their work, they are not doing their job, and at the same time they are incurring high costs for the company. *(Ren Zhengfei: Being Performance-focused and Result-oriented, and Striving to Increase Per Capita Efficiency, 2002)*

Currently, we do not lack bold and capable heroes. But why don't we have great generals? The reason is that we are not educating them properly on systematic and standardized operating methods. Such training is not based on Western training materials. We need to customize these materials based on business scenarios in our company. We must learn what is urgently needed and flexibly apply what we have learned. We must combine systematic and comprehensive training with real-world problem solving. *(Ren Zhengfei: Huawei University Must Become the Cradle of Generals, 2007)*

During this CFO training session, we will not adopt the cramming approach that was often used in the past. Instead, we will adopt the case discussion method initiated by Harvard Business School: We will thoroughly discuss cases that actually occurred at Huawei, review various types of materials from different sources, and work together to find appropriate solutions. However, attending the training session today does not guarantee that you will become a qualified CFO tomorrow. After the discussion, you will need to apply what you have learned to practice to see if the solutions work. It is impossible for us to teach you everything you need to know about being a qualified CFO. You need to learn how to be a CFO through hands-on work. *(Ren Zhengfei: Timely, Accurate, High Quality, and Low Cost Delivery Calls for Professional Process-compliant CFOs, 2009)*

High-quality HR management means having the right person in the right position, rather than having a lot of talented people who are not suitable for their positions. All these years our definition of high-quality HR management, such as selecting the best people, has been wrong. What matters is to ensure the right people in the right positions. *(Ren Zhengfei: Speech at the Regular Meeting of the Reserve Pool, June 24, 2009)*

The Core Engineering Department must cover all regions and develop managers. The developed managers will rotate from one place to another as a team to help every place improve performance. The HR department will be responsible for daily work related to selecting and developing members of the Core Engineering Department, while Huawei University will provide training services. As for courses which Huawei University finds challenging, we can invite external experts to give lectures, which can help employees learn effectively. *(Ren Zhengfei: Speech at the EMT ST Meeting, August 31, 2012)*

I think, at the current stage, Huawei University needs to focus more on organizational development. Take leadership as an example. One doesn't need to have the leadership skills required in a head of state. Huawei University should not focus on all those big things that are not useful for hands-on operations. Instead, it can give instructions on how to lead a small project or team. If you teach trainees all those big things about leadership that are not practical, they will need to customize what they have learned, and the customization may not be appropriate. Therefore, you need to train them on exactly what they need. Therefore, instructors need to adjust the macro views of experts and adapt them to projects. *(Ren Zhengfei: Minutes of the Meeting with Staff from Huawei University Institute of Education, 2012)*

8.2.2 Focusing on methodologies rather than knowledge

At Huawei, our training focuses on knowledge transfers. I don't think a lack of knowledge was the only problem for employees who have been dismissed. In my opinion, the primary problem is with their work attitude. The second problem is that they lacked relevant knowledge. So for CFO and CSO training, we don't have key courses, standards, or textbooks. Trainees need to think about how to be a CFO or CSO on their own. If they cannot figure it out, they should not work in those positions. If trainees don't know what a CFO is all about, they can first have a discussion in the way discussion is organized at Harvard Business School. Through the discussion they can understand the mission and specific responsibilities of a CFO, as well as the responsibilities regarding internal controls, planning, bonus calculation, and HR management. After understanding all these things, they can try to improve the CFO function. Finally, they will give an oral defense. Due to time limits, mere knowledge transfers cannot achieve our training goals. We therefore had better help trainees master methodologies rather than knowledge. Only in this way can we identify the managers we need. Different people might understand the same methodologies differently. Leaders are those who can master *huidu*. If we overemphasize classification of qualifications, the management of the Reserve Pool will become more complex and too fine-grained, and its major goals and principles will be ignored. Such management will be very costly and cannot achieve good results. Training of the Reserve Pool should not focus on content, but on methodologies. We value two things when selecting managers. The first is dedication and the second is methodology. We cannot overemphasize knowledge. At Huawei, higher-level organizations do not have the required management capabilities, and are unable to coach and accept high-performing subordinates. In addition, field managers do not follow rules or regulations. When this happens, we will be unable to achieve great success. Currently, some of our field managers have done a very poor job regarding the commercial authorization of contracts worth hundreds of millions of US dollars, as their aim is just to beat competitors. These managers are not doing the right thing, and are not the type of managers we expect. We will develop managers who master the correct methodologies. *(Ren Zhengfei: Speech at the Regular Meeting of the Reserve Pool, June 24, 2009)*

Huawei University needs to adopt the case method during training. In general, there are two types of cases: cases in a story format and cases with various tables, forms, and sheets. The former is easy to understand and the latter is helpful for trainees to master the right methods and put them into work. *(Ren Zhengfei: Minutes of the Meeting with Staff from Huawei University Institute of Education, 2012)*

The slogan for the managerial candidate team is "broad vision, strong will, and good character". Managers must first have broad vision; strong will and good character come next. A strong will that is not supported by broad vision is useless. The slogan for the new employee team is "endure mental and physical hardships and assume heavy responsibilities". We have to distinguish between our expectations for these two teams. Although broad vision is also important for new employees, it is not as important as practice and establishing personal goals. *(Ren Zhengfei: Speech at the EMT ST Meeting, October 30, 2012)*

8.2.3 Studying corporate documents to learn from the wisdom of the senior management team

We need to ensure that our managers study our corporate culture and carefully read relevant corporate documents. Otherwise, they will not be promoted. *(Ren Zhengfei: Remarks at a Meeting with Administrative Management Staff of Huawei Telecommunications, 1997)*

Mechanisms and processes are the main driving forces behind the company's development. Managers at all levels need to be clear about the future direction and focus on building management systems at all levels. They should always keep the big picture in mind and avoid simply seeing trees and losing sight of the forest. Improvement is a summary of the company's best management practices. In a sense, it is like a key to promotions. Whoever understands what is in this newspaper will have a better chance of making progress. *(Ren Zhengfei: On Transforming the Management System and Developing Managers, 1998)*

Whether managers at all levels have carefully read the Huawei People and Improvement newspapers should be considered during their performance appraisals. If they don't even read the newspapers, then they are unqualified to hold their positions. In addition, they need to write a brief review each month to talk about their thoughts and how they may put what they read in the newspapers into practice. We may even list the names of those who don't read the newspapers in *Improvement*. *(Ren Zhengfei: Remarks at a Meeting with Staff of the Huawei People Editorial Board and CEC, 2006)*

To me, the number of books one reads is not as important as the number of times one reads a book. If one reads a lot of books but does not review them, he or she may not gain a thorough understanding of any of them. At Huawei, many corporate documents are the result of extensive research and embody the wisdom of the senior management team. So reading those documents is a great way to learn. The more you read them, the deeper your understanding will become. For example, you can read corporate documents once a week. If you want to become a manager in the future, it is important to learn from other people's experience. It doesn't matter if you can't understand the documents after your first reading. The more you read them, the more accurate your understanding will be. *(Ren Zhengfei: Famous Battles Do Not Automatically Produce Generals, but All Generals Were Once Heroes, 2006)*

Many senior managers simply do not study our corporate documents. They do things based on their own experience. Such managers must step down; otherwise, the company will be doomed. The resolutions and documents drawn up by the EMT embody the wisdom of our senior management team. Yet, many senior managers don't bother to read them. Perhaps, we need to test their knowledge on the 400+ EMT documents. Those who don't pass the test cannot receive pay raises. We need to let them know that they are on the verge of being demoted. Those who have made outstanding contributions cannot assume that they will never be demoted. That's not necessarily the case. Everyone needs to keep learning and improving themselves. *(Ren Zhengfei: Speech at the EMT ST Meeting, 2009)*

We need to ensure that our senior managers carefully study our management culture, actively participate in establishing systems, and strictly follow relevant processes. We will not force ordinary employees to study our corporate culture, as this may increase their burdens. Their main job is to work hard and earn money. Some senior managers don't spend time learning new things and instead ask their subordinates to do it. As a result, many of their subordinates have become senior managers and they themselves may gradually be left behind and demoted. *(Ren Zhengfei: Success Is Not a Reliable Guide to Future Development, 2011)*

8.2.4 Using the case method to extract theory from practice

Knowledge is static and focuses on what is common among different things. It is very general and may therefore have limitations when applied to practice. Work often has its own unique features. Learning from specific cases is preferred by those who are good at learning, as it enables them to make rapid progress. We need to constantly summarize lessons to enrich our knowledge. To some extent, making summaries is similar to knitting a fishing net. The more efforts we put in this area, the bigger our net will be, which will enable us to catch more fish. We need to make summaries of both successes and failures. *(Ren Zhengfei: Shifting from the Realm of Necessity to the Realm of Freedom – Preface for the Book Titled Summary of the UAE 3G Engineering Project, 2004)*

In the future, case-based training will be an important method for advanced training. We should not hesitate to use cases during training even if they are problematic. All the cases will be recorded for future use, and even be used by prestigious universities as part of their teaching materials. Cases are based on practice, which is the best instructor. *(Ren Zhengfei: Training – An Important Path Leading to Huawei's Future, 1996)*

We need to standardize the templates for cases, but the content of the cases needs to be based on management or business practice in field offices. Both key employees and middle and senior managers need to prepare cases. Those who are good at developing cases can receive good assessments. Huawei University can assist field people in preparing cases. Nowadays, IBM can no longer tell us much about its supervision system. The reason is as follows: After dozens and hundreds of years of operation, this system has been deeply integrated into IBM's processes and operations. At Huawei, we need to promptly summarize our Integrated Product Development (IPD) and Integrated Supply Chain (ISC) processes to save ourselves trouble in the future. *(Source: EMT Meeting Minutes No. [2005] 049)*

To ensure high-quality training, we can invite experienced field employees to be instructors and discuss cases. Internship for engineering installation can be done in any place that meets specific requirements. During evaluation, we need to emphasize the importance of skills. We can ask employees to memorize relevant criteria first so that they can start working and then understand the reasoning behind the criteria when there is enough time. *(Source: EMT Meeting Minutes No. [2005] 037)*

I think everyone needs to learn how to summarize lessons learned from past experience. If employees can't even summarize what they learned from key events they experienced, they won't be competent for a managerial position. If managers cannot thoroughly understand their own business, can we expect them to understand those of others? We expect every employee to constantly make summaries based on their key events, which is the key to improving capabilities. During the process, one's thinking will become more systematic. We emphasize theory-guided practice, and encourage extracting theory from practice. All managers need to write about their successful experience, which needs to be publicized for feedback and recognized by others around them. If what they wrote is not recognized, I may suspect that the story is totally made up. The ability to summarize lessons from experience is a great indicator of one's capabilities. Successful experience is contributions, and assessment is a process of collecting feedback. Summary reports must be made public and recognized by everyone.

(Ren Zhengfei: Human Resources Must Be Oriented Towards Forging Ahead and Refrain from Being Dogmatic and Rigid, 2009)

Practice without a clear understanding may not get you anywhere. We should not practice for the sake of experiencing the process. Instead, we need to understand what we are doing and combine standard learning and careful practice. Practice is only valuable when we learn and understand past experience summarized by others, validate it through practice, and summarize our own experience. *(Ren Zhengfei: Comments to Staff from Finance, 2011)*

Practice without any theoretical support will only produce workmen, who may not know what to do when things are different from what they are familiar with. Engineers can enable batch production, but workmen cannot. Practical experience needs to be enhanced and enriched by theoretical understanding. Otherwise, one will not be able to adapt to project changes. During the learning and training process, instructors should emphasize practice while trainees need to extract theory from practice. *(Ren Zhengfei: Minutes of the Meeting with Staff from Huawei University Institute of Education, 2012)*

We should meet more often to discuss a project before it starts and to summarize it after completion. During the wrap-up sessions, we should compare our expectations for the project and the actual results achieved to see how much they overlap. No matter whether or not there is overlap, we are learning something in this process. If we do this for every project, we will make huge progress after two or three projects. To me, our mind is composted of lots of separate threads. If we summarize every project we do to think about lessons learned, we are tying a knot in the threads. Over time, our mind will become a net, with which we can catch fish. It's a fact of life: More thinking and more reflection mean more knots in your net. And the bigger your net becomes, the bigger the fish you can catch. You have done a good job in making systematic designs. However, you need to apply them to projects and then compare the outcomes with the designs to see if they are consistent and why. If we keep doing this, we will be able to knit a big net and then catch big fish with it. *(Ren Zhengfei: Speech at a Report Meeting of the Eastern and Southern Africa Multi-country Management Department, November 15, 2012)*

8.3

Establishing a System to Ensure Manager Mobility

8.3.1 Middle and senior managers need to rotate among different positions

I think a certain degree of mobility is a good thing. We should ensure our middle and senior managers rotate among different positions in the end-to-end processes. If there is no mobility, our project management capabilities will not improve, and we will not have sufficient senior managers. The promotion of senior managers in the same department will lead to nepotism. *(Ren Zhengfei: Speech at the Management Training Class, 1996)*

Job rotation is a must for our middle and senior managers. Those without relevant work experience cannot be promoted to managerial positions, and those without field experience cannot become team leaders. At Huawei, we have two types of rotations: business rotations and job rotations. One example of the first type is R&D engineers going to work in development & pilot, manufacturing, and services to better understand what products are needed in the market. Only with such experience will they become senior experts in their fields. If they don't have experience in other domains, they will not be considered senior or experienced. Job rotation means rotating middle and senior managers to other positions to transfer management capabilities across the company and achieve balanced development while facilitating the growth of outstanding managers. *(Ren Zhengfei: Remarks During the Report to the China Telecom Survey Group and at a Meeting with Managers Above the Section Chief Level at China Unicom Headquarters, 1998)*

317

We employ a "red team and blue team" method. Similar to modern war games, the blue team plays the role of a competitor, always challenging the red team and exposing its faults to help the red team improve. The blue team can help managers develop dual perspectives and approaches, broaden their strategic thinking, and is therefore a very important field for middle and senior managers to practice and learn to think outside the box. *(Source: EMT Meeting Minutes No. [2007] 014)*

The purpose of transferring managers from business departments to the finance department is to help the latter better understand business operations and adjust the way they think and work. Through this, the finance department can change its past practice of being simple and stubborn, and begin working smarter. By doing so, we are adding sand into cement to make concrete, rather than simply replacing old cement. Those who want to transfer to the finance department will need to pass accounting exams. For middle managers, job rotations are conducive to their career development and comply with our zigzag development program, and outstanding employees should be glad to be rotated to other positions. For those who voluntarily transfer to the finance department, they have seen new opportunities for them. The departments to which they previously belonged need to be willing to welcome them back to their original positions if they do not achieve high performance in the finance department. In this way, they are providing strong support for the development of other departments. They are keeping the big picture in mind and considering the overall interests of the entire company. Senior managers should also act in this way. *(Ren Zhengfei: Comments to Staff from Finance, 2011)*

Through strategic reserves like the elite teams, the Key Project Department, and the Project Management Resource Pool, we aim to expedite the circulation of organizations, talent, technologies, management approaches, and experience during project operations. We can also identify more outstanding managers and experts to help our company achieve continuous progress. *(Ren Zhengfei: Speech at Huawei Annual Management Conference, 2013)*

8.3.2 Managers need to follow a zigzag development path

In the past, our managers grew along a linear path, without knowing anything about other fields. We need to emphasize a zigzag development path for managers and implement this policy, starting with newly promoted junior managers. Managers must have successful field experience. Today, we have placed high-potential employees from each department in the most challenging positions and regions, so that they will cultivate a stronger will, become more capable, and develop more rapidly. They will also receive preference during future manager selection. Those who want to become managers must walk this path. Our purpose is to cultivate managers. *(Ren Zhengfei: Comments to Staff of the Core Engineering Department, 2009)*

Many of our senior managers are promoted along a linear path and lack a wide variety of experience. They are outstanding in certain fields, but may not be capable enough in tasks that require strong and comprehensive coordination skills. *(Ren Zhengfei: Speech at the Regular Meeting of the Reserve Pool, June 24, 2009)*

A zigzag development path is applicable only to senior managers and experts with comprehensive skill sets, not to junior managers and employees. I think junior managers are unlikely to become leaders in a short period of time. Nowadays, it is not realistic to expect a junior manager to become a great leader overnight. I am not saying it is impossible. But at present, it is becoming increasingly unlikely. We expect our junior managers and employees to love what they do and excel in their given fields; we don't encourage them to transfer to other positions. Currently, the proportion of underperformers who are dismissed is not high. If an employee transfers to a new department, but cannot fulfill the new job's responsibilities, this will incur extra costs. In addition, processes that involve him or her will not function properly, which will also impact the work efficiency of his or her colleagues. *(Ren Zhengfei: Comments to Trainees of the Tenth Session of the Senior Management Seminar at Huawei University, 2011)*

Junior managers and employees can only move and be promoted within a specific domain. I don't think they should transfer across domains. Take junior secretaries as an example. We can create a junior secretary resource pool for outstanding clerks who have passed appraisals. The same approach can also be applied to other positions, such as dispatchers, planners, accountants, and bookkeepers. A resource pool has many criteria. Key employees with outstanding performance can also be placed in such resource pools after completing exams and receiving promotions, so that they may have the chance to be selected by other departments. This approach is fairer than relying on recommendations. We should not overemphasize the importance of educational background. Those who are well educated are not necessarily more capable or smarter than those with hands-on experience. We should assess employees based on the capabilities they have demonstrated in real-world settings, rather than their academic degrees. We don't expect everyone at levels 13-15 to be a strategist or leader. The zigzag development path is only applicable to senior managers and experts with comprehensive skill sets. In fact, it has already been implemented during succession planning. *(Ren Zhengfei: Comments to Trainees of the Tenth Session of the Senior Management Seminar at Huawei University, 2011)*

The zigzag development path should vary according to the levels of managers. Junior managers with successful experience can be promoted to positions two levels higher than their current ones, because new managerial positions will be the same, except for the size of teams. *(Ren Zhengfei: Speech at the EMT ST Meeting, July 27, 2012)*

The zigzag development path is intended to cultivate senior managers. The work location of the leader of a cooking team won't have much impact on his or her future development. So what is the point of sending him or her to a different department? If an employee has difficulty getting along with other people in his or her current department, it is understandable if he or she wants to transfer. But after being transferred to a new department, he or she must be assessed according to the requirements of the new position and be paid accordingly. *(Ren Zhengfei: Speech at the Meeting Regarding the Report on the Pilot Program for Absolute Appraisals of Junior Employees in Operational Positions, 2012)*

8.3.3 Creating career development paths for managers

All departments need to think carefully on how to ensure the mobility of outstanding managers to help them improve their capabilities through rotation and prepare them to support the company's high-speed development. As for junior and middle employees who have no potential, job rotation would be a waste of time and resources. *(Ren Zhengfei: Speech at the Meeting Regarding the Report by Marketing & Sales on Its Organizational Restructuring Solution, November 1, 1996)*

We believe the rotation of managers is normal. When doing this, we try to ensure that each manager finds positions where they can best unleash their potential. The most important thing is whether he or she can do a good job, rather than whether or not he or she is working in a good department. *(Ren Zhengfei: Speech at the Meeting for Sending off the Third Batch of HQ Managers to Field Offices, 1997)*

We need to mix employees together, such as by introducing non-Chinese employees into teams solely composed of Chinese, placing customer service employees in R&D teams, and sending R&D managers to work in customer service for six months or one year. When R&D engineers analyze customer needs, they need to consult marketing experts. It is necessary to strengthen the horizontal and vertical rotation of managers among different departments. *(Ren Zhengfei: Being Open Is the Only Way Out, 2001)*

Through rotation between different departments, we can help certain employees acquire more management knowledge and become managers; we can also help certain employees acquire more technical knowledge and become experts. I don't think it is a good idea to forbid manager mobility. Managers who are not allowed to rotate to other positions may choose to leave the company. Talent can only be identified during the rotation process. *(Ren Zhengfei: Speech at a Meeting with Key Employees of the Optical Network Product Line, April 18, 2002)*

We should develop policies to mandate two-way job rotations between R&D engineers and employees from departments such as technical sales, marketing, technical support, and turnkey. R&D managerial candidates must actively apply to work in field positions for upstream and downstream departments to gain hands-on experience. In principle, business and technology managers in the R&D division, who are above the Leader of Product Development Team (LPDT) and system engineer levels, must have successful experience in technical sales, marketing or technical support. *(Source: EMT Resolution No. [2006] 023)*

HR directors at all levels in the products and solutions division need to better understand the company's management requirements in order to better fulfill their job responsibilities. To that end, they must take turns working in field offices overseas, especially in hardship regions, for three to six months to gain hands-on experience. *(Source: EMT Resolution No. [2007] 020)*

To strengthen the internal control awareness among managers, we need to establish career development paths and job rotation systems for managers, and send managers with extensive experience in business operations to work in auditing and supervision. We also need to send high-performing auditing and supervision personnel who have experience in internal controls to work in managerial positions of business departments. *(Source: EMT Resolution No. [2007] 045)*

We encourage employees to become experts in their given fields and constantly improve their expertise and performance. The purpose of job rotations and manager development is to help managers perform better at work. We will not conduct job rotations simply for their own sake. *(Source: EMT Meeting Minutes No. [2008] 013)*

I think it is very important to maintain a certain degree of mobility within the company, both vertically and horizontally. Some people may become generals in the rotation process. Generals have a strong sense of direction and good judgment. Without hands-on experience, they will remain uninspired. *(Ren Zhengfei: Speech at the EMT ST Meeting, 2009)*

We need to establish a mechanism for horizontal job rotations and an internal talent market to maintain a proper degree of talent mobility. As for managers who have been working on the same position for a certain period of time, we need to pay attention to their needs and communicate with them to see if they want to work in a different position. If they have this desire and there are suitable positions available, we should help them with a transfer so as to avoid career fatigue. The purpose of establishing an internal talent market is to help employees find vacant positions within the company. Its main target is to provide alternative opportunities to those who want to make bigger contributions in more suitable positions and those released from their previous positions due to organizational restructuring. Eligible employees can enter the internal talent market without obtaining approval from their current department. As for those who have worked at Huawei for a long time and want to work in a lower-level position due to poor health, we need to respect their decisions and help them make the change, as long as they are competent for the new positions and are willing to accept a lower salary. We should view such decisions as normal instead of negative. *(Ren Zhengfei: Uniting as Many People as Possible, 2013)*

It is our policy to transfer the managers in key managerial positions in one region to other regions and require them to rotate on a regular basis. This will affect the career development of certain local managers. As a result, we need to research and specify related policy requirements, and communicate with local managers regarding the policy to prevent misunderstandings. In principle, job rotation doesn't apply to local employees, with the exception of certain high-end professionals involved in global business support and managers involved in global business management. This is to prevent costs from increasing. *(Ren Zhengfei: Uniting as Many People as Possible, 2013)*

8.3.4 Promoting manager development via a competitive internal environment

When developing managerial candidates, we need to learn from West Point to continuously demote unqualified managers. In this way, all candidates will feel a sense of urgency. Of course, the selection methods, criteria, and candidates will change as time goes by. We need to continuously select those with huge potential while eliminating those who are unqualified. *(Ren Zhengfei: Speech at a Meeting with Huawei University and the Strategic Reserve Pool, 2005)*

When selecting members of the Reserve Pool, we need to focus on outstanding employees who are responsible, devoted, willing to make sacrifices, loyal, have a sense of mission, and have made exceptional contributions. We will send them to Huawei University to receive training and help them develop their integrity, competence, capabilities, leadership, and, more importantly, the appropriate ways to learn and work. We need to ensure that they are well-prepared for the positions where they are needed. We also expect them to voluntarily work in the most challenging positions. *(Ren Zhengfei: Speech at a Meeting with Huawei University and the Strategic Reserve Pool, 2005)*

When developing junior employees to senior managers, we should apply stricter criteria, as we only select the most outstanding ones. We will select talent from among those with hands-on practice as well as trainees from Huawei University. We will implement a policy of managing managerial candidates through separation of the rights of nomination, review, and examination. This policy will make manager selection more accurate and reduce the chances of selecting unqualified employees. *(Ren Zhengfei: Speech at a Meeting with Huawei University and the Strategic Reserve Pool, 2005)*

Capabilities are not the only requirement for manager selection. Candidates must have successful experience and have made contributions in their jobs. The top 25% will be recommended as managerial candidates.

Contributions refer to the extent to which employees have met their Personal Business Commitments (PBCs) rather than just sales performance. We will also organize assessments of employees' competence through training at Huawei University, management teams' communication, and self-assessments of key events. Although every candidate recommended by business departments will be required to perform a self-assessment, only the top one third of the top 25% will be assessed at an organizational level and placed in our resource pool of managerial candidates. We will give them opportunities whenever appropriate. Last but not the least, we will assess candidates' integrity. If a candidate has moral or ethical issues, he or she will be immediately excluded from the selection process. *(Ren Zhengfei: Speech at the Annual Meeting of the Domestic Market Finance Department, 2006)*

Apart from selecting managers, the Reserve Pool is also responsible for developing managers. For instance, it will send employees, who are released from their previous positions after organizational and process adjustments, to various manager training programs or training sessions for CSOs and CFOs. Training of managerial candidates needs to help in their personal development. Before we promote managers, we need to first place them in the Reserve Pool to provide them with opportunities to learn something about installation, engineering, and manufacturing. Mere knowledge about coding is not enough. *(Ren Zhengfei: Speech at the EMT ST Meeting, 2009)*

Another important role of the Reserve Pool is to objectively reevaluate managers. In the future, managerial candidates will need to be evaluated by the Reserve Pool before they begin working in a managerial position. Currently, the biggest problem with our junior and middle managers is that they are all just playing it safe. Sometimes they dare not ask questions even though they don't understand what their superiors are saying. They ask their subordinates to do their jobs without clear instructions. This leads to low efficiency and wasted resources. Those who are afraid of communicating with their bosses or asking their bosses about their goals or expectations cannot work in managerial positions. Through the Reserve Pool's objective assessment mechanism, we need to remove from managerial positions those who are incompetent and transfer them to other positions. *(Ren Zhengfei: Speech at the Regular Meeting of the Reserve Pool, June 24, 2009)*

I think we need to promote those who work effectively in field offices and produce results. We need to cultivate a group of team leaders, and send them to work in field offices. So, when selecting them, we need to focus more on their ability to work in real-world settings rather than their competence. If we provide opportunities to them, they may be promoted to higher-level positions. But if they don't study corporate documents carefully and fail to understand their essence, it will be better for them to stay where they are and retain the basic authority and responsibilities of team leaders. The opportunities for personal development totally depends on themselves. The Reserve Pool needs to recruit more trainees, and develop a payment model for trainees. It should be fair for all employees. Allowances can only be provided to those who work in hardship regions such as Afghanistan or the Arctic. With such an operating support system, manager conduct system, and learning system, we will be able to succeed anywhere in the world. *(Ren Zhengfei: Comments on the Reserve Pool, 2010)*

We will select a large number of managers with a strong sense of mission, strategic thinking, business acumen, strong motivation, and successful experience around the world, and place them in management teams at all levels. We need to pay attention to our succession plans and create mechanisms that encourage healthy competition among managers. *(Source: EMT Resolution No. [2012] 030)*

At Huawei, talent are selected rather than trained. We only promote to managerial positions talented people who have proved their capabilities and potential through outstanding performance. Huawei's managers must understand the company's relevant processes and IT tools. They can gain credits by taking online exams and pass certifications. As to specific processes and IT tools, senior managers need to have the required knowledge; middle managers need to have the required knowledge and basically master the required skills; junior managers must have the required skills. *(Source: EMT Meeting Minutes No. [2012] 025)*

To achieve success, we should be willing to promote outstanding managers through a fast-track process even during times of smooth development. We will place outstanding managers, who are released from their previous positions due to organizational restructuring, on elite teams in field offices to gain practical experience and improve operating capabilities. This is a great way to inspire passion across the organization. As a special position established by the company, the JCR must work with BGs to effectively manage and deploy managers. *(Source: EMT Meeting Minutes No. [2012] 026)*

Developing Managerial Candidates to Ensure Huawei's Sustainable Development

8.4.1 Managerial candidates are a bottleneck that hinders Huawei's sustainable development

Middle and senior managers need to improve their management capabilities and business qualifications to meet the requirements of the rapidly changing environment. After the ten years of development since our establishment, I think our middle and senior managers have become very responsible, enterprising, self-critical, and restrained. However, some may have been placed in managerial positions due to historical reasons. In that case, they may not have the skills or capabilities required for their positions. But as long as they are loyal and dedicated, they may well stay in their positions after improving their skills. They need to try their best to close the gap in management skills to support the company's rapid development and to express their gratitude for the company's trust. *(Ren Zhengfei: Speech at the Meeting and Awards Ceremony Regarding the Report on the Achievements of Quality Control Circles, 1998)*

We are now faced with an important mission, but we lack sufficient qualified managers who have been well-trained and tested in field offices. Our key task now is to cultivate managerial candidates to prepare for a worldwide boom in business in 2007, 2008, and 2009. Managers at all levels must shoulder heavy responsibilities in cultivating more managers. Right now, we are like a huge dumpling with a very thin wrapper, and can easily fall apart. It is hard to believe that we will be able to build a large 3G network when nobody in the company has truly learned from our mistake in the project at AIS (a Thai telecom operator). If we fail to deliver a single big contract, no customers will believe in us anymore. If that happens, the company may indeed fall apart. So now our top priority is developing a large number of outstanding managers and sending outstanding managerial candidates to field offices to help them gain practical experience and develop their skills. Actually, I'm worried that we will be unable to rapidly deliver large contracts each worth billions of US dollars. *(Ren Zhengfei: Seeing the Situation Clearly and Accelerating Organizational and Reserve Pool Development to Embrace Huawei's New Development, 2005)*

The priority of management is to focus on bottlenecks. Currently, our company has two bottlenecks: managerial candidates and management transformation. We need to put more emphasis on developing managerial candidates. The more candidates a department has, the better job the department head and HR department have done. *(Source: EMT Meeting Minutes No. [2005] 009)*

Currently, one of the big problems we face is poor management. I expect HR departments at all levels to focus on the problem and try their best to improve the management system and develop key managers. We cannot exaggerate our capabilities; if we do so, we will lose valuable growth opportunities. *(Ren Zhengfei: Seeing the Situation Clearly and Accelerating Organizational and Reserve Pool Development to Embrace Huawei's New Development, 2005)*

Many managers at Huawei lack adequate management knowledge and capabilities. They were placed in managerial positions due to historical reasons. If they don't work hard to improve themselves and keep pace with the new environment, they may be removed from their positions. In fact, in these past two years, many senior managers have been removed from their positions because of this. I will by no means leave difficult issues to my successors. To ensure the success of our current financial transformation, we need to remove many obstacles that block our path. I hope everyone can move forward and keep pace with the company. The company will abandon the guerrilla tactics we grew up with, and transform into a modern organization. If a senior manager is incompetent, he or she will need to transfer to a non-managerial position rather than being demoted level by level. Our company is developing rapidly. We will not waste our time convincing managers to improve themselves. *(Ren Zhengfei: Speech at the Meeting Regarding the IFS Project Report, August 8, 2007)*

A major problem we are currently facing is that our current managers are not as competent as we expect them to be and we don't have enough managerial candidates. We don't have sufficient managers that can make market breakthroughs. In markets where breakthroughs have been made, we don't have sufficient managerial candidates to consolidate our gains. We don't have enough professionals to carry out fine-grained management in the markets we have won to increase profitability. *(Source: EMT Meeting Minutes No. [2007] 025)*

We should have a plan to cultivate large numbers of managers and send them to operating teams. We need large numbers of managers in field offices, and cannot keep positions vacant until more qualified candidates appear. Currently, business departments, rather than the HR department or HRC, are in charge of developing managerial candidates. The HR department and HRC have to listen to business departments when it comes to developing managerial candidates, because they do not have sufficient manager resources, cannot enable manager mobility, and therefore cannot establish a positive climate. I think developing managerial candidates is critical because we will have enough people to be assigned to field offices at any given time. In addition, we will be able to place higher requirements on managers who are already working in field offices. Those who are not dedicated will be replaced with the managerial candidates we have developed. Therefore, the Reserve Pool must play an important role. *(Ren Zhengfei: Comments on the Reserve Pool, 2010)*

During this workshop on our HR management philosophy, we found that many people never read the materials beforehand and did not know why we have compiled this book. This indicates that they are relying solely on their experience during work and are not learning. However, we are not opposed to relying on experience. We should establish new rules before discarding the old rules, not vice versa. The Reserve Pool should do the same thing, and develop many managers at different levels who have mastered modern management approaches and skills. When there is a problem in a field team that the current leader can't handle on his or her own, we can send someone over to serve as the deputy leader and help the leader solve the problem. The leader will be replaced only when the problem cannot be solved. I don't mean to arrange for someone to replace the leader immediately after discovering that he or she cannot do a good job. If the person we dispatch successfully helps the leader achieve their goal, he or she may be promoted later due to his or her talents. If he or she manages to replace the leader, I may be a little concerned about his or her ambition. I will still use this person, though with some oversight. *(Ren Zhengfei: Comments on the Reserve Pool, 2010)*

We need to have the courage to place junior employees with huge potential on our senior management team. Otherwise, where will our generals come from? Throughout history, many people became generals in their thirties or forties. Why not at Huawei? I think we should offer some membership opportunities to high-potential junior employees. Such employees who join our Board of Directors, Supervisory Board, management committees, and ATs may not get the equivalent C&Q levels, and their shares may not increase because of such membership, either. The current rotating chairperson may be replaced in the future, but he or she will have gained some experience. *(Ren Zhengfei: Speech at the EMT ST Meeting, May 31, 2011)*

We welcome individuals who aim high but might be poor to join us and serve as a strong force for Huawei. These individuals will give Huawei the power to generate more revenue, and with more revenue Huawei will make more investments, which will in turn help Huawei gain even more power. This is the virtuous cycle we desire. *(Ren Zhengfei: Success Is Not a Reliable Guide to Future Development, 2011)*

We need to strengthen the development and self-nomination of managerial candidates. We are badly in need of a large number of young people who are highly motivated, passionate, capable, and willing to sacrifice and work in places where they are needed. Currently, we are trying to achieve diversity, which requires a lot of outstanding employees. Also, we need to make sure that no incompetent but well-connected managers are selected. *(Ren Zhengfei: Success Is Not a Reliable Guide to Future Development, 2011)*

We welcome employees to voluntarily work in hardship regions and challenging positions. We provide opportunities to help them achieve better performance and get promoted. We need to respect employees' choice of their jobs and the bosses they work for. We will also need to establish an internal talent market to allow employees to change jobs when they want, though they risk not being hired by any department or having to accept a reduced job level and compensation. Currently, we have some managers who are incompetent and do not behave properly at work; these managers may have very competent subordinates who are staying in the team merely for the sake of a high salary. If we have an internal talent market in place, these employees can suspend their current jobs after obtaining approval from the Learning and Development Department and find a new job through this market. They may have more choices and be able to create more value for the company. However, it is also possible that they may not find a suitable position and may have to accept a salary cut in the end, which is, in my opinion, not a big deal. They may well be promoted in the future as long as they work hard. *(Ren Zhengfei: Success Is Not a Reliable Guide to Future Development, 2011)*

The next three to five years will be critical for Huawei's development because it is the period when we will need to fight for a favorable strategic position. Here, I think there are several important factors: First is a clear strategic direction. Second is enhanced succession planning for managers. Right now, our managers have to take part in numerous meetings and handle many issues, which take up too much of their time and energy when they should have been thinking about more important things. When we make new succession plans, we need to decrease coordination between departments and the number of additional roles managers are taking on, so as to help them focus on their main responsibilities and provide more opportunities to other employees. To successfully seize the strategic high ground within three to five years, we will need a huge operating team. Right now, we always appoint familiar faces to our operating team. This is a sign of poor organizational development. The Carrier BG must develop a bigger and stronger team over the next three to five years to work together and seize a favorable strategic position. *(Ren Zhengfei: Speech at the EMT ST Meeting, October 30, 2012)*

8.4.2 Providing more challenging opportunities to managers with successful experience

Currently, it is the best time to develop a large number of managers. If our sales revenue increases dramatically, we will be presented with numerous opportunities. We are now in a critical period of development. So everyone needs to study hard, be open at work, and communicate more with others. *(Ren Zhengfei: Speech at the Meeting Regarding the Work Report of the Asia Pacific Region, 2006)*

I think learning and development are a minimum requirement on qualification. If you cannot meet this requirement, I will not bother to assess your competence. You need to take responsibility for your own learning and development. If you are qualified, I will give you an opportunity. If you succeed, I will give you a better opportunity. If you meet my expectations again, I will provide you with even more opportunities to gain more practical experience and learn during practice. We need to put what we have learned into practice and then learn theory during practice. *(Ren Zhengfei: Human Resources Must Be Oriented Towards Forging Ahead and Refrain from Being Dogmatic and Rigid, 2009)*

We need to transfer some employees to the finance department to make the department stronger. This process can be compared to creating concrete with pebbles, sand, and cement to achieve higher quality. We also need to recruit more talent from outside the company. The finance department can't simply recruit people when there are vacancies. In that case, those who are incompetent will never be removed from their positions. *(Ren Zhengfei: Speech at the EMT ST Meeting, July 28, 2011)*

High-potential employees need to prove themselves through practice. If the employees demonstrate outstanding performance during practice, we can provide them with opportunities to work on key projects and assume greater responsibilities. In about ten years, they will become senior managers. The Human Resource Management Department and Huawei University will need to further improve the management of high-potential employees and ensure they are constantly tracked and cultivated, and promoted to higher-level managerial positions after working in field offices for several years. If we succeed in developing managerial candidates in this way, we will have a proven method for developing sales and other types of talent. However, we must ensure that the manager development model works. *(Ren Zhengfei: Speech at the EMT ST Meeting, October 30, 2012)*

8.4.3 Establishing mechanisms and systems that encourage managerial candidates to emerge continuously

The separation of rights must be ensured during the nomination, selection, and assessment of managerial candidates. Huawei University and the Human Resource Management Department will need to work out related processes and the CEC will manage the archive system. *(Source: EMT Meeting Minutes No. [2005] 022)*

The management team of each business department selects members for the Reserve Pool. The director of the management team is the primary owner who must assume responsibility for the selection process and results. *(Source: EMT Meeting Minutes No. [2005] 040)*

Strategic reserves can be established at different levels. Huawei University needs to create training plans for each level with training materials and cases specifically designed for that level. In addition, Huawei University will implement a mentorship system to allow employees with successful experience and leadership potential to coach less experienced employees. Mentors may be divided into different levels and will take turns coaching employees for a certain period, such as one year. There should also be incentives for mentors. For instance, outstanding mentors should be prioritized for promotions. *(Ren Zhengfei: Speech at the Meeting Regarding the Work Report of the Asia Pacific Region, 2006)*

The HRC needs to take responsibility for selecting managers, and focus on high-potential talent that have not been identified by the senior management team or ATs. High-level ATs should also nominate managerial candidates from among junior and middle managers. We have to combine regular and fast-track selection mechanisms to ensure we have a sound manager selection system. *(Source: EMT Meeting Minutes No. [2007] 025)*

The HRC mainly manages managers, so as to place the right managers in the right positions and create more value. At Huawei, the rights of appraisal and execution are separated to help junior and middle managers develop. I think right now we need to focus on selecting managers and replace them if they are incompetent. Those who are not selected can be placed in the Reserve Pool to look for new opportunities. We will not promote employees based on their educational background. Instead, we will make sure their career development is determined by their actual competence and contributions to the company. We should make the best use of our talent, not simply stress the importance of talent. *(Ren Zhengfei: Speech at the Regular Meeting of the Reserve Pool, March 25, 2009)*

We need to emphasize the principles and mechanisms for selecting managers. How does the HRC select managers? How are young managers promoted? The answer is simple and clear: Those who make contributions in field offices will be promoted. At Huawei, we do not select managers based on seniority. Those who work at the HQ, but don't have experience in field offices, will not be promoted to managerial positions or receive high salaries. Managers must have successful practical experience such as project management. We can become invincible if we adhere to this principle. *(Ren Zhengfei: Speech at the EMT ST Meeting, May 31, 2011)*

At Huawei, we have two pyramids: managers and experts. The two pyramids share the same bottom layers. At the middle layers, job holders can be rotated back and forth. But when it comes to higher levels, it is better to maintain separation. Those who are at the top of each pyramid should focus on directions for future development. I think this talent model proposed by Ken Hu is very good. It would be great if we can use our understanding of philosophy to enrich and improve the model so as to build a future talent system for both managers and experts. *(Ren Zhengfei: Criticism and Self-criticism, 2011)*

Huawei's administrative management organizations were established through top-down appraisals, selection, and development, based on authorization by the Board of Directors. This is different from how the CEC was created. Selection by organizations and open supervision are implemented in our administrative management organizations. Although managers are selected by the upper-level organization through collective discussions, there may still be biases involved, and open supervision is needed to correct any possible mistakes. We are opposed to manager selection through voting in administrative management organizations. Managers should effectively fulfill the responsibilities assigned by the Board of Directors, and use their authority to achieve high performance. If a voting system is adopted for manager selection, managerial candidates may seek to please the voters, which may lead to an unbalanced welfare system that is harmful to the company's sustainable development. *(Ren Zhengfei: Comments to Staff of the CEC, 2011)*

The JCR is a special position established by the company. It takes a neutral stance and is not the leader of regions. The JCR must coordinate between BGs and regions on the company's behalf. In particular, it must effectively manage the selection and allocation of BG's managers at BG's HQ offices. It must promote those with successful experience in field offices to the BG's HQ offices and send high-potential employees, including outstanding managers, to field offices to gain hands-on experience. *(Ren Zhengfei: Speech at the EMT ST Meeting, October 30, 2012)*

We need to establish a mobility system that sends those who have practical experience in field offices to work in BGs' HQ offices, and, at the same time, sends young talent with high-potential in BGs' HQ offices to the field to gain practical experience. We will allocate high-quality resources to valued customers, and enable the talent to grow through hands-on operations. Such mobility will help the company realize a promising future. *(Ren Zhengfei: Remarks at a Meeting with Staff of the Guangzhou Representative Office, 2013)*

We need to develop a system which can provide opportunities to young and high-potential employees. Who will take on the heavy responsibilities at Huawei? Currently, new technology is developing very quickly. Huawei is in a field with cutting-edge technology. Due to these rapid changes, young people may be in a more advantageous position to address the associated challenges. As a result, our system needs to help such people stand out and play a more important role. *(Ren Zhengfei: Speech at the EMT ST Meeting, March 29, 2013)*

Currently, we lack managers. Why is this? In the past, our managers had no authority. What they did was to make phone calls and apply for approvals. As a result, our managers were not mature at that time. Real authority is now delegated to managers, and they will become mature after about two years. In this way, we will see many senior managers emerge in three to five years. By then, we may have a huge number of outstanding managers and successors. *(Ren Zhengfei: Remarks at a Meeting with Staff of the Guangzhou Representative Office, 2013)*

The purpose of delegating authority to field offices is to give more opportunities to outstanding employees who can work independently and let them leverage their potential based on existing processes and policies. We expect our leaders in field offices to be proactive and creative in our core businesses and work together toward a common goal. *(Ren Zhengfei: Remarks at a Meeting with Staff of the Guangzhou Representative Office, 2013)*

Why are we restructuring the Reserve Pool now? Huawei University doesn't have the authority or capability to manage managers. Instead, the JCR needs to have this authority and capability. The allocation of managers needs to be managed by the Human Resource Management Department and JCR under the guidance of the HRC. Since you have already worked out the structure and quality requirements, what needs to be done is to send numerous managers and employees to field offices. *(Ren Zhengfei: Speech at the EMT ST Meeting, March 29, 2013)*

ACRONYMS

CHAPTER 1

PSST: Products & Solutions Staff Team

EMT: Executive Management Team

ST: Staff Team

CIMS: Computer Integrated Manufacturing System

PIRB: Product Investment Review Board; later changed to IRB for short.

CHAPTER 2

C&Q: Competency & Qualification

HRC: Human Resources Committee

BG: Business Group

BCGs: Business Conduct Guidelines

ISC: Integrated Supply Chain

CHAPTER 3

AT: Administrative Team

GSM: Global System for Mobile Communications

IFS: Integrated Financial Services

PBC: Personal Business Commitment

CHAPTER 4

GTS: Global Technical Service

IPD: Integrated Product Development

CHAPTER 6

CC3: Customer Centric 3: a project-based cross-functional team, consisting of three roles: Account Responsible (AR), Solution Responsible (SR), and Fulfillment Responsible (FR).

CHAPTER 7

CEC: Committee of Ethics and Compliance

JCR: Joint Committee of Regions

AT: Administrative Team

BCGs: Business Conduct Guidelines

BG: Business Group

CC3: Customer Centric 3: a project-based cross-functional team, consisting of three roles: Account Responsible (AR), Solution Responsible (SR), and Fulfillment Responsible (FR).

CIMS: Computer Integrated Manufacturing System

C&Q: Competency & Qualification

EMT: Executive Management Team

GSM: Global System for Mobile Communications

GTS: Global Technical Service

HRC: Human Resources Committee

IFS: Integrated Financial Services

IPD: Integrated Product Development

ISC: Integrated Supply Chain

JCR: Joint Committee of Regions

PBC: Personal Business Commitment

PIRB: Product Investment Review Board; later changed to IRB for short.

PSST: Products & Solutions Staff Team

ST: Staff Team